IDENTITY CRISIS

& THE RISE OF QUEBEC

CANADA IN THE 20TH CENTURY
1953 TO 1982

LINK BYFIELD

CanMedia Inc.
Edmonton
2009

Author and Editor
LINK BYFIELD

Layout and Design
DEAN PICKUP

Proofreading
KIRK MARLOW

Index
MOIRA CALDER

Published By
CanMedia Inc.

President
CURTIS STEWART

Suite 202,
10479 - 184 Street,
Edmonton, Alberta.
T5S 2L1
Phone (780) 486-6735
Fax (780) 486-6726
Toll Free: 1-888-301-2664
www.cdnhistory.com

Printed in Canada
By Friesens Corporation, Altona, Manitoba

IDENTITY CRISIS & THE RISE OF QUEBEC
CANADA IN THE 20TH CENTURY
1953-1982

© Copyright 2010
CanMedia Inc.
First Printing

Identity Crisis & The Rise Of Quebec
Canada In The 20th Century
Includes bibliographical references and index.
ISBN 0-9736530-7-8
ISBN 978-0-9736530-7-6
EAN 9780973653076

1. Canada - History - 1953-1982
11. Byfield, Link, 1951-

FOREWORD

In the first half of the 20th century, Canada was hammered and shaped on the anvil of courageous undertakings and cataclysmic events: the surge of settlers into the western wilderness, two world wars and the worst depression in history. These huge challenges and achievements demanded of ordinary Canadians a level of personal sacrifice and determination that is, in hindsight, awe-inspiring.

These great events constituted Canada's heroic age, and they were the focus of Volumes 1 and 2 in this series, "Birth of a Nation" and "Tragedy & Triumph."

Since that era our national narrative has been, more than anything else, political. Canadians have done all kinds of other interesting things. But as a nation, our common enterprise has been the quieter achievement of self-government in an increasingly complex and dangerous world. Even in prosperous times – and recent generations have been blessed with unprecedented abundance – governing a federal union as diverse and dispersed as ours is difficult.

This volume has been titled "Identity Crisis," for that is what characterized Canada in the third quarter of the 20th century. For three decades the question perplexed us. Were we in essence and attitude still British – or were we now American – or anything except American – or some unique bicultural or multicultural hybrid? It was a time of soul-searching.

Very little of that self-absorbed discussion – so common at the time, and yet, let's be frank, so terribly tedious – appears in this book. It was probably necessary; but a nation is known in the end by what its citizens do, not by narcissistic self-reflection among its intellectual elites. What continued to define Canada was the building of cities, the extraction of resources, the arrival of hopeful newcomers with no interest in our past quarrels, and the enduring Canadian urge to advance and improve.

Yet at the same time, no nation can entirely escape its past. More than any other factor, history influences how people think, feel and act, whether they are aware of it or not. And as the thought settled on English Canadians after the Second World War that they were no longer British in political loyalty because the British Empire had vanished, they suddenly realized that the glue holding the pieces together was gone. In our regional experience and prospects we were all in reality quite divergent – the Atlantic from the rest, Ontario from the West, and everyone from Quebec.

As Alberta thinkers John Barr and Owen Anderson put it at the time, we found we were not "two solitudes but many." In all areas of Canada, including Quebec, the challenge became to establish why and how to continue as a single entity.

The need to reconcile past and future, region with region and culture with culture became a political, economic and constitutional struggle that began in the 1950s and climaxed with the National Energy Program and the Queen's proclamation of the new Canadian Constitution in 1982. At a lesser level of intensity, it continues to the present day. For so it must in a nation in which there is no one common language, economy or heritage.

The post-war, pre-Charter era was striking for two things.

It was characterized by strong leaders of impressive integrity – John Diefenbaker, Lester Pearson, Pierre Trudeau, René Lévesque and Peter Lougheed, among others. Though radically different in their aims, these men were driven to a remarkable degree by deep and principled convictions about what was right for Canada.

It was also an era of profound social change, even turmoil – the youth rebellion and the more lasting "rights" revolutions. The results, both good and bad, are still being felt and still being tallied half a century later.

In its main narrative, this book recounts the national political story. In numerous smaller sidebars it recounts other events and trends which, each in its own way, helped make Canada what it is – from the turbulent expansion of the National Hockey League, to the thrilling Canadian rescue of American hostages from Iran, to the amazing personal odyssey of Terry Fox.

Canada is an interesting and unusual country – probably less virtuous than we like to imagine, but more significant than we are left to feel in the shadow of the superpower across our border.

It was not leadership alone that held us together in the centrifugal chaos of the 1960s and 1970s. Leaders succeed only if they have followers. It was a shared refusal among ordinary citizens in all regions to allow Confederation to come apart.

Why the prospect of disunion should fill Canadians with dread is hard to say. It just does.

Link Byfield

Edmonton, Alberta
August 2008

TABLE OF CONTENTS

Part One – 1953-1967

Part Two – 1968-1979

PART THREE – 1979-1982

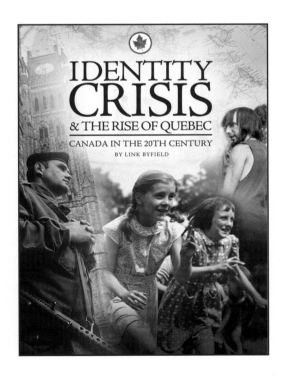

The Cover:

Youth, energy and profound change marked the postwar 1950s to 1980s. Politically, Quebec emerged from its long isolation to make demands that shook the nation. Socially, the first television generation burst from the orderly and prosperous confines of a growing suburbia to overturn age-old assumptions about virtue and propriety. Graphic designer Dean Pickup illustrates the kaleidoscope mood with a collage spanning the period.

PART ONE

1953-1967

The 1950s marked the climax of the "baby boom", bringing a post-war birth surge after the impoverished 1930s, and war-preoccupied 1940s. In Canada, the fertility rate peaked in 1958 at an average of four children per woman. Children here are racing in an Ottawa schoolyard in 1957.

Photo - National Archives of Canada

The new colossus

*As the British Empire recedes into history, Canadians
must decide if they love or hate the United States*

Canada, in many ways, had hit a high point by the summer of 1953.
The Korean War was over. Except for the Cold War with Communism, which
didn't feel very warlike, the country was at peace. A popular and respected
French-Canadian was prime minister, and Canadians felt united. Economically, all regions were making solid progress, including the Atlantic. Even the prairie grain
carryover of 1952 had been sold off, and a new bumper crop was growing in the fields.
Work on the mammoth St. Lawrence Seaway project was about to begin. Manufacturing
in Quebec and Ontario was booming.

Across Canada average personal incomes, with more purchasing power than ever before, were still rising. Taxes and unemployment remained low. The post-war "baby boom"
was in full career, and there were now mobs of young children everywhere. Women were
staying home in growing numbers to raise them – something that could be done on a husband's income alone. Mile upon mile of new suburban streets were rolling out, flanked by
modern and spacious bungalows, playgrounds, parks, schools and churches.

For the first time since pioneer days, it was now assumed that most Canadians would
own their own home. Crime was uncommon, public discourse was civil, divorce was rare,
sex outside of marriage was considered shameful, and children were, on average, healthier
than their parents had been – and better fed, better clothed and better educated. Canada
had a world-class navy, close ties to the mighty United States, and 10,000 military personnel and 12 air squadrons in Europe holding back the Communist menace.

Though it probably didn't seem so at the time, the early '50s were an idyllic moment. But
it was brief.

Over the next three decades, the nation would be rent by Quebec separatism and western resentment, the crime rate would quintuple, half of all marriages would end in divorce,
the tax load would quadruple, single-earner family incomes would shrink, sexual diseases

The 1950s were a time of unprecedented Canadian prosperity and rising
consumption. Here are Christmas
shoppers in an unidentified Ottawa
department store in 1955. It was an
era of low taxation, little inflation and
an expanding economy. A man with
an average salary could single-handedly support a modest house and a
growing family.

Photo - National Archives of Canada

would become epidemic, the birth rate would plunge, one-third of students would leave high school classified as functionally illiterate, relations with the U.S. would deteriorate, the Canadian military would fall into feeble disarray, whole regional economies would stall, and revolutionary new ideas would divide political parties, Parliament and Canadian society.

But in 1953, all that lay in the future, entirely unforeseen and probably unimaginable. Canadians went to the racy Oscar-winning movie *From Here to Eternity* at their new neighbourhood drive-in theatres to see how much the censors had left in of Burt Lancaster and Deborah Kerr scandalously entwined on the beach. Then they drove home listening to that year's popular radio hits, "I Saw Mommy Kissing Santa Claus" and "How Much Is That Doggie in the Window?"

Societies blessed by a golden glow of prosperity rarely show much interest in politics, and compared to the 1930s Canadians had politically fallen asleep. All major regions, from the Atlantic to the Pacific, were comfortably, complacently and overwhelmingly Liberal. A crushing 191-seat victory for the Liberals in 1949 had reduced the Conservatives to a mostly-Ontario rump of 41 seats, and the CCF (later the NDP) to 13.

In fact, the only province to swim against the Liberal tide in 1949 had been Alberta, opting instead to give two-thirds of its 15 federal seats to the federal Social Credit Party.

Everywhere else was a sea of Liberal red: 68 of Quebec's 73 seats went to the Grits; in Ontario, it was 55 out of 83, and so on through the Atlantic and the West.

The mobs of growing children in the 1950s needed homes, causing an unprecedented boom in suburban development. Miles of new, Spartan bungalows appeared along new streets, flanked by new cars. Seen here are new homes in Edmonton's Parkview district, 1956. Children loved cars too, of course: two generations of mobility in one Toronto garage, 1960.

Photos - National Archives of Canada (right), Provincial Archives of Alberta (below)

Louis St. Laurent, pictured here (left) with PM Mackenzie King at the Liberal convention in 1948, was the first Canadian prime minister to have a manufactured public image. He was portrayed as a kindly, doting homebody, as in this 1948 Easter dinner photo with two granddaughters. In reality he was as elitist and partisan as any politician of that era, and as he aged prone to irritation and melancholy.

Photos - National Archives of Canada

The leader of this massive Liberal majority was Louis St. Laurent – "Uncle Louis," as he had been dubbed and defined by a Montreal advertising agency, becoming in the process the first Canadian prime minister to have a professionally manufactured public image. Outwardly, he appeared patrician, avuncular and calm, and his dark, soulful eyes appealed to the better part of human nature. He was said to be a doting grandfather when the pressures of office allowed. In reality he could be demanding, aloof and irritable. But he had led the country well since Mackenzie King's resignation in 1948.

St. Laurent was one of that small minority of Canadians lucky enough to grow up bilingual. Born in 1882 at Compton in Quebec's Eastern Townships, as a child he had spoken French to his storekeeper father and English to his Irish mother. Not until his teens, he later recalled, did he realize this was unusual. His own father had been a staunch Liberal in a Tory era, but times were about to change. In 1896, at age 14, Louis shook the hand of Wilfrid Laurier, the year Laurier became Canada's first French-speaking prime minister. One-half century later, Louis Stephen St. Laurent would become its second.

Though connected to politicians all his life, St. Laurent's own political career came late. After graduating in law from Université Laval in 1905, his practice as a bilingual Montreal corporate and constitutional lawyer often took him to Ottawa (as well as London and Washington), where he was well regarded by Liberals. So when Prime Minister King's close friend and long-time

Quebec in 1948 became the first province to adopt its own flag; other provinces continued to fly the British Union Jack or its Canadian derivative, the Red Ensign. By the 1950s, French nationalism had become a major force in provincial politics, as evidenced by this Union Nationale youth march in Montreal proclaiming Quebec pride in the new flag.

Photos - Canadian Press Images (inset), National Archives of Canada (bottom)

Quebec lieutenant Ernest Lapointe died in 1941, King appealed to St. Laurent to replace him.

In fact, King could turn to no one else. Most Quebec Liberal MPs in those days were uneducated, uncomplicated souls – local distributors of judgeships and postal jobs. They dispensed patronage with an unabashed blatancy that King found distasteful and subsequent Quebec generations would consider embarrassing. King needed someone with more class.

Though at 59 St. Laurent was within sight of a comfortable retirement, he ran for a seat and won, and joined the cabinet in 1942. He steered King's wartime government through the Quebec Conscription Crisis of 1944, and by the time King retired in 1948, two years before his death, there was widespread agreement that "Uncle Louis," old though he was, should succeed him.

Until then, the Liberal Party had had only four leaders since Confederation – compared to ten for the Conservatives, all of British descent. Since Laurier's great success, the Grits had conceived the idea that their leadership should alternate between English and French. Just as King had been the obvious successor to Laurier, now St. Laurent looked like the perfect candidate to follow King.

"Our nation," St. Laurent said in 1948, "was planned as a political partnership of two great races. It was planned by men of vision, of tolerance, as a partnership in which both of the partners would retain their essential characteristics, their religion, their culture."

Strong undercurrents were pulling it apart, even after the wartime Conscription Crisis had passed. In 1948, for example, Quebec replaced the Union Jack on its provincial Legislature with a new blue provincial flag bearing a white cross and four fleurs-de-lys – a sign of things to come. No other province did such things, at that time.

By the 1950s, the terms "Liberal leader" and "prime minister" had become synonymous. Except during troubled times – the First World War and the Depression – the Liberals had run Canada since 1896. For as long as anyone could remember, good times were Liberal times. And times had never been better than in 1953.

Besides, who else was there?

By the 1950s, with the quiet Cold War against Communism in full force, most Canadians considered the left-wing Co-operative Commonwealth Federation (CCF) as suspect in its ideology as it was incomprehensible in its name. Though not Communist itself, it upheld Communism's egalitarian ideals instead of denouncing its barbarities. The CCF had entered Parliament from the West in the Depression. It peaked in the Gallup poll in 1943, and reached its parliamentary zenith in the election of 1945, winning about 30 percent of the western vote, and 27 seats. It broke into Ontario that year, pulling almost 15 percent of the vote, though it took no Ontario seats. It even won a seat in Nova Scotia.

Then it declined. In 1949, as the Soviets exploded their first atomic test-bomb, back came the post-war Liberals, stronger than ever, and down went the hopes and fortunes of populist socialism. As "Uncle Louis" called for freedom abroad and free enterprise at home, Canadians reduced the CCF to 15 seats.

The CCF's main problem was that most people associated the party with pre-war social conflicts – union strikes, farm boycotts and class struggle. Liberals, by contrast, were seen as centrist conciliators. Most Canadians were quite open to social programs as a practical matter, but showed scant interest in egalitarian ideology. Despite honest and principled MPs

Wartime memories were still fresh in the 1950s, and the possibility of Soviet bombers invading from the north was very real. Civil defence exercises like the one below in Arnprior, Ontario, and evacuation planning for major centres like the one on the right for Edmonton in 1952, were a normal part of Canadian life until larger, more destructive intercontinental ballistic missiles of the 1960s rendered such civil precautions irrelevant.

Photos - Department of National Defence (below), National Archives of Canada (opposite)

who were, by all accounts, masterful parliamentarians – J.S. Woodsworth, M.J. Coldwell and Stanley Knowles – the CCF's ideological harangues consigned it to third place, and left it in constant danger of vanishing.

But if the Co-operative Commonwealth Federation had problems, those of the Progressive Conservatives were, if anything, worse.

The Tory party's origins predated Confederation, but not since the end of the Sir John A. Macdonald era in 1891 had it been popular for very long. It had become seen as the party of British reaction to Canadian aspirations, of English hegemony in Quebec, of troubled times, and of rich capitalists in "Tory Toronto."

Even western Conservative national leaders such as Arthur Meighen, R.B. Bennett and John Bracken were dismissed as impractical and elitist – too deferential to Britain, and not interested in developing Canada as an independent nation. Whether this was fair or not, it was the popular perception. By contrast, King had devoted his career to quietly ridding Canada of elitist British authority, and most post-war Canadians, to whatever degree they were aware of it, generally approved.

When St. Laurent led the Liberals into an election in the summer of 1953, the Conservative leader, George Drew, was seen by the newspapers and most voters as true to the Tory

type – a First World War officer (therefore pro-British and authoritarian) and a Bay Street tycoon (and therefore elitist and unsympathetic). He was widely and wrongly assumed to be rich – just as St. Laurent was widely and wrongly assumed to be a man of the people.

What was known to all, however, was that Drew had been premier of Ontario, and the Conservatives had not yet discovered that Canadians never elect as a prime minister a former provincial premier. It was not the last time the party would make this mistake.

In the election of 1953, St. Laurent and the Liberals did almost as well as they had in 1949. With 169 seats (of a total of 265), they retained a strong majority. Drew's Tories and M.J. Coldwell's CCF regained 10 seats each, and the Social Credit edged up to 15. But there was no sense, even among opposition parties, that anything had really changed. The Liberals were still the Natural Governing Party – the party of pragmatism, national consensus and managerial competence – as they had been for most of the past 60 years.

In this frame of mind, they pushed ahead with the St. Lawrence Seaway and the steady centralization of Canadian social programs.

It was smooth sailing at first. However, by 1956 things had started to change. Beneath the placid surface of Liberal acceptance, the tide of Canadian political opinion had begun running in other directions. For one thing, age was clearly taking its toll on St. Laurent. He was becoming forgetful, depressed and irritable. Besides, the Liberals had been in power without interruption for 21 years, and most senior cabinet ministers were still from the King era. Meanwhile, the Liberals had lost one provincial government after another – seven in all since 1943.

Two memorable things happened in 1956 which sealed their fate. One was the Suez Crisis, the other the Pipeline Debate.

The Suez Canal Crisis was ignited by Egyptian president Gamal Nasser's announcement on July 26 that his government was nationalizing the strategic Red Sea shipping link between Europe and the Far East which was owned and operated by the Franco-British Suez Canal Company. Alarmed that they would be denied affordable access to what they regarded as an international passage, England and France made a secret pact with Israel.

By mutual arrangement, Israel attacked Egypt along the canal on October 29. As secretly agreed, France and England then ordered both armies to withdraw. Both refused, so after waiting two days France and Britain bombed Egypt's airfields, and a week later landed their own troops via the Mediterranean port of Said. All this caused an earthquake in international affairs, a run on the British pound, and two Soviet submarines to head towards the area from the Baltic Sea.

If nothing else, the attack proved how much the world had changed since 1939. No longer was the Middle East the sphere of European colonial powers. It was now dominated by the competing interests of the United States and the Soviet Union, both of which felt threatened by the Suez confrontation.

In Canada, St. Laurent was alarmed as well. At a minimum, he feared Britain's action would split the Commonwealth, and at worst might start a Third World War. Caught in a rare crossfire between Britain and the U.S., Canada's two wartime allies, he told his foreign minister, Lester Pearson, to go to New York and find a solution.

Pearson conducted whirlwind negotiations with members of the United Nation, and met with U.S. Secretary of State John Foster Dulles. On November 3, 1956, he successfully proposed a United Nations emergency force consisting of troops from 10 nations, led by Canada, to replace the British and French. Egypt consented, and 1,000 Canadian troops joined 5,000 others in November to patrol the area and keep the combatants apart. The emergency force remained there until war broke out again in 1967.

Canada's initiative made the world aware of the need for global "peacekeeping," and it earned Pearson the 1957 Nobel Peace Prize (see page 20).

Prime Minister St. Laurent wearing Calgary's trademark white Stetson in 1953 greeting local candidate Harold Riley Jr. at the airport. Alberta and Saskatchewan were the only provinces that resisted the red Liberal tide that year, and Riley was defeated. Most Alberta seats went to the Social Credit, and most of Saskatchewan's to the CCF.

Photo - Glenbow Museum

The Suez Crisis

Pearson makes Canada a "peacekeeper" and wins the Nobel Prize

by Craig Docksteader

For 21 days in November of 1956, the world faced a crisis that threatened to escalate into another world war – possibly even a nuclear war. Britain, which was in the process of decolonization, had recently relinquished control of the Suez Canal after 72 years of British occupation. The excavated channel between the Indian Ocean and the Mediterranean Sea was still a vital world shipping lane.

The older colonial powers, in fact, now had little influence in the region. The real issue was security of U.S. oil supplies, as Arab countries became more nationalist and the Soviet Union worked to turn them against Israel and the United States.

In 1955, Egyptian President Gamal Abdul Nasser, tired of the Americans, signed an arms deal with the USSR. The United States and Britain subsequently cancelled their financial aid for Egypt's Aswan Dam, a massive irrigation development. Nasser announced that he would nationalize the canal to use its toll revenue to finance the project.

Britain and France were alarmed by this, as was Israel. Israel had been suffering attacks from Egypt's militia and wanted control of the Gaza Strip, east of the canal, as a security buffer.

The three countries entered into a secret pact to attack Egypt. Israel was to begin with a ground assault, and Britain and France would follow with air strikes under the guise of re-establishing neutrality in the region.

On October 29, 1956, the assault began. Israel moved its

Canadian troops rolling south from Port Said in January 1957. The Suez Crisis marked the eclipse of Europe in the Middle East and the hegemony of the two global superpowers, the U.S. and the USSR. Canadian diplomat and External Affairs minister Lester Pearson finessed the deployment of an international force headed by Canada to keep combatants away from the vital sea link between Asia and Europe.

Photo - Department of National Defence

troops into position, occupying Gaza and the Sinai.

The conflict prompted an emergency meeting of the United Nations Security Council to restore peace. Britain and France vetoed the efforts, ensuring that no consensus could be reached. With the USSR threatening military intervention, international fears soared.

On November 3, Canadian External Affairs Minister Lester Pearson proposed to the UN General Assembly that a peace-keeping force be established, called the United Nations Emergency Force (UNEF).

Pearson, who would soon become Canada's next prime minister, envisioned "a truly international peace and police force...large enough to keep these borders at peace while a political settlement is being worked out." The presence of peacekeepers would create a buffer zone be-

tween the parties, and allow for withdrawal of British, French and Israeli troops.

After some significant international pressure, Britain and France agreed. Within two weeks, the first peacekeepers landed at Port Said, at the north end of the Suez Canal. By late December, the occupying French and British forces had withdrawn, and by early March of 1957, the Israeli forces were gone as well. With the withdrawal complete, the UN peacekeepers continued to serve as a buffer between Egypt and Israel, and to ensure the ceasefire.

Canadians were divided over Pearson's initiative. He was attacked by some for not supporting Britain and for siding with the United States. But a volatile international crisis of significant proportions had been defused, and Pearson's proposal was the key to the resolution. For his efforts he was awarded

Above, Canadian soldiers from the "Vandoos" Regiment in Cyprus, April 1964, among the first of 25,000 Canadian troops to keep peace between Cypriot Greeks and Turks from 1964 to 1993. A total of 28 Canadians died keeping the peace in Cyprus. Below, Canadians patrolling the Suez.

Photos - Department of National Defence

the Nobel Peace Price in 1957, and gained recognition as the "grandfather of peacekeeping."[1]

Peacekeeping became an enduring Canadian specialty – a welcome follow-up to our military prowess in two world wars.

It requires two things: a peace treaty – or, at least, a voluntary ceasefire – and enough neutral nations contributing soldiers and/or supplies for the mission to monitor, and sometimes enforce, the truce. Peacekeepers might be unarmed neutral observers, or armed referees who would shoot back – as in Cyprus in 1974, when a small contingent of Canadians, standing their ground, persuaded a much larger force of the Turkish army to withdraw from the airport in the island's capital, Nicosia.

Besides soldiers, peacekeepers are often electoral officials, armaments experts or police – especially members of the Royal Canadian Mounted Police.

Towards the end of the century, peacekeeping often switched to "peacemaking," as in the former Yugoslavia and Afghanistan.

The United Nations is not the only organizer of missions. Others are the North Atlantic Treaty Organziation (in Afghanistan and Yugoslavia), the European Union (in Yugoslavia and Chad), the African Union (in Sudan) and ad hoc, single-purpose international bodies (in the Sinai and Sri Lanka).

1. The first international peacekeeping mission was not in the Suez, but was a United Nations intervention to protect an Arab-Israeli ceasefire in 1948.

Photos - Department of National Defence (below)
National Archives of Canada (inset)

Peacekeeping patrol in Cyprus in 1973. By the turn of the century, Canada would lose 114 soldiers, policemen and civilians killed while on mission with the United Nations. An estimated one million personnel from 130 countries had served, though by century's end Canada's military was too depleted to contribute large contingents. Inset, Lester Pearson, with his wife Marion, receives the Nobel Peace Prize in Oslo, Norway, 1957.

However, the Suez affair had an unforeseen political consequence in Canada. The Liberals were angrily accused by many in English Canada of "betraying Britain." Canadians had mixed attitudes towards both the British and the Americans. Many still felt a nostalgic obligation to Britain, and thought Canada should have sent in troops alongside the Mother Country, not acted against them at the behest of the Americans.

People were reminded that the Liberals had always been friendlier to the Americans than the Tories had been – all the way back to their origin as Ontario's Clear Grits in the 1840s. Every so often, the Liberals were punished for being too openly pro-American, just as the Conservatives were sometimes punished as too pro-British.

Although it was eroding, fondness and loyalty to Britain were far from spent in English Canada, whose cultural memory, governing institutions and political language derived from the Mother Country. There was probably more resentment towards Pearson about the Suez in English Canada than there was even in Britain.

The Liberals, however, had to deal with the reality that Britain was now geopolitically irrelevant. Any buffer or brokerage role for Canada lay between the United States and the Soviet Union. St. Laurent and Pearson had played that role well with the Suez, but they paid a political price.

Even more damaging to the Liberals in 1956 was the Pipeline Debate.

By now, Alberta's oil boom was nine years old, and the industry was in need of markets. In reality, Alberta had far more natural gas than oil, and the only way to get it to the large markets of central Canada was to build a pipeline. With a secure supply of natural gas, consumers and industries could then rely less on imported oil. Building a pipeline would be expensive, but the Liberals had been working with Alberta's Social Credit government and private companies to make it happen.

Construction of the TransCanada Pipeline in 1956 opened essential eastern consumer markets for Alberta natural gas. It was the first major national infrastructure project tying east to west since the railway boom. Much like the railways, an all-Canadian route required federal and Ontario government assistance to traverse the vast, empty expanse north of the Great Lakes.

Photo - Provincial Archives of Alberta

There were two main obstacles. One was the disinterest of eastern Canadian investors – a perennial problem for western resource development. Only U.S. companies were interested in oil and gas, or in pipelines. The second problem was that, as with the Canadian Pacific Railway 75 years earlier, the shortest and cheapest route from west to east ran south of the Great Lakes through the American Midwest. Building a pipeline across the empty and rugged expanse of northern Ontario was not commercially viable.

The Liberals, therefore, had to choose between a federally subsidized line through Canada or an unsubsidized line through the U.S. owned by Americans and giving Americans first claim on its contents.

Under famously autocratic Trade and Commerce Minister C.D. Howe, Ottawa chose the Canadian route, relying on U.S.

Clarence Decatur Howe, famously the "Minister of Everything" during the Second World War, was the driving political force behind the national pipeline. Until the 1960s, the Liberals pursued continentalist policies in matters of resource development, such as the expanding western oil and gas industry, and provincial governments across Canada relied on U.S. capital investment.

Photo - National Archives of Canada

investment and western Canadian management. The TransCanada Pipeline would be 2,200 kilometres long and cost $375 million to build. One-third of that amount would be contributed by the Ontario and federal governments to offset the extra cost of running it through northern Ontario.

Howe wanted to begin construction in June of 1956, but the pipeline company could not get its American capital in place that quickly. Howe announced to Parliament in early May, therefore, that (in addition to the grants) the government would loan TransCanada Pipeline Company Ltd. (TCPL) $80 million to start in June, and that the loan would be repaid when the money was raised privately.

The Opposition objected, arguing that between the government grant and the government loan, Canadian taxpayers were on the hook for over half of a project, 80 percent of which was owned by Americans.

To start on schedule, the Liberals introduced an enabling bill in early May, giving notice of "closure" (restriction of debate) before the opposition MPs had even a chance to speak. The House erupted. Closure, though legal, had been imposed only seven times since 1867, and never since 1932.

Led by Conservative George Drew and M.J. Coldwell of the CCF, opposition MPs called more than 70 time-consuming recorded votes over the next three weeks to hold up proceedings.

Drilling for oil and natural gas at Peers, Alberta, 1955. Gas was more abundant than oil, but needed a big pipe to reach market. C.D. Howe had the answer.

Photo - Provincial Archives of Alberta

Alberta's 10 Social Credit MPs, along with Tory MP Carl Nickle from Calgary, voted with the Liberal government. Albertans wanted the pipeline. In fact, Nickle at one point crossed the chamber to congratulate Minister Howe for holding firm.

Tempers rose as Howe's June 7 deadline neared. Drew accused the Liberals of "one-man government" (referring to Howe, not St. Laurent), and the normally civil Coldwell strode into the aisle and faced the Speaker, shouting and shaking his fist. By the end, the Speaker, an agreeable Quebec MP named René Beaudoin, looked to be in danger of having a heart attack as furious MPs yelled "traitor," "fascist" and "coward" at him for having reversed an earlier decision to allow more time. Conservative MP Donald Fleming was thrown out of the chamber, and was greeted on his return to Toronto as a hero by several hundred cheering supporters.

Canada's Parliament had never seen anything like it before, and has seen nothing like it since.

Howe got his way, as usual. The bill cleared Parliament by its June 7 deadline, the pipeline got built, and TCPL's loan was repaid. But the Liberals had damaged themselves – probably more than they realized.

■ ■ ■ ■

There was a conscious self-satisfaction to suburban life in the 1950s, and widespread conformity to social norms: three kids, decent bungalow, nice car, plenty of food. Here is an unidentified Alberta family in 1958, and a newly opened IGA supermarket in the Edmonton community of Beverly that same year. Such explicit materialism would soon inspire rebellion among the Baby Boomers, but they themselves would return to it in the 1970s.

Photos: Provincial Archives of Alberta

120

Soon after this, Conservative leader George Drew fell ill with meningitis (from which he later recovered), and the party called a leadership convention for December. The most obvious candidates were two solid and accomplished party men of the standard Tory stamp. One was Donald Fleming, a lawyer from Toronto, and the other was the Rhodes Scholar Davie Fulton, a lawyer from Kamloops, B.C.

A third suitable candidate was George Hees – "Gorgeous George" – a prosperous, gregarious Toronto businessman. He was a former Toronto Argonaut linebacker, champion amateur boxer and Second World War army major.

Hees crossed the country to measure his support, but concluded that the party rank and file, and a growing swath of its establishment, wanted someone else – John Diefenbaker.

"Dief" was, in many Conservative minds, not suitable. Mainly, he lacked social and family connections to the Canadian establishment in Montreal and Toronto, and the proper spirit of deference to its interests.

In fact, Diefenbaker was an enigma. As a prairie populist with left-wing economic values, he would probably have fit comfortably into the CCF.

But he was also classically Conservative in his passionate adherence to Britain, the monarchy and the Commonwealth, all of which he saw as a necessary counterbalance to the growing power and assertiveness of the United States and Soviet Union. In many ways, he shared the anti-American patriotism of Conservative contemporary intellectuals Donald Creighton and George Grant, whose nationalism was coming into fashion after decades of Liberal lock-step co-operation with the Americans. But Dief was not only anti-American. He was also staunchly anti-Communist – though he thought the American approach to the Communists was too confrontational.

Diefenbaker had been a lightning rod in the House of Commons ever since arriving as MP for Lake Centre in Saskatchewan in 1940, at age 39. A First World War army veteran, he had later graduated in law and carried on a criminal practice in Prince Albert. Of the 20 accused murderers he had defended, only two were hanged. He had also tried and failed five times since 1925 to get elected as a Tory in Grit Saskatchewan, impelled by a boyhood intuition that he would one day be prime minister.

Such an ambition by someone with a German surname in the first half of the 20th century, especially in the Tory party, was laughable. Every Conservative leader since Macdonald had been of

Diefenbaker, a staunch Conservative defender of British tradition, ran five times before winning a seat in Liberal Saskatchewan. That a social unknown with a German surname from the Liberal prairie hinterland should aspire to lead the Conservatives seemed patently ridiculous at first to almost everyone except Diefenbaker himself.

Photo - Diefenbaker Centre

When he arrived in the House of Commons in 1940, Diefenbaker's mastery of debate more than compensated for his lack of social pedigree.

Photo - National Archives of Canada

British descent – not French, and certainly not German. Dief found this attitude ridiculous. He was a fourth-generation Canadian, he said, and if his parents' names had been reversed – had his father had been born "Bannerman" and his mother "Diefenbaker" – the issue would never have arisen.

He held in equal scorn St. Laurent's notion that Canada consisted of "two nations" – French and English. Throughout his career, Diefenbaker emphasized "one Canada," unconnected by a hyphen to French, English or anything else. On any other basis, he insisted, Canada was bound to break apart.

Diefenbaker's two earlier attempts to become party leader, in 1942 and 1948, had not been taken seriously, but by 1956 the world had changed, and after four straight defeats Conservatives were becoming more open-minded.

From a lifetime of courtroom and political practice, Diefenbaker had honed oratorical skills nobody in Parliament could match. His electrifying attacks in the Commons had left numerous Liberal ministers unhappy. As a mark of respect, they gerrymandered his riding early on, leaving him centred in the socialist bastion of Moose Jaw; but he was re-elected, regardless. In 1953, he ran and won in his home area of Prince Albert.

By the time of the Conservative leadership convention in December 1956, Diefenbaker had the backing of party stalwarts such as Gordon Churchill in Winnipeg, Major-General George Pearkes in B.C., and the party's acknowledged strategist, Toronto public relations pro Allister Grosart. George Hees had joined his camp, too, and Diefenbaker handily won the convention, with 774 votes to Fleming's 393 and Fulton's 117.

At the convention, Dief set the theme that would characterize his entire political career, and would set him apart from Louis St. Laurent and so many others: "one Canada." "The Conservative party will be the national party," he declared. "It is the party which founded Confederation and the party that will save Confederation…It is my intention to unite all Canadians from the Atlantic to the Pacific, under the banner of patriotism." Diefenbaker, though by far the most lethal Conservative debater in the House, had taken little part in the pipeline melee – presumably so as not to alienate Albertans. All the same, the imbroglio would serve him well as leader now that it was over.

The Pipeline Debate had been so over the top that it jarred Canadians into thinking about the purpose of Parliament, and how long the Liberals had been running the government.

High arctic anxiety

Fear of a Soviet attack leads to a North American technological marvel

by Craig Docksteader

The nuclear ashes at Nagasaki, Japan, had scarcely cooled after the Second World War when the Cold War broke out between western nations and Soviet Russia and her conquered satellites. For almost half a century, North America lived under a real threat of Soviet attack. Soviet citizens felt a reciprocal fear.

By 1949, it was known that the Soviets were developing nuclear bombs and aircraft capable of delivering them to North American targets. With Canada and Russia separated in the north by only a few hundred miles of icy ocean, the Canadian and U.S. governments were keenly aware that such an attack would come most easily from over the pole.

As a protective measure, they built a string of radar stations across the northern United States and southern Canada at about the 50th parallel. Known as the Pinetree Line, the radar system was to provide early detection of a Soviet bomber attack on North America.

But construction of that line had just started when the designers began to doubt it would be of much use. Faster, more powerful bomber jets were being developed, which meant that by the time attacking bombers were detected, it would be too late to stop them. Furthermore, the system used older radar technology that was easy to jam, and it could not detect low-flying targets.

To combat the increased threat, another line, known as the Mid-Canada Line, was built further north, running from Dawson Creek, B.C., across the north end of James Bay to the middle of the Labrador coast. Construction began in 1956, and by January 1, 1958, the line was fully operational.

But, once again, improvements in Soviet technology rendered the system less than effective before it was finished. An even earlier, costlier and more northern warning system was necessary.

In response, the Canadian and U.S. governments built a

third line – an integrated chain of 63 radar and communication systems stretching almost 10,000 kilometres along the continental coast of the Arctic Ocean, from Alaska to the eastern shore of Baffin Island. This became known as the Distant Early Warning Line, or DEW Line. (There are some stations further east, in Greenland and Iceland.)

More than 25,000 people were employed in the construction of the DEW Line in the harshest of conditions. Summers were short, winters were dark and long, temperatures were unbelievably cold and the amenities rustic.

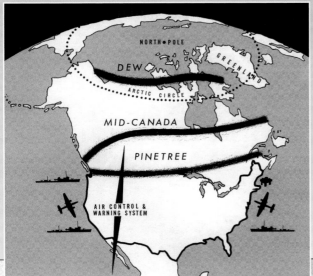

Construction crews lived in tents which housed up to four employees. Heat was provided by gravity-fed kerosene heaters, and washroom facilities consisted of outhouses. The line was built entirely within the Arctic Circle, and for much of the distance it crossed country that had not yet been explored.

The DEW Line was declared fully operational on July 31, 1957. It was the first line of air defence for the North American continent, and was considered an engineering marvel.

Quite quickly after its completion, however, the line lost much of its purpose. Fear of Soviet bomber attacks had given way to fear of intercontinental ballistic missiles. Most stations were retained, however, to monitor Soviet air activities and to assert Canada's sovereignty in the Arctic.

In 1985, eight Canadian DEW Line stations, along with five new ones, were upgraded into a North Warning System (NWS), and the rest were decommissioned and dismantled. After the Cold War ended in 1990, U.S. military personnel were pulled out, and the system was handed over to the Canadian Forces.

When the Distant Early Warning (DEW) Line was commissioned in 1957, it was a communications engineering marvel and the first line of defence against Soviet nuclear bombers. Within a few brief years it was rendered largely obsolete by the development of intercontinental ballistic missiles.

Photos - Wikimedia Commons / U.S Federal Government

It's time for a DIEFENBAKER Government

The polls didn't show it, but at a deep level public attitudes were shifting.

There was a growing sense – much expressed at the time – that the Liberals had become arrogant. What had looked like quiet confidence under King now smacked of unaccountable disregard. Perhaps voters were starting to resent the subtle Liberal trick of presenting themselves as defenders of the people against big business when talking to the people, and defenders of big business against the people when talking to big business.

But, above all, the Liberals had become the party of the civil service, if only because so many of them, starting long ago with King himself, had risen to political office through its senior echelons: Mitchell Sharp, Lester Pearson and Jack Pickersgill, to name only the most prominent at the time.

If there was one thing Diefenbaker wasn't, it was a representative of either big business or big government. With his arresting voice, fierce blue eyes, shaking jowls and long, accusatory finger, he would verbally flay his opponents.

"I'm not one of the Bay Street boys," he was wont to declare. "I'm not one of those six-bucks-a-month boys." (This was a reference to Liberals who argued the country could not afford to pay better old age pensions.) "I represent the average Canadian."

It was not an attitude people had associated with the Conservative party before, but in Dief's case they knew it was true. As a small-time criminal lawyer from a small city in a small province, Diefenbaker championed individual freedom, racial equality, one Canada and reasonable material security for all citizens.

■ ■ ■ ■

Dief hits the hustings in Toronto. As the Diefenbaker tide built across the country, crowds became ever younger and ever larger, culminating in the highest voter turnout in Canadian history.

Photo - Diefenbaker Centre

In Liberal hindsight, it might have been better if St. Laurent, now 75, had retired before calling an election in 1956. Perhaps he couldn't. Having been so successful for so long, the Liberal Party was suddenly revealed as hollowed-out and top-heavy, softened by easy victories. Dief and his grassroots Conservatives stormed the country with new ideas, new energy and a new sense of righteous rage.

Even then, media and pollsters did not expect the upset. The overall Canadian economy was strong, and St. Laurent adopted a serene tone. Opening the 1957 campaign in Winnipeg, "Uncle Louis" recited a well-known couplet by the poet Robert Browning: "Grow old along with me. The best is yet to be."

But in saying it, he may only have reminded people that he had been born before the Riel Rebellion. By 1957, most Canadians were watching news on television, and they were struck by how old he looked.

Indeed, everything the Liberals did reinforced the Tory message that the Grits had been in power too long. They appeared not to care, for example, that prairie grain had once again backed up, leaving huge piles of rotting wheat in farmyards, exposed to the weather, and leaving farmers – and the whole prairie economy – strapped for cash.

Newspapers across Canada reported a telling campaign incident. Trade minister C.D. Howe, confronted by a distraught farmer in Carman, Manitoba, patted the man on the belly with the back of his hand and replied, "You look pretty well fed."

C.D. Howe (second from left) in 1955, meeting in Alberta with the president of Rolls Royce, Ernest Hives (left), Canadian Pacific Air president Grant McConachie (centre right) and Trans-Canada Airlines president Gordon McGregor. By the summer of 1957, grain was again backing up, where it often had to be piled in the open field, as at this Barons, Alberta, farm.

Photos - SAGM (top)
Provincial Archives of Alberta (bottom)

Throughout the 1950s, Canadians continued their love affair with the automobile. Here a family on holiday is checked by an Ontario Provincial Police officer for unrecorded reasons. Between 1950 and 1980, personal vehicle ownership rose from less than one car per five people, to more than one car per two people. It would remain at the higher level until the next century.

Photo - National Archives of Canada

In nearby Morris, Howe had to explain to an angry assembly of farmers why Canada could not afford to loan them cash against undelivered grain, as the Conservatives were promising. The meeting disintegrated into jeers and derision. When Howe invited the chairman of the local Liberal association to speak, the man launched into a tirade against the government. When someone else confronted the weary 71-year-old minister as he tried to leave the hall, Howe said, "Look here, my good man, when the election comes, why don't you just go away and vote for the party you support? In fact, why don't you just go away?"

Pundits were still predicting a minority Liberal government before the June election, but when ballots were counted, the unthinkable had occurred. The Conservatives had doubled their seat count to 112, compared to the Liberals' 104. The Liberals had lost.

Diefenbaker's 1957 victory came mainly from increased support in Ontario. Alberta stayed with the Social Credit, and Quebec with the Liberals. Incapable of speaking even passable French, Dief had ignored Quebec in the campaign, and with his constant "one-Canada" emphasis, was taken to be anti-French. His few Quebec seats were in English-speaking areas.

Diefenbaker immediately assembled a cabinet with impressive regional balance and parliamentary experience, and legislation poured from Parliament as it had never done under the Liberals: cash loans for prairie farmers and an aggressive grain-sales campaign in Europe, revitalization of Cape Breton coal mines, a 2-percent cut in personal income tax and an increase in exemptions for low-income Canadians, a pay raise for the civil service, more support for veterans, pensioners and the disabled, low-interest housing loans, and competition in airline services.

The Liberals were left stunned by their loss, and had forgotten how to oppose in Parliament, especially against such a torrent of activity. In September, at age 75, St. Laurent at last retired, and in January of 1958 Lester ("Mike") Pearson took over. He was opposed by former Cabinet colleague Paul Martin Sr., but few doubted that Pearson was the best man available. Howe had already been defeated, and a number of other war-era heavyweights would soon retire or lose.

Lester B. Pearson returning from Norway in December 1957, having won his Nobel Prize for his masterful work solving the Suez Crisis. On the left is former Health and Welfare minister Paul Martin Sr., on the right former prime minister Louis St. Laurent. All three now found themselves quite unexpectedly in Opposition. Martin was Pearson's main rival to succeed St. Laurent the following month, but came a distant second.

Photo - National Archives of Canada

Prime Minister Diefenbaker addresses the House of Commons, October 1957. Though he commanded only a weak minority, Pearson gave him the chance he was seeking for a second election.

Photo - National Archives of Canada

However, old attitudes die hard. Pearson's first act in Parliament was to introduce a remarkably ill-advised motion that rather than call another election, the Conservatives simply return the government to the Liberals, because only they (Pearson argued) knew how to run it. Diefenbaker was both outraged and elated. He went immediately to the Governor General, and was granted a second election.

Canadians had learned enough about Diefenbaker by now to be interested in him. Interest soon grew to enthusiasm, and enthusiasm to wild approval. While his cabinet ministers crossed the country making one aggressive policy promise after another – wheat sales to China, new roads to northern resources, and more – Canadians turned out in hundreds and then thousands to hear "Dief the Chief."

In many ways, it was a return to an earlier era of stump speeches. In other ways, it was a harbinger of the "Trudeaumania" that swept Canada a decade later. The whole country, including Quebec, came onside.

Even Dief's harshest critics acknowledged that he was, if nothing else, an absolutely brilliant campaigner. "I don't think he ever recognized the line between campaigning for votes and running the country," recalled NDP leader David Lewis in his 1981 memoirs entitled *The Good Fight*, "but he was a spell-binder on the platform, mixing indignation, vision and wit into a powerful brew."

The Springhill Mine Disaster

Amid a Nova Scotia tragedy, a daring rescue thrills the world

by Craig Docksteader

They said the older miners could feel it coming. The coal mines of Springhill, Nova Scotia, had experienced disaster before – twice – and some were anticipating a third.

Springhill is a town north of Halifax, on the land bridge connecting Nova Scotia and New Brunswick.

The first disaster, back in 1891, had been a fire. Coal dust had ignited, causing fire to sweep through the mine, killing 125 miners and injuring dozens more. It was the largest disaster in Canadian mining history up to that time. (A worse one in 1914, at Hillcrest in southwest Alberta, killed 189.)

The second tragedy came in 1956. A mine train hauling a load of coal dust to the surface met a draft of air coming down, spreading the highly explosive dust through the shaft. This alone would have passed without incident, had several of the cars not broken loose at the same time, rolled backwards, derailed and hit a power line. Sparks ignited the coal dust, creating an enormous blast which trapped miners and destroyed buildings on the surface. Thirty-nine men died.

This time, in 1958, the disaster would come as a "bump" in Colliery 2. Bumps are seismic shifts – like minor earthquakes – which would rattle the windows in the town. A heave in the earth below the mine shaft would cause the rock floor to break upwards, destroying support beams and caving in tunnels. At a depth of 1.2 kilometres, with sloped tunnels more than 4 kilometres long, Colliery 2 was one of the deepest coal mines in the world. The coal wall was being mined along high underground galleries opening off the entrance shafts.

Bumps were common. In the seven months prior to the 1958 disaster, there had been 17 of them in Colliery 2, injuring 49 miners and killing one. For the most part, they were small tremors, but occasionally there would be a larger one, such as one on December 7, 1954, which killed five men.

The worst came on October 23, 1958, beginning with a small bump around 7 p.m. The miners were startled, but when nothing came of it they resumed work. Then, at 8:05 p.m., the most severe bump in North American mining history hit the Springhill mine.

Blackened by coal dust and plainly exhausted, mine rescuer John Totten reports progress to his brother William in the 1958 "bump" that killed 75 men at Springhill. William was caught in the original cave-in, rescued, and then joined the rescue effort.

Rescuers carry out one of the survivors of the 1956 explosion.

Photos - Canadian Press Images

As described by Melissa Fay Greene in her book *Last Man Out* (2003), it was not that there was a cave-in, but that the floor heaved upwards. "The deepest stone floor rose faster than an elevator…Men found themselves riding toward the ceilings upon the surging floors. They closed their eyes and held their breath against impact and instant death. In a few odd sections, the floor shot up and then stopped just shy of the roof. It was the only reason anyone survived."

One hundred and seventy-four men were in the mine that night. Only 100 got out alive, and one of them died later of his injuries.

Rescue workers went in immediately, even though the danger remained extreme. Another bump could cave in more of the mine, or they could be caught in a pocket of deadly methane gas released by shifting rock. More than once, rescue managers from outside the community tried to stop the search. But the miners refused.

News of the disaster spread quickly, the media arrived, and it became an international news story that gripped viewers around the world. After four days, the chance of finding survivors was becoming remote. Eighty-one miners had been rescued so far, and the remaining 93 were probably dead. The mood was grim. With hope fading, the media began to pull out.

As long as there were men in the mine, the rescuers pressed on. Two days later, they were rewarded when they heard voices.

Twelve men were discovered more than three kilometres in. They had been trapped for six days without food or water. The media rushed back to the mine, and people around the world rejoiced. Two days after that, seven more miners were found alive.

These were the last men saved. The last body was recovered on November 6. The mine was then sealed and never reopened.

Coal mining, however dangerous, provided badly needed economic opportunity. Not far away, at Stellarton, Curragh Resources of Toronto opened the Westray Mine in 1991. Miners complained almost immediately about dangerous levels of coal dust and lax safety standards, and eight months later a methane explosion killed 26 men. Eleven bodies were not recovered before the mine was sealed. Two managers were criminally charged with manslaughter, but after much legal manoeuvring the charges were dropped for lack of sufficient evidence.

1. Media coverage of Springhill was so heavy that the governor of Georgia, Marvin Griffin, seeking to promote state tourism, invited some of the surviving Nova Scotia miners for a free visit to his state. One of the invitees was Maurice Ruddick, who, upon reaching the surface of the mine, had said all he wanted was a cold 7Up. Governor Griffin, whose state was still racially segregated, was appalled and embarrassed to learn that Ruddick was black.

Diefenbaker's win in 1957 was dismissed by some, even in his own party, as fluke luck. This was clearly not the case as he steamrolled to the biggest victory in Canadian electoral history in 1958. The more people heard about him, the more they wanted to see him, and he drew crowds everywhere, here in the Regina armoury, and in a Prince Edward Island schoolyard.

Photos - Diefenbaker Centre

"For all his oratorical spellbinding and talent for political guerilla warfare," observed UBC poet and literary critic George Woodcock in *Canada and the Canadians* (1970), "Diefenbaker belonged to an age that was already past. He was – in spite of the Conservative label – the last of the great prairie radicals."

On March 31, 1958, Canadians voted the Conservatives back into office with the biggest federal majority of all time – 78 percent of the seats (208 out of a total of 265), with 54 percent of the popular vote. (The closest parallel would come in 1984, when another Conservative, Brian Mulroney, led the party to take 75 percent of the seats, with 50 percent of the popular vote.)

Diefenbaker's campaign brought out the highest percentage of eligible voters in Canadian history – 79.4 percent, compared to a middling 75.7 percent in the Trudeaumania election of 1968.

"An examination of the returns shows that the Liberals and the CCF in their best strongholds mustered as many votes as they had previously," wrote Milton MacKaye in the *Saturday Evening Post*. "Sometimes more. Yet they went down to defeat. Obviously, thousands of young new voters, and older people who had never voted before, turned up at the polling places to go on the record for Diefenbaker."

With nine former ministers defeated and only 48 seats, the Liberals found themselves as weak as George Drew's Conservatives in 1953. The CCF had been crushed to a mere eight MPs, and the Social Credit had vanished from Parliament entirely. Bringing in so massive a majority presented perils, however, especially for a party that had spent most of the century opposing rather than governing.

Most hazardous was the problem of inflated expectations – the natural assumption that someone so popular will perform extraordinarily well. Such hopes were soon dashed. Diefenbaker's majority, which had germinated with such vigour as a minority, almost immediately encountered a series of calamities, not all of its own making. Yet even sympathetic chroniclers such as Thomas Van Dusen, in *The Chief* (1968), later conceded that Diefenbaker too often mismanaged key issues and people.

When Pearson the year before demanded the government step aside, Diefenbaker had rounded on him, accusing the Liberals of having hidden a warning emanating from their finance ministry that the economy was heading into recession. It was true.

As with R.B. Bennett in 1930, Conservatives had once again risen to power just as the economy took a prolonged dive. It didn't crater completely as it had in 1930, but the long post-war boom was now over. As unemployment rose from 3.4 percent in 1956 to 7.4 percent in 1961, the CBC routinely ran dismal footage of soup kitchens while the opposition Liberals, as oppositions do, blamed the government alternately for not spending enough and for spending too much.

However, the Diefenbaker government could hardly be accused of underspending. It ran a series of annual deficits running some 10 percent over revenues. Yet the employment situation just got worse. When Diefenbaker raised Unemployment Insurance benefits to $36 a month from $30, the Liberals accused him of bankrupting the federal plan. Had he not,

By 1959, when Diefenbaker was made an honorary chief of the Sioux near Outlook, Saskatchewan, he had already been nicknamed Dief the Chief, for reasons of his flamboyant egocentrism. But Dief felt a strong obligation to Canadian aboriginals, an unusual sentiment for that time. In 1958 he appointed the first aboriginal senator, James Gladstone of the Bloods in Alberta. In 1960 his government extended the right to vote to treaty Indians.

Photo - Diefenbaker Centre

Diefenbaker, now commanding the biggest majority in Canadian history, welcomes Governor General Vincent Massey to Parliament to deliver the Throne Speech, May 1958.

they'd have accused him of letting the unemployed starve.

The Social Credit premier of Alberta, Ernest Manning – among others – chided the government for borrowing such ruinous amounts of money, and a large portion of Dief's Cabinet silently agreed. But the deficits continued.

With the economy shrinking, one of the first things Diefenbaker had to do was cancel the Avro Arrow, a cutting-edge interceptor jet developed by A.V. Roe Canada Ltd. in Toronto. It was now ready for production, and would employ 13,000 workers. This was another matter the Liberals had neglected to mention before the 1957 election. Newly designed surface-to-air missiles had rendered the Arrow obsolete. Allied governments didn't want it, and without foreign sales Canada could not afford to build it. (see page 42)

When Diefenbaker announced that A.V. Roe would be given other procurement contracts to cushion the blow of cancellation, company president Gordon Crawford took that to mean the project would continue, and began running ads to ensure it did. When the government then stated clearly that the Arrow project was finished, an enraged Gordon announced over the plant loudspeaker that all 13,000 workers were now laid off. Ontario politicians and newspapers then complained that Diefenbaker had not provided the promised alternative work.

It was a public relations disaster for the government, though plenty of commentators at the time congratulated Diefenbaker for having the courage to deal such a hard blow to the only part of Canada that had reliably voted Conservative for longer than anyone could remember.

The third Liberal land mine to blow up in Diefenbaker's face was the curious affair of Bank of Canada governor James Coyne. The bank had been a government-owned but generally autonomous institution that had quietly overseen Canadian currency and credit since 1938. In 1955, St. Laurent's government appointed Coyne, a long-time senior employee with an impressive resumé, to run it.

Coyne was a westerner from Winnipeg, a Rhodes Scholar and a Second World War air force

An arrow falls to earth

The bitter demise of Canada's cutting-edge jet fighter

by Craig Docksteader

On October 4, 1957, the Royal Canadian Air Force (RCAF) rolled out the very first Canadian supersonic airplane. Dubbed the Avro Arrow, the jet fighter was in a class of its own, capable of flying at twice the speed of sound and packed with cutting-edge technology.

Over the four years it had taken to become a reality, the Arrow had fired the military pride and imagination of Canadians. It had become a symbol of our national ambition in technological leadership, military power and political relevance in the post-war era.

Few Canadians understood, however, the speed and escalating cost of Cold War technological innovation.

The Soviets had detonated their first atomic bomb in 1949, and were building heavy bombers capable of reaching targets in the United States. The U.S. and its allies felt they were facing a very real threat of Soviet nuclear attack.

In April of 1953, the RCAF issued specification requirements for a new fighter jet surpassing anything in the western world. It commissioned A.V. Roe Canada Ltd., an impressive wartime military aircraft company in Malton, northwest of Toronto, to embark on a $118-million development and testing program that would produce 40 new CF-105 "interceptors." Avro had already designed, and was producing, a smaller and slower jet fighter, the CF-100 Canuck. It produced almost 700 of these, but by 1953 they were already becoming obsolete. The Avro Arrow was the logical next step.

Within months of the program's inauguration, the Soviets unveiled a new jet-powered bomber, the Myasishchev M-4 "Bison," which was soon followed by the "Bear" – the Soviet's most formidable bomber of the Cold War era. This development sharpened the sense of urgency for Canada to develop a supersonic interceptor.

Unfortunately, the Avro Arrow soon became dogged by escalating costs and lengthening development times. That summer, Avro revised its cost estimates upwards to $153 million, and later to $298 million. To spread the costs out, Liberal Defence Minister Ralph Campney began slowing the program down, and reducing the number of aircraft on order. It was about this time that the first rumours of cancellation began to circulate.

On June 10, 1957, Canada had its first change of government in 22 years. Conservative Prime Minister John Diefenbaker

The first Avro Arrow emerges from production in October 1957. By September 1958 it was clear to the Diefenbaker government that the cutting-edge interceptor jets were already obsolete. The sixth aircraft was a week from completion when the government scrapped the program.

Diefenbaker paid a heavy political price for terminating a high-tech aeronautics program so heavily invested with Canadian hope and pride. Though Canada retained an aviation-manufacturing industry, most of the best talent was soon drawn to the U.S. and Britain.

Photos - National Archives of Canada

defeated the Liberals, capturing 111 seats out of 265. Even though the Conservatives had campaigned on a promise to reduce defence spending, they let the Arrow project proceed, knowing how popular it was.

The official rollout of the Avro Arrow followed on October 4, 1957. Among 12,000 onlookers were throngs of media, government and industry representatives. But, as it turned out, media coverage was overshadowed by a more ominous event: the Soviet launch of *Sputnik 1* on the same day.

Six initial Arrow jets performed reasonably well during 71 hours of test flights. There were technical problems, but they were surmountable. However, even had landing gear and other problems been fixed, the aircraft was now doomed.

Though federal politicians would be blamed, the doom of the Arrow program was sealed by Sputnik. It meant that the Communists would soon be able to deliver nuclear weapons by unmanned rockets in mere minutes. The Avro Arrow, designed to intercept bombers, could not stop warheads from space.

The following March, Diefenbaker's Conservative party defeated the Liberals again, this time winning 208 seats in the 265-seat House of Commons. Now Diefenbaker could make a decision on the Arrow, and he did.

With the threat of a Soviet missile attack growing, the U.S. was automating its air-defence system. It had established radar and control systems along its northern border to detect and intercept

Soviet missiles. Nuclear-tipped anti-aircraft missiles would be launched from the U.S. and intercept incoming Soviet missiles.

The problem was, from the Canadian perspective, that the interception would occur over Canada.

The solution was straightforward: launch defence missiles from Canada, pushing the interception point further north. The U.S. proposed that if Canada would install new radar, control systems and defensive Bomarc missiles, it would share the cost. With the use of the Bomarc missiles, Canada would need only 100 interceptor jets instead of 300, which the U.S. offered to sell to Canada at a price lower than the Arrow.

On September 23, 1958, Diefenbaker announced that the government had decided to build two missile bases in Canada, and that the Arrow program was going to be reviewed. In spite of the ensuing intensive public relations campaign by Avro, the government terminated the Avro Arrow program on February 20, 1959, and subsequently instructed Avro to destroy anything and everything related to its production. The project that had vaulted Canada to the front ranks of military aircraft design and brought together some the best engineering minds on the continent was over in less than a year after the Arrow's maiden flight.

With no work left to do in Canada, hundreds of aeronautics and weapons specialists moved to the U.S. and Britain. Many Canadians never forgave either Diefenbaker or his party for the decision.

veteran. Unbeknownst to the Liberals or anyone else, however, he harboured unorthodox, very nationalist ideas and opinions. While Finance Minister Donald Fleming did what all governments do in a recession and borrowed money, Coyne should have lowered interest rates to stimulate consumption and capital investment. But this would have devalued the Canadian dollar, and Coyne feared that a weak dollar would allow even more Canadian industry to be bought by Americans. He insisted on maintaining high interest rates and a strong dollar. Ottawa should keep the dollar strong, he argued, even if it meant restricting foreign investment, nationalizing industry and enforcing disciplined levels of productivity and consumption. Otherwise, the country would be purchased and eventually annexed by the United States.

By 1961, the issue had escalated into a full-blown crisis, with Coyne going on an unprecedented speaking tour, leaving large numbers of people either baffled or alarmed. Twenty-nine prominent economists published a letter saying he should be fired. Most sensible people agreed, but Diefenbaker and Fleming said only Parliament had the power to do it. The House of Commons then did vote to fire him. Though the bill stalled in the Senate, Coyne resigned anyway.

Coyne may not have been entirely wrong. Within a year, the Canadian dollar had sunk to US$.925, and some of the austerities Coyne was demanding of governments had to be implemented to save it from sinking further.

All these crises – unemployment, the Avro Arrow cancellation, the deficits, the devaluaton – took a heavy political toll. In too many minds, Diefenbaker still appeared to be in opposition, not government. By the time an election loomed in 1962, public confidence, especially in Ontario and Quebec, had been shaken.

Finance minister Donald Fleming and Bank of Canada governor James Coyne. Though the eccentric ideas and behaviour came from Coyne, a Liberal appointee, the Diefenbaker government ended up bearing the blame.

Photo - National Archives of Canada

In addition to the obvious, there were subtle but serious problems in the background. The Conservative government was seen as an intruder by the public sector. The CBC, for one, took an openly antagonistic stance, which Diefenbaker chose to ignore. Moreover, when the government cleaned up the Liberals' blatant patronage system in Quebec and the Atlantic, spending discretion went by default to the public service, which was itself heavily Liberal and behaved accordingly, causing political loss to the Conservatives in those regions. There was frequent miscommunication between the Conservative Cabinet and Ottawa's civil-service mandarins, who did not think the same way; the latter did not understand or sympathize with the new government's political imperatives. Perhaps unavoidably, this made the Conservatives appear inept.

Dief took to the hustings in April with his trademark thunder, energy and personality, but with far less success than four years earlier. When the votes were counted, he was reduced to a 116-seat minority government, facing 99 Liberals under Pearson.

One significant result of the 1962 election was the revival of the CCF, which in the previous year had joined forces with the Canadian Labour Congress to form the New Democratic Party. Under the leadership of former Saskatchewan premier Tommy Douglas, it now boasted 19 seats. The Social Credit were back in Parliament too, with four seats from the West and 26 from Quebec.

■ ■ ■ ■

The Co-operative Commonwealth Federation (CCF) party, which had languished during the prosperous 1950s, took advantage of labour unrest during the economic downturn to reconstitute itself as the New Democratic Party in 1961. Its first leader was Tommy Douglas, long-time Premier of Saskatchewan.

The St. Lawrence Seaway

Canada pushes an impressive mid-century mega-project to completion

by Craig Docksteader

From the deck of his small vessel in 1541, the wilderness cataract blocking his two ships can't have looked to French explorer Jacques Cartier much like the Orient, but he called them "China Rapids" anyway. Seeking a navigable route to the riches of Cathay, he had sailed up (and named) the St. Lawrence River, until the Lachine Rapids at present-day Montreal forced him to turn around.

For the next two centuries, men dreamed of opening a shipping route, or seaway – if not to China, then at least to the industrial heartland of the New World.

The upper half of the St. Lawrence, from Lake Ontario down to Montreal, lies between Ontario and New York, making it an international waterway. In 1954, a long-awaited agreement between Canada and the U.S. made the seaway possible.

Negotiations had been ongoing for over 62 years, but U.S. politicians faced intense opposition from a range of railroads, port facilities and even automakers. Eventually, mineral discoveries in remote Labrador caused the Canadian government to threaten to build the seaway entirely within Canadian territory, and so the American government moved ahead.

It was one of the largest civil-engineering feats ever tackled, taking almost five years to complete. It employed more than 22,000 workers, and utilized enough cement to build a highway 1,000 miles long and enough steel to encircle the globe. Bridges were built without interrupting the existing flow of traffic. Tunnels, dikes and roads had to be constructed. Entire communities had to be relocated, displacing 6,500 people.

Existing canals, built since the early 1800s, would have to be deepened to 8.2 metres, permitting the passage of ocean-going vessels up to 225.5 metres long and 23.8 metres wide. Seven locks would have to be built – two on the U.S. side and five on the Canadian. In total, seaway locks could raise and lower ships a total of 270 metres, and each new lock could do its job in seven minutes. The size of the project surpassed anything in operation around the world.

On June 26, 1959, President Dwight D. Eisenhower and Queen Elizabeth II, on board the royal yacht *Britannia*, officially opened the St. Lawrence Seaway. The cost was US$470 million (about $4 billion in 2008) – 70 percent of which was paid by Canada.

Two heads of state, Elizabeth II and President Dwight D. Eisenhower, meet in 1959 to open one of the biggest civil-engineering projects in history.

Both the U.S. and Canada wanted the Seaway to repay its cost over 50 years by collecting tolls. However, for many years toll revenues consistently fell far short of annual operating costs and interest payments. Instead of paying off its debt, the Seaway was going in deeper.

It never did repay its capital cost, and it wasn't until the 1970s that tolls began to keep pace with the operational costs. In 1977, the Canadian government converted the Canadian Seaway Authority's debt to equity held by Canada, but required that toll revenues cover all operating and maintenance costs. This change was successful, bringing stability to the Seaway's financial position.

The seaway at Montreal when opened. This is one of seven locks that could raise and lower saltwater freighters a total of 270 metres.

Photos - National Archives of Canada (opposite); Canadian Press images (above)

D iefenbaker's third government soon faced even worse problems than his second. Costly Conservative election promises had to be quickly abandoned as the dollar sank. That was bad enough, but worse was the deterioration of relations with the United States.

As far back as Prime Minister John A. Macdonald, Conservatives – unlike Liberals – had viewed the Americans as rivals more than as allies, and now increasingly as bullies. This had continued under Diefenbaker, who was more devoted to the British Empire – now the Commonwealth – than were the British themselves.

Washington had been particularly angered in 1961 when Canada contracted a large portion of its wheat surplus for sale to Communist mainland China, contrary to U.S. trade policy. Relations were further strained by an intense personal dislike between Diefenbaker and U.S. president John F. Kennedy. Diefenbaker privately considered Kennedy a brash Yankee blowhard who was deliberately offensive, and Kennedy privately considered Diefenbaker a crank and "a platitudinous bore."

U.S. president John F. Kennedy and his wife Jackie visit Ottawa, May 1961. The two leaders disliked each other, and had very different approaches to global defence against the Communist threat.

Photo - National Archives of Canada

Such personal pettiness attained terrifying public significance on Monday, October 22, 1962, when the Cuban Missile Crisis erupted.

Aware that the Soviet Union was shipping ballistic missiles to its Cuban ally, in easy striking distance of the North American mainland, President Kennedy ordered a U.S. naval blockade of the island republic, and ordered a continental state of military alert known as Defence Condition 3, meaning complete readiness to engage the enemy.

Defence Minister Douglas Harkness, a Calgary MP and decorated army commander in the Second World War, was obliged by mutual defence protocols to make the order, and was ready to do it. However, Diefenbaker and his External Affairs minister, Howard Green, were ill-disposed to being ordered about by the Americans on 90 minutes' notice, and refused to comply. In general, they disapproved of the confrontational U.S. approach to Communist countries. Though Dief had no sympathy himself for Communists – in the UN, he excoriated the Soviets for their human rights atrocities – he nevertheless preferred negotiation to belligerence.

For four long days, Soviet warships cruised towards Cuba, Dief urged Parliament not to panic and Canadians lived in waking fear of all-out nuclear war. It remained unclear whether the Canadian forces were on DEFCON 3 alert or not. This, by itself, alarmed and infuriated the American government, and dismayed many in the Canadian Cabinet – not least Defence Minister Harkness and his associate minister, Pierre Sévigny.

The U.S. warship *Vesole* intercepts the Soviet freighter *Polzunov* off the Cuban coast on November 10, 1962, loaded with what appear to be covered missiles. The Americans already had aerial intelligence photos of Soviet vessels in Cuba's Mariel Naval Port offloading nuclear infrastructure. Washington did not take kindly to Diefenbaker's reluctance to declare a state of maximum alert, and his proposal for a "fact-finding" mission. The Americans said they had already found out the facts, and expected Canada to stand ready for nuclear war.

Photos - Canadian Press Images

The Americans were further exasperated when Diefenbaker suggested that an international team visit Cuba to ascertain "the facts." Washington felt it had already published the facts, and that the showdown with the Kremlin demanded the unanimous support of all free nations, especially its northern neighbour. To many Canadians, Diefenbaker appeared impractical and irresolute. That impression lasted long after the Soviets backed down and turned their ships around.

The Cuban crisis was soon over, but the Cold War nuclear faceoff kept escalating.

In December, Diefenbaker further disconcerted domestic and foreign opinion by dropping in uninvited on a mini-summit in Nassau, Bahamas, between Kennedy and British Prime Minister Harold Macmillan, who had met to discuss nuclear strategy. Diefenbaker warned them that Canada would not be anyone's geopolitical pawn, and upon his return to Ottawa announced to the world that the two leaders had quietly decided to install nuclear arms in India. (The Indian government had not yet been told.) The U.S. State Department publicly rebuked Diefenbaker, and Diefenbaker recalled Canada's U.S. ambassador – a move just short of breaking off diplomatic relations.

Driving all this was a spreading public dread of global nuclear war. Intercontinental ballistic missiles (ICBMs) with multiple warheads were already being

After the Cuban crisis, Dief showed up uninvited at a Nassau meeting between Kennedy and British prime minister Harold Macmillan. More international diplomatic turbulence followed. Behind much of the friction was the Bomarc missile, pictured here with Canadian insignia in 1962.

developed for deployment from both land and sea. The Cuban confrontation had demonstrated that the fate of the whole northern hemisphere was in the grip of a terrifying strategic stalemate between the superpowers called "mutually assured destruction."

In 1962, however, aircraft crossing the Arctic – not ICBMs – still posed the most viable delivery threat from the Soviet Union. The Americans had developed an unmanned interceptor missile, the Bomarc, to prevent bombers from reaching U.S. cities. It was the imminence of the Bomarc missile that had doomed the Canadian interceptor jet, the Avro Arrow.

Canada did not want the Americans blowing up nuclear-armed Soviet bombers over Canadian cities en route to New York and Los Angeles. After scrapping the Arrow, Diefenbaker had agreed in 1959 to allow 56 Bomarc missiles on Canadian soil at two bases well north of population centres – North Bay, Ontario, and several hundred miles to the east near Mont Tremblant, Quebec.

Urgent questions, however, remained unresolved. Would the Bomarcs, armed merely with sandbags for the moment, be equipped with conventional warheads or nuclear ones? If nuclear, would the decision to fire them remain in Washington? Given the receding nature of the bomber threat, as the superpowers shifted to ICBMs, was there any point deploying interceptor missiles at all?

A split already apparent in Diefenbaker's cabinet rapidly widened, with Harkness demanding to install nuclear Bomarcs, and Green and Diefenbaker balking and waffling.

It came to a head in January of 1963, when the U.S. State Department again publicly criticized the Canadian government – this time for indecision. This statement, later seen by many as sealing the doom of the Diefenbaker government, required Canadians to decide whether they were more afraid of the Americans or the Soviets, and by extension whether they felt more secure under the Liberals or the Conservatives.

The Liberals, accurately gauging the direction of public thinking, switched position to favour nuclear Bomarcs. The government remained indecisive.

The fortunes of the Diefenbaker government now collapsed. Harkness announced that the Bomarcs would be nuclear, while Diefenbaker announced that they would not. Harkness

Defence minister Douglas Harkness quit the Diefenbaker Cabinet over the Bomarc impasse, precipitating a steady exodus of ministers.

Photo - Glenbow Museum

went into a Cabinet meeting on February 3, rebuked Diefenbaker, resigned his Cabinet post and quit the caucus to sit as an independent MP. Associate Defence minister Pierre Sévigny – never a Diefenbaker enthusiast – quit too.

Dief had already had to squelch a fairly public caucus rebellion in mid-January. Four days later George Hees quarrelled with the leader over a minor difference, and resigned as trade minister. Davie Fulton then quarrelled over a similarly minor disagreement about deploying more RCMP to keep order in a Newfoundland strike, and he too made it clear he would quit, though not immediately. The chief commissioner of the RCMP, Leonard Nicholson, resigned too. Finally, long-time Finance minister Donald Fleming announced that for personal reasons he would not seek re-election.

It fell to Social Credit leader Robert Thompson of Alberta – silently backed, it is believed, by Alberta Social Credit Premier Ernest Manning – to deliver the final blow. He said his small caucus could no longer support Diefenbaker, and on February 5 he moved a motion of non-confidence that defeated the government by 142 votes to 111.

Diefenbaker, throughout the ensuing campaign, presented himself as a figure of tragic greatness, defiant against titanic forces and betrayed by fickle friends. The role, no doubt sincerely felt, made good theatre but ineffective politics. The Conservatives were defeated, especially in Ontario and Quebec, and would remain in opposition for two long decades.

Unhappily for the Liberals, however, Lester Pearson had proven as bad at campaigning as Diefenbaker was bad at governing.

Pearson was 66 years old, a career diplomat and natural conciliator, and was by nature affable and self-deprecating. He could not even begin to match the bombastic witticisms and stormy appeal of his opponent. Diefenbaker attacked and entertained, while Pearson lectured and explained. Although the Liberal Party had reorganized during its sojourn in the Opposition wilderness, several of its new American-style campaign tactics backfired, and it had not lost its old arrogant attitude of "Seriously, what other choice do you have?"

The Grits had gone into the 1963 campaign polling 44 percent support – 11 percent ahead of the Conservatives. In the April 8 election, they received 42 percent of the vote, missing the 7-percent campaign gain that had won them so many resounding victories in the past. Conservative support, meanwhile, held solid at 33 percent instead of evaporating, as the Liberals had expected.

As a result, the Liberals felt almost disappointed by their 1963 minority victory. Given how spectacularly the Diefenbaker government had failed, they had been confident of a strong majority. Though they had a fairly sturdy minority, their leader was a parliamentary featherweight compared to Diefenbaker, and though Diefenbaker was under serious internal attack, no very convincing leadership rival stood poised to replace him.

■ ■ ■ ■

End of an Era

By the campaigns of 1962 and 1963, Diefenbaker personified the end of an era. He was the last of the great prairie populist orators (though Preston Manning would come close 25 years later), and the last national leader to conduct his campaigns mainly by train. But even though he was clearly losing and increasingly out of date, he remained a formidable election-fighter. In small towns and large cities, crowds would invariably turn out, as in Quebec at right, Medicine Hat, Alberta (further right), and Nova Scotia (furthest right). The locations at bottom are unrecorded.

Photos - Diefenbaker Centre

From motorized dogsleds to jet aircraft

A Quebec entrepreneur founds a global transportation giant

by Craig Docksteader and Link Byfield

Joseph-Armand Bombardier of Quebec was a practical, determined innovator of a kind for which 20th-century Canada was justly famous.

Born to a large farming and storekeeping family in the Eastern Townships in 1907, his boyhood ambition was to create a mechanized sled that would float on snow. His original idea was to produce a motorized dogsled to replace the light dogsleds used by trappers, missionaries and prospectors in the North.

He failed at that – engines and tracks, in those days, were too heavy.

He was not alone. Others had been trying to design vehicles for snow travel. Adolphe Kégresse, a Frenchman and technical director in the imperial garage of Czar Nicholas II of Russia, is credited as being the first. In 1904, he installed a track drive around the rear wheels of a car, and put a pair of skis on the front for steering. In 1913, Virgil White, a Ford dealer in New Hampshire, devised a track-and-ski conversion kit for the Model T, and later the Model A. He succeeded in selling 20,000 of these in the 1920s, and patented the term "snowmobile."

But the designs were clumsy, and prone to breakage, belt slippage and plugging with snow. Bombardier, who apprenticed as a mechanic in the 1920s, wanted to do better. Working out of his small repair shop in Valcourt, Quebec, he designed a sprocket device that would resolve many of the earlier problems. The result, in 1937, was his first successful snowmobile, called the B7.

His original machines were large, multipassenger vehicles, built on a Ford chassis, with a plywood cabin shaped like a mighty Volkswagen Beetle. They were priced at just over $1,000 – the cost of a low-end automobile – and, at first, were purchased primarily by rural doctors who needed a more efficient means of transportation so that they could call on their patients.

Bombardier sold 12 units in 1937, and decided to go into production. Sales increased to 25 units in 1938, and 50 units in

Quebec innovator Joseph-Armand Bombardier and his large early-vintage snowmobile.

Photos - Canadian Press Images

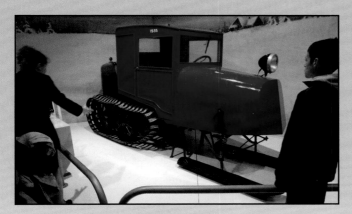

Touring Quebec students examine a 1935 prototype of the famous Ski-Doo. Success would have to wait for better small-engine technology and synthetic track materials in the 1950s.

1939. The customer base expanded to include taxi drivers, bus operators, innkeepers, funeral directors, milkmen and travelling salesmen. In the years to come, larger designs would be produced for a broadening array of applications, including public transport, freight transport, ambulance services and mail delivery.

There were setbacks. The first one came with the onset of the Second World War, when the government passed regulations to redirect national production away from civilian needs to military requirements. Bombardier's customers now had to demonstrate that a snowmobile was essential to their livelihood before the Department of Munitions and Supply would allow them to purchase one. Over the next year, production plummeted from 70 units to 27. To stay afloat, Bombardier began producing vehicles for the military, and he incorporated as L'Auto-Neige Bombardier Limitée to limit his personal liability.

The second setback followed the end of the war, when governments, including Quebec's, began plowing roads in winter, enabling people to drive their cars year-round. Once again, Bombardier's sales fell by half, prompting him to diversify again – this time into all-terrain vehicles designed for the mining, oil and forestry sectors. Soon, long trains of bobbing, growling blue Bombardiers hauling huge sleds along winter roads became a familiar sight all across the Canadian North.

But Bombardier's personal dream remained to develop a motorized dogsled – a fast, lightweight snowmobile for carrying one or two people. The emergence of smaller, more efficient engines in the late 1950s made this possible. After developing several prototypes with his oldest son Germain, the Ski-Doo hit the market in 1959. Its name was supposed to be the "Ski-Dog," but a typo in an early promotional brochure had it as "Ski-Doo," and Bombardier liked that better.

The Ski-Doo was a huge success. Sales started at 250 machines in the first year of production, and grew rapidly to 8,210 by year four. But Bombardier's enjoyment of his dream was to be cut short by his battle with cancer. He died on February 18, 1964, at the pinnacle of his career, leaving the thriving business to Germain.

With their domineering founder gone, Bombardier's sons and in-laws reorganized the company, computerized its production systems and went public in 1969. In 1970, they bought into rail transportation, and in 1986 into aerospace, buying in short succession Canadair, de Havilland and Learjet. By the turn of the century, Bombardier had become the third-largest civil aircraft manufacturer in the world, and a Fortune 500 company with over $15 billion in revenue and 50,000 employees.

In 2003, the Bombardier family came full circle when it bought back from the public company, Bombardier Inc., the recreational-vehicles division – the one that had started it all.

A Bombardier 90-passenger CRJ-900 jet takes off from Calgary.

There had been much soul-searching among Liberals since their ignominious double defeat in 1957 and 1958. Many older Liberals had quit in disgust. Meanwhile, a clique of younger, energetic newcomers, calling themselves Cell 13, had been holding earnest weekly strategy meetings to rebrand and rebuild. They were mostly men, mostly from Toronto and mostly lawyers and accountants.

They included people who soon became well-known, such as Gordon Dryden, Royce Frith and Keith Davey. They knew the party could not regain power unless they could recast it in a more contemporary mould, capable of capturing the increasingly fluid vote in Canada's expanding suburbs. In this, they were guided and encouraged by several key Liberal elder statesmen – chiefly, a Toronto financial power-broker named Walter Gordon, and, to a considerable degree, Gordon's close friend, Lester Pearson.

By 1960, as the Diefenbaker tailspin gathered speed, the Liberal new guard were organizing large national party assemblies, first in Kingston and then in Ottawa.

The Liberal Party, they were certain, could no longer succeed as the loose alliance of provincial patronage bosses it had been under Mackenzie King and St. Laurent. Patronage, said Davey, must be centrally controlled and dispensed by the party, not by regional Cabinet

Liberals promoting the party at the 1960 Calgary Stampede, and (opposite) Liberal strategist Keith Davey in the early 1960s. Despite obvious self-contradictions, the "new Liberalism" gradually caught on.

Photos - Glenbow Museum (above)
National Archives of Canada (opposite)

heavyweights. Liberalism must henceforth be grassroots-driven and genuinely democratic – more willing to undertake bold new national social measures, more open to the rising aspirations of Quebec, and more organized, centralized and professional.

That these new imperatives all contradicted each other did not discourage the widening circle of the new guard. It may not even have occurred to them. This was the "new politics."

As would become clear, however, the new Liberalism would prove even less democratic than the old Liberalism. It was designed in Toronto by Walter Gordon and executed from Ottawa by party organizer Keith Davey. It relied heavily on jargon and euphemisms such as "participation" and "manufactured consent" (manipulation), national recruitment of "star" candidates, and practical new methods of centralized party management.

As the Diefenbaker nova briefly lit the heavens and then faded, the new guard recruited vigorously and effectively, discovering, cajoling and promoting others like themselves across the country – John Turner and Maurice Sauvé in Quebec, James Coutts in Alberta, academic and journalist Tom Kent in Manitoba, Jack Davis and Jack Nicholson in British Columbia, and a small army in Ontario – Mitchell Sharp, Edgar Benson, Judy LaMarsh, Eugene Whelan, Pauline Jewett, Herb Gray, and dozens of others who soon took control of the party and then the country.

What most strikingly distinguished new Liberalism was its anti-American bias (previously a Conservative trait) and its faith in "progressivism": the idea that government – especially the national government – can and should lead and shape society. This set it apart from the Liberalism of King and St. Laurent, who were pro-American and still accepted that the main tasks of the national government were to defend the country, issue currency, set tariffs and deliver the mail.

Only three national social programs had been established during the long King-St. Laurent era: unemployment insurance (1941), family allowance (1944) and a minimalist federal old age pension (1952). Each had been undertaken carefully, parsimoniously and only after much negotiation with the provinces, who under the Constitution held exclusive responsibility for social affairs.

Before these three were created, provincial governments had been running rudimentary "mothers' allowance," poverty relief and old age annuity programs. But when the Depression of the 1930s threw 25 percent of Canadians out of work and 20 percent of Canadian families onto relief, a whole generation of policy-makers had concluded that the original 1867 Constitution didn't work. It came to be widely assumed in English Canada – though not in Quebec – that Ottawa was a better guarantor of social security than were the provinces on their own. The competence of the federal war effort confirmed this belief.

However, the Depression may have been more an excuse than a reason for overriding the Constitution. In a few years, the Depression was over and there was full employment again, and by the 1950s more prosperity than ever before. By now, provinces were funding an ever-larger share of an ever-costlier education system, as well as supervising and subsidizing various doctor-run health- and hospital-insurance schemes.

Complex calculations and bargains to divide fields of taxation and spending had been ongoing since the Rowell-Sirois Commission of 1937. Of necessity, Ottawa had almost doubled its share of taxes to fight the Second World War – from almost half of all Canadian taxes in 1937 (federal, provincial and municipal) to 81 percent in 1943.

Afterward, rather than reducing its take and returning "tax room" to lower levels so provinces could fund their own expanding programs, the federal government had been pushing into the social field itself. This had two effects. The first was to create a surge of taxation, starting in the 1950s and peaking in the 1970s. The second was to provoke separatism in Quebec.

Some – principally Alberta, Ontario and Quebec – wanted Ottawa to reduce its taxes

This class of Grade 3s in Edmonton's Strathearn elementary school, photographed in 1954, could have been taken anytime until the mid-1960s. By then an increasingly expensive education system was funded in less prosperous provinces by a new federal program called "equalization" Rather than restore "tax room" to the provinces after the Second World war, Ottawa – supported by provincial governments with below-average revenues – chose to spend its way into provincial social responsibilities, especially health, education and welfare.

Photos - Provincial Archives of Alberta

and let the provinces continue to make their own social provisions. The smaller and poorer provinces supported Ottawa providing equalized levels of funding which provinces could then administer. Ottawa, for obvious reasons, agreed with the smaller provinces, and the psychology of "national social programs" evolved steadily, almost inexorably, regardless of which federal party was in power.

In 1957, Ottawa came up with a complex formula, later dubbed Equalization, using federal funds to bring all provinces up to a common level of per-capita spending on health, education and welfare.

Whether "new guard" Liberals thought much about these constitutional matters is doubtful. They took it for granted that central management was "progressive," and that their minority win in 1963 gave them a mandate to go much further.

In addition to "national social programs," two themes would dominate the Pearson years: Canadian nationalism – a holdover from Diefenbaker – and Quebec nationalism, which was a new factor in federal politics. Both marked a departure from Liberal tradition.

Pearson came into office facing huge disadvantages. Scandals in his Quebec caucus soon dominated Parliament, opening the government to withering scorn from Diefenbaker. There was tense division in his own party between "old guard" and "new guard," continuing weakness in the economy and a serious budget deficit.

The disciplined arts

Culture gets a huge government boost to go in unpredictable directions

Culture, in the narrower sense of that very broad word, fairly exploded with new activity after the Second World War, right through to the 1980s.

The phenomenon reflected the prosperity, increased education, new attitudes, new technologies and youthful energy of the era.

Popular culture – i.e., that which is willingly paid for by its audience, such as rock music – flourished as never before (see page 74). But even the more elevated and aesthetic branches of culture – those subsidized by corporate and state patronage, such as theatre, dance, film, written music and literary publishing – thrived as well.

Professional theatre and symphony orchestras had been a normal part of life in Canada's larger cities since before the First World War. They now spread with astonishing vigour and determination to smaller centres, which hitherto had relied on amateur efforts or had gone without.

Between the late 1940s and early 1960s, professional symphony orchestras sprang up, for example, in Winnipeg, Victoria, Halifax, Edmonton, Moncton and Calgary.

Folk art and ethnic cultural festivals began popping up everywhere, especially with the adoption of official multiculturalism in the 1970s. Serious aboriginal artists, for the first time, found public appreciation for something other than phony tourist trinkets.

Theatre also burgeoned. In Ontario, the highly successful Stratford Festival opened in 1953, and the Shaw Festival at Niagara-on-the-Lake in 1962. Numerous smaller outdoor theatres were started, many of which, such as Winnipeg's Rainbow Stage (1954), were still going strong into the 21st century. By the end of the period, no significant Canadian city lacked a professional theatre troupe, and most had several.

The Royal Winnipeg Ballet, founded in 1939, started touring

Above, Governor General Vincent Massey, whose 1951 royal commission on the arts set the policy for half a century. Below, National Gallery director Alan Jarvis, left, views a Tom Thomson painting with Group of Seven artist A.Y. Jackson.

Photos - Canadian Press Images

Left, a meeting of the minds in the Royal Ontario Museum, 1959. Right, a new and struggling Montreal novelist, Mordecai Richler, promoting his 1957 book *A Choice of Enemies*.

Photos - National Archives of Canada

after the war. It was such a hit in Toronto in 1949 that the city started its own company, the National Ballet, in 1951.

Two post-war milestones could be said, in hindsight, to have set the tone – one official, and the other quite scandalous.

The official one, very significant at the time, was a vast federal royal commission report on the arts chaired by the austere Vincent Massey, a one-time amateur actor, former president of the Massey-Harris farm equipment company, a patron of artists and a future Governor General.

The thrust of his extensive report in 1951 was that only the public support of key cultural media and the disciplined arts could defend Canada from the materialist pathologies pouring north from the United States. That led to the formation of the Canada Council for the Arts as a national funding agency in 1957, and the notional conscription of cultural enterprise, from broadcast giants to mad sculptors with welding torches, to defend national culture. Whether it was to defend Canadians from American republicanism or just from American bad taste was never made clear. Neither has it ever been possible to

assess how much difference it has made.

The unofficial milestone was the publication, in 1948, of a wild, 3,300-word Quebec manifesto entitled *Refus global* ("Total Refusal") by 16 overexcited Quebec artists and intellectuals, deriding and condemning religion, reason, private property, war, consumerism and traditional morality – in Quebec and around the world.

Though it's hard to take it seriously over half a century later, it caught a lot of attention at the time – in Canada, the U.S. and France. In considerable measure, its celebration of "glorious anarchy" set (or at least anticipated) the tone of much of what taxpayers would end up subsidizing in the 1960s and long thereafter.

It could be said that Vincent Massey provided the canvas, and *Refus global* the painting.

Not that Canadian arts have ever been primarily state-financed, or entirely dedicated to anarchism. They have become far too diverse for any simple statement of purpose, or any cost-benefit calculation.

Lester Bowles "Mike" Pearson was personally as underwhelming as Diefenbaker was the opposite. Yet in five years his two minority governments, despite many stumbles and scandals, accomplished an astonishing list of achievements. In both social and language policy, Pearson more than anyone could claim to be the architect of modern Canada.

Parliament opened in the spring of 1963 with "sixty days of decision," an unabashed Liberal plagiarism of Kennedy's "one hundred days of decision" three years earlier.

The Liberals' arch-nationalist was Toronto strategist Walter Gordon, the man who had worked so long and hard with Keith Davey to reorganize and revitalize the party. He was now rookie MP for the Toronto riding of Davenport, and Pearson's finance minister.

In May, on Day 53 of the 60, he brought down a budget introducing, among other nationalist measures, a new 30-percent tax on foreign takeovers of Canadian companies. But like the departed Bank of Canada governor James Coyne, Gordon would soon discover the political limits of economic nationalism.

Provincial governments, all of which were courting American capital to develop their resources, were infuriated. So too were Canadian businesses anxious to preserve their capital value. So too were the federal mandarins, schooled on the King-St. Laurent doctrine of continentalism. Pearson himself was skeptical. Such a tide of opposition arose that the budget had to be rescinded, stripped of its most egregious measures, and reintroduced. Had the Opposition wanted an election, it probably could have forced one.

The budget fiasco was followed by provincial rejection of another grand innovation by another rookie minister, Niagara Falls MP Judy LaMarsh: a new federal Canada Pension Plan. It too angered the provinces, especially Quebec, and had to be withdrawn and redesigned. That rejection in turn delayed – and could have killed – another touted Liberal invasion of provincial constitutional turf: Medicare.

Measures such as these prompted many to brand Pearson a socialist. But in his heart of hearts, he was neither a socialist nor an economic nationalist. According to one who knew him well – Jack Pickersgill, a civil service and Cabinet fixture since 1945 – Pearson was a "status nationalist."

Pickersgill meant that Pearson cared more about the symbols of national sovereignty than the substance of it. "Nationalism" to him meant erasing the British symbols of Canada's past, not about preventing American influence in the future. Pearson assumed American influence was here to stay – and that it was generally good.

In fact, the first thing he did as prime minister was to restore friendly relations with President Kennedy, and give way on Bomarc missiles. He allowed NORAD (i.e., the U.S.) to arm the missiles with nuclear warheads, and control them. They remained in place, and unused, until 1971.

Pearson's reversal on nuclear warheads had come on January 12, 1963, before the election. It cost the Liberals

An early star of the Liberal restoration was Finance minister Walter Gordon, a personal friend and an ardent economic nationalist. His attempts to fence out American investors created a furor among provincial governments and business lobbies, forcing Pearson to backtrack.

Photo - National Archives of Canada

support in Quebec, at least briefly, infuriating such potential star Liberal candidates as labour leader Jean Marchand. It also inspired a scathing attack from a socialist University of Montreal law professor named Pierre Trudeau, who denounced Pearson as a "defrocked priest of peace." (This essay soon enough came back to haunt Trudeau. In it, he branded the Liberal Party a "spineless herd," and added that "Power beckoned to Mr. Pearson. He had nothing to lose but honour. He lost it. And his whole party lost it too.")

Pearson, however, was content to ignore the rising tide of anti-American pacifism within the party and across the country. Though he had begun life as a university lecturer fully convinced of British superiority, his wartime experience as a diplomat in London and Washington had changed his view entirely. Where he had started, like Diefenbaker, upholding the British legacy, by the 1950s he had come to see Canada's future as being a bicultural union in a North America dominated by the United States.

His instinct to work with the Americans rather than against them had its benefits. One was the 1965 Canada-U.S. Auto Pact. The principle was simple: for every U.S. car sold in Canada, a car (or its equivalent) had to be made in Canada. This closed a yawning trade imbalance between the two countries, and turbo-charged Ontario's manufacturing base (and to a lesser extent Quebec's) with high-paying jobs for the next 30 years. Although the Auto Pact survived the free trade treaties of the 1990s with the U.S. and Mexico, it ran afoul of the rules of the World Trade Organization and was scrapped in 2001. By then auto manufacture had become a global enterprise far more difficult for nationalist governments to police than it had been with North America's Big Three in the 1960s.

It was not English Canadian nationalism that disturbed Pearson, it was the Quebec version, which by the early 1960s had become overtly separatist. He set out to create a new Canadian polity by erasing the vestiges of British rule which, he was convinced, made it impossible for French Quebeckers to become equal partners in the national life. Pearson's complete U-turn from earlier years in this regard prompted many anglophones to accuse him of political treachery – prominent among them his one-time student associate at Oxford, Toronto historian Donald Creighton.

Over the next three years, Pearson had Paul Hellyer and a francophone general, Jean-Victor Allard, "unify" and homogenize Canada's army, navy and air force – all heavily grounded in British military symbols and memories – into a single, bilingual defence operation run by the civil service.

Pearson also immediately set about creating a new national flag to replace the Red Ensign (a small British Union Jack cornered in a red field) (see page 70).

In due course, he would establish the country's first sovereign national honour, the Order of Canada. Until then, Canadians of distinction (like Pearson himself) had been awarded the Order of the British Empire.

By opposing the British heritage, Pearson set himself against the older generation, and by supporting the U.S. he set himself against the young. Perhaps this was why he never received a national majority. Nonetheless, he persisted.

As he explained to the Empire Club in Toronto in October of 1964: "We have a part – but only a relatively modest part – to play in preventing [a global nuclear] tragedy…"

Of far greater risk to Canada, he went on, was internal division. "Canada is a federation of provinces based on two founding peoples, English-speaking and French-speaking. Canadian national unity rests on the recognition and the acceptance of this dualism in our origin. This dualism must not be permitted to weaken or destroy us. Inside this entity, however, there is a French-speaking sector which, socially, culturally and historically, has the nature of a national community, with the Province of Quebec as its heart and centre."

By 1964, that "heart and centre" had become a boiling political cauldron of mailbox and armoury bombings, wildcat strikes, anti-monarchy riots and left-wing nationalist manifestos from a new terrorist group calling itself the Quebec Liberation Front (Le Front de libération du Québec, or FLQ). A 1964 first ministers' conference in Quebec City on the new pension plan required heavy security due to bomb threats, and the plan collapsed under a provincial attack led by an angry Quebec premier, Jean Lesage.

To Canadians in neighbouring provinces, Quebec's growing turmoil was perhaps a source of concern, while in the more distant West it was shrugged off as incomprehensible and probably a passing fad. But as seen from the Prime Minister's Office on Parliament Hill it had become a lethal threat. Under Pearson, the Great Question now entered federal discourse: "What does Quebec want?"

"Mike" Pearson – affable, ineffectual, but persistent as ever – set out to answer it.

In 1963 lethal political violence erupted in Quebec with the first bombing attacks of the Front de libération du Québec (FLQ). Pearson's answer was a Bilingualism and Biculturalism Commission (inset right) headed by Montreal journalist André Laurendeau (seated at left) and former CBC mandarin Davidson Dunton. Though easily dismissed by French and English alike, the commission laid the groundwork for the sweeping Official Languages Act six years later.

Photos - National Archives of Canada

Pearson's first act was to appoint a Royal Commission on Bilingualism and Biculturalism chaired by two Quebeckers. They were Davidson Dunton, an anglophone native of Montreal and career federal civil servant, and André Laurendeau, associate editor of the influential nationalist newspaper *Le Devoir*. Laurendeau had first proposed the commission idea to Diefenbaker, but he wasn't interested.

This "By-and-By" Commission, as it was soon dubbed – given how long it lasted – set the federal course and tone for the next half-century. Over seven years, its recommendations led to the bilingualization of the federal service, federal funding of French education in all English school systems, and the general acceptance that Canada is more a partnership of "two founding nations" than a confederation of 10 equal provinces.

These developments, of course, lay in the future. For the present, the "By-and-By" Commission was mostly ignored in English Canada, and dismissed in Quebec as window dressing.
Undaunted, Pearson then set about raising Quebec's profile in his Cabinet.
Liberal cabinets had always included francophones, and Pearson's had more than any before.

The maple leaf forever

Canada's great flag flap of 1964

Conservatives, whose historic memory is probably as poor on average as anyone's, recoiled at Lester B. Pearson's 1960 promise as Opposition leader to push for a new national flag. Canada already had a national flag, they objected – the Red Ensign, beneath which Canadian troops had fought and died in two world wars.

Except that they hadn't.

Canada's first official flag was actually the Blue Ensign, assigned for use by the British Colonial Office in 1865. That was followed in 1892 by an earlier version of the Red Ensign, solely for use by Canada's merchant marine. (An "ensign" usually means the adaptation of a national flag for specific uses.) Canadian soldiers in the Riel Rebellion, the Boer War, the First World War and half of the Second World War fought under the British Union Jack, which had always been Canada's national flag.

Certain reactionary MPs, most notably Tommy Church of Toronto, made regular political hay in the 1920s deploring the increasing but illegitimate substitute of the Red Ensign for the Union Jack for reasons of national pride. They lost the argument. The Red Ensign was approved for use on land by military directive in November 1943 (to distinguish Canadian army and air force units from British), and confirmed for use by the whole country under a Cabinet order of September 1945.

Mackenzie King had twice become unwillingly and terrifyingly embroiled in controversy about Canada adopting its own national flag – once in 1926 when he became prime minister and again in 1945-6, just before he retired. On the second occasion, Parliament devoted significant research to heraldry, protocol and design before abandoning the issue.

Two factors drove the recurrent interest. One was a traditional resentment towards any version of the Union Jack in Quebec, where it was seen by many (understandably) as a symbol of their defeat by General Wolfe in 1759. This feeling

The maple leaf figured prominently among thousands of flag designs proposed by famous and not-so-famous Canadians. Above is Pearson's original suggestion, and below one from someone else trying to preserve continuity and bicultural respect. The one point Pearson was firm on, however, was that the flag be entirely new and entirely Canadian.

abated with the winning of responsible government in the 19th century, but returned with the rise of 20th-century Quebec nationalism.

Equally at work was a new Canadian nationalism growing in English Canada between the First and Second World Wars. Before 1945, the Red Ensign was deplored by conservatives as a move away from Britain. By the 1960s, nationalism had so eroded Canada's imperial loyalty that the Red Ensign was defended by conservatives and deplored by progressives as a symbol of continued colonization.

Pearson was determined to avoid the trap of tinkering with the crest on the Ensign and leaving the Union Jack in the corner, thereby offending everybody. He wanted a whole new flag. His own preferred design, he said, would be three red maple leaves on white flanked by two blue bars.

The ensuing bitter debate, in Parliament and across the country, was rich with ironies.

John Diefenbaker – the great champion of "unhyphenated" national unity – ended up defending to his political death a flag whose symbols identified Canada's diverse Old Country origins and ethnic identities. The Royal Canadian Legion ended up opposing the Maple Leaf, the national badge they had worn on their shoulders and berets in both world wars, and which was graven on tens of thousands of military tombstones in France, in defence of a flag few outside the Navy had actually fought under.

This came to a head when Pearson – the only Canadian prime minister ever to have served in active combat (in the First World War) – faced down the 1964 national convention of the Legion. Pearson, the career federal bureaucrat, ended up arguing for Parliament's right to decide on a flag, while Diefenbaker – a champion of Parliament – sought to preserve a flag Parliament (as distinct from the Cabinet) had never approved.

It took six months and 308 speeches in Parliament, but in a December 1964 free vote, the Commons approved the new flag – by now reduced to the single stylized maple leaf flanked by red bars we have today. (The combination of red-white-red had been approved as Canada's official colour scheme in 1921, and dated back to the opening of the Military College of Canada in Kingston, Ontario, in 1876.)

The new flag was raised above the Peace Tower on Parliament Hill on February 15, 1965. It hung listlessly against a leaden sky for a while, but soon the sun came out, the wind blew, and the red and white stood proudly against the blue heavens.

Changing the flag was probably the riskiest action of the Pearson government. Whether it united the country, or simply erased Canadians' dwindling sense of a connection with their own history, is a question that can never be certainly answered.

A French-speaking RCMP constable raises the new flag on Parliament Hill for the first time, February 15, 1965

Photos - Canadian Press Images

1. A thorough account of the flag debate can be found in the 1980 book by John Matheson, *Canada's Flag: A Search for a Country*. As an Ontario MP, Matheson spearheaded the flag issue for Pearson, to whom he dedicated his book. He is openly partisan, but formidably backgrounded.

But, for the most part, they occupied the same fairly minor patronage-dispensing posts favoured by, and often reserved for, Quebec ministers.

The main prize was postmaster general, which for a year went to Mackenzie King-era Quebec stalwart Azellus Denis before he was further rewarded with a retirement seat in the Senate. Another traditionally francophone pork barrel was Immigration, which went to René Tremblay. He later became postmaster general, as in turn did Jean-Pierre Côté. Another plum portfolio was Defence, which went to Lucien Cardin. A fourth patronage hub was Public Works, which fell to Jean-Paul Deschatelets before he was retired to the Senate in 1966.

Had the ministry confined itself to patronage-as-usual, little more would or could have been said. The Diefenbaker Tories had tried to clean up patronage, and their reward was to lose almost all their Quebec seats in 1962. But under Pearson, it didn't stop at mere patronage. Tory vigilance soon uncovered corruption.

One scandal involved long-time provincial Liberal Yvon Dupuis, who had entered Parliament in 1957 and was now a junior minister. He was accused of taking a bribe to ensure the award of a race track licence in his riding of Saint-Jean-Iberville-Napierville. In 1965, he became the first cabinet minister in Canadian history to resign due to criminal charges. He was later acquitted, but the damage was done.

Far worse for the government was the fate of Justice Minister Guy Favreau. He was one of the new guard from Quebec – a Montreal lawyer of distinction, a rookie MP and prominent in

Liberal Premier Jean Lesage (left), father of Quebec's "Quiet Revolution," pictured here with his then-Resources minister René Lévesque. The sudden burst of secularization and modernization Lesage's government unleashed drew the same political talent from Quebec the Pearson Liberals were so anxious to recruit. Most chose to stay in Quebec.

Photo - National Archives of Canada

constitutional negotiations with the provinces. In late 1964, Yukon Tory MP Erik Nielsen charged that one of Favreau's parliamentary assistants, along with one of René Tremblay's, had offered a $20,000 bribe to a Quebec lawyer.

The lawyer was applying on behalf of the American government to extradite a Montreal mobster named Lucien Rivard, who was wanted in the U.S. for running drugs and guns out of a Cuban casino. The bribe was to induce this lawyer not to oppose bail for Rivard, so he could skip the country. After the scandal erupted, Rivard remained in prison. However, on a night well above freezing, his guards mysteriously allowed him to go outdoors to flood the prison rink. He used the water hose to scale the prison wall, and vanished.

Bedlam broke loose in Parliament, a public inquiry followed, Favreau resigned in disgrace in 1965, and Diefenbaker used the episode to huge advantage in the 1965 election. (Rivard was recaptured after four months, convicted in the U.S. of drug smuggling and sentenced to 20 years.)

Such incidents were doubly damaging to the Liberals. Not only did they reveal the Liberal Cabinet as corrupt, but they also persuaded many English Canadians that all this new kowtowing to Quebec was a bad idea.

It wasn't just Conservatives who felt this way. Doug Fisher – the NDP MP who had defeated C.D. Howe in Port Arthur in 1957 – probably voiced the thought of many anglophones while addressing a 1961 student congress on independence at Laval University. He declared that if Quebec wanted to separate, English Canada would be only too happy to see it go, because its contribution to Canada consisted mainly of hockey players and strippers, and its MPs did nothing useful in Parliament.

English bigotry combined with French Liberal corruption kept reputable French Quebeckers away in droves. Crusading left-wing journalist Gérard Pelletier called the federal Liberal Party "the garbage can of Montreal." René Lévesque, a provincial Liberal at the time, later branded it "the biggest whorehouse in the western world."

By 1965, Pearson was growing desperate for credible francophones. The honest ones in his Cabinet, such as Maurice Lamontagne, Jean-Luc Pépin and Maurice Sauvé, were neither numerous nor strong enough to establish bicultural equality. Most of Quebec's best political talent, meanwhile, had been drafted into the "Quiet Revolution" – men such as Lévesque, Pierre Laporte, Jacques Parizeau, Claude Castonguay and Jean Lesage. Maurice Duplessis, the premier who had led the Union Nationale and ruled Quebec with an iron hand since 1936, had died in 1959. In 1960, Lesage had left the federal Liberal Cabinet to lead Quebec's provincial Liberals to unexpected victory.

So who else was there? Well, there was Jean Marchand. A talented and determined labour organizer, he had supported the Lesage reform movement, but had stayed out of provincial politics. He and a small handful of other 1950s-era Quebec reformers did not trust the growing drift in all Quebec parties towards ethnic nationalism. Instead, they advanced the unlikely idea that rather than leave Canada, Quebec should take Canada over.

■ ■ ■ ■

Turn on, tune in, drop out

A generation with new ideals and no experience takes over everything

The Swinging Sixties was the decade of youth – the one when the post-war "baby boom" burst from its suburban high schools to take over the world. It brought with it new beliefs, sentiments and expectations that changed Canada, radically and permanently.

In 1961, half the Canadian population was under 25 years of age, compared to one-quarter almost half a century later.

More significant than their raw numbers, perhaps, was the cavalier impatience with which the young demanded change, and the irresolute resistance to their demands by those in positions of authority.

In reality, of course, all of post-war society – not just its youth – had been reoriented by new products, new mass-marketing techniques and new social ideas incubating since the 1920s in universities, government, professions and business.

But, unlike their elders, the '60s kids had no experience of sterner times.

They were the first people incubated in a society where everything was provided by someone else – processed food, canned music, sophisticated medicine, military security, and happiness on the instalment plan. The only requirement was that someone – in their limited experience, that meant someone else – had to pay for it. In the new consumer economy, nobody needed to make anything for themselves, or even decide anything. That's how the children of the '50s – with their hula hoops, pocket radios and Elvis Presley records – had been raised.

They were, in fact, the first distinct and self-contained "youth culture" that had ever existed. Before that, there had been only two recognized estates in life: childhood and adulthood. You were either a provider or a providee, and the social expectations demanded of both were known and enforced. Now, there emerged an intermediate stage, lasting from the mid-teens to the mid-twenties, for which the expectations were undefined. In the end, it was mainly the youth who decided them.

The change over 15 years – from the mid-1950s to about

The "fab four" Beatles, Paul McCartney, Ringo Starr, George Harrison and John Lennon at a press conference before a concert at Maple Leaf Gardens in Toronto.

Photos - Canadian Press Images

1970 – had three aspects to it: music, manners and morals.

Music was foremost. It suddenly shifted from emphasizing melody (the tune) to emphasizing rhythm (the beat). Rock and roll was more Afro-American in origin than anything else, but young white Canadian society happily embraced it. Though Canadians were as good at producing it as Americans, success and significance – as ever – were determined by the American market.

Before it fractured, the new music followed a 15-year

progression. It began as simple rock-and-roll dance music in the mid-'50s, with Elvis Presley, Jerry Lee Lewis, Chuck Berry and Buddy Holly. Driven by electric guitars and loud drums, it was rollicking good fun, but by traditional standards disturbingly sexual and unmelodic. It soon crossed the Atlantic and produced the Beatles and the Rolling Stones in the early 1960s. But the art form remained mainly white in market and black in origin – and mainly American.

About 1960, Rock was gradually joined by an acoustic, older, quieter form of white music called Folk. Being more serious, it was the preference of liberal intellectuals and melancholy people. Folk was more political than Rock, and had begun much earlier, among champions of the American working-class such as Woody Guthrie and Pete Seeger. By the 1960s, Folk was (among other things) the art form of social protest, performed by Peter, Paul and Mary, Tom Paxton and Joan Baez, and in Canada Ian Tyson, Joni Mitchell and Gordon Lightfoot.

In the mid-'60s, Folk and Rock were melded by Bob Dylan, who is widely considered the greatest singer-songwriter of the era. In the later 1960s, most Rock music turned "psychedelic," or drug-related.

Music was the heart and soul of the new youth culture, and its temples of pilgrimage were the great outdoor Folk and Rock festivals of the late '60s. These were mostly American: Newport, Rhode Island, when Dylan went electric in 1965 before an audience of 70,000; Monterey, California, in 1967, drawing 50,000 people; Miami in 1968, with 99,000; and the granddaddy of them all – Woodstock, in upper New York state in 1969, with 500,000.

Canada's festivals were smaller and less iconic, but just as important to youth culture north of the border. One of the most famous was the Rock and Roll Revival in 1969 at the University of Toronto Varsity Stadium, featuring Beatle John Lennon with his fellow British superstar Eric Clapton, Jim Morrison and the Doors, and some of the great original rock-and-rollers – Chuck Berry, Little Richard and Jerry Lee Lewis.

By 1970, the golden era had passed, and the genre fractured

Outside the confines of Quebec, the youth revolution was American, led by the likes of folk rocker Bob Dylan, interviewed here in 1965 on a Canadian tour. Canadians such as folk singer Joni Mitchell were an exception to the rule, but their status depended heavily on whether they had made it big in the U.S.

into numerous more contrived derivatives: among many others, Disco, Metal, Punk, Industrial, and, by the century's end, Rap, which eliminated melody entirely to leave only beat combined with crude, angry slum talk.

Because of the rock-and-roll music which took the airwaves by storm in the 1950s, the new youth culture was mostly liberal American in taste and interests. It took its political inspiration from the racial civil rights crusades of the post-war southern U.S. It was not at its core anti-American, although it sounded that way – it *was* American, and drew its ideas from the anti-war, anti-capitalist, anti-racist idealism of American post-war activists and folk singers.

The exception was in Quebec. There, the youth culture was

The Hippies begat the Yippies, revolutionary activists of the New Left. Head Yippie Jerry Rubin drew a standing ovation from a thousand York University students in 1969, where he spoke of the "Unfair struggle between the forces of the past and the forces of the future." Ten years later, he was a New York stockbroker.

Photos - Canadian Press Images

still quite French, but no longer Catholic. Across the country, the new culture brought with it a deep antipathy to organized religion, and an impatient "do your own thing" demand for self-gratification rather than self-restraint.

This brought about a marked change in manners and morals. Traditional courtesies and conventions vanished – rejected as outmoded, unnatural and unnecessary. Hair was not cut and often not washed, dress became casual, bizarre and often unsightly, males stopped shaving and females stopped wearing makeup. What percentage of young people fully embraced this "hippie" culture is unknown – it was certainly a minority – but, nevertheless, they set the tone.

Hippies were said to have originated in San Francisco in the mid-1960s, but the lifestyle popped up all throughout urban North America in the later 1960s. It was heavily immersed in mind-altering drugs, especially marijuana, LSD, amphetamines, cocaine and heroin. This generated immediate conflict with police – a struggle which continued long after the hippies had shorn their hair in the 1970s and found jobs.

Though far from forming a majority, hippies were an extreme expression of the new and different values overtaking Canada and the entire developed world, seeping even into Communist Eastern Europe.

The new culture offered mixed blessings. It reduced the sometimes overt racism traditional to Canadian society, and restored an appreciation for nature. But it fell far short of its naive aspiration to create a peaceful, egalitarian, non-materialistic world. Many said then, and have said since, that the destruction of traditional values left society much the poorer.

At a superficial level, simple confidence-building social courtesies and decorum, especially between the sexes, fell victim to a quest for spontaneity. More significantly, the traditional emphasis on family and civic duty, and respect for private property and personal responsibility, gave way to assumptions of common entitlement and moral latitude, if not lassitude. Tolerance, elevated to the status of a virtue, began to excuse a multitude of social pathologies. The crime rate soared in all categories, divorce and abandonment soared, illiteracy soared, drug addiction soared, and welfare dependency soared.

How all these social failures occurred during a time of unparalleled prosperity will probably puzzle sociologists for a long time to come. The situation remained little changed by the end of the century.

Demographics alone can't fully explain the sea change in mood and morals. The percentage of youth in Canadian society (those aged 15 to 24) increased only from 15 percent in 1951 to 18.5 percent by 1971. That was when the great change took root. The aging of Canada's population came later, and only gradually.

It's hard to conceive that so small an increase in the proportion of teenagers would have caused all this change by itself. Other, more powerful factors must have been at work.

An obvious contributing factor was the birth control pill, first legalized in 1960, and the combination of sexual permissiveness and demographic implosion it brought with it. The Canadian fertility rate (the average number of births per woman in her lifetime) peaked at almost four children in 1958 – its highest level since settlement days – and then plunged dramatically to an unprecedented low of less than two children per woman by 1970.

The '60s kids were hardly the only ones who used birth control to separate sex from pregnancy. That attitude quickly pervaded all social strata, reinforced by illusory concerns about overpopulation. From contraception, it was a small step to legalized abortion in the 1970s, ending one pregnancy in four in the last quarter of the century. Along with that came a permanent epidemic of new sexual diseases, and aggressive

Beneath its left-wing, planned-economy rhetoric, the youth revolution was highly entrepreneurial. This was particularly true of the legal music business and the illegal drug trade, on which two hinges the entire subculture turned – as can be seen among the 55,000 young people attending the Strawberry Fields music festival east of Oshawa in August 1970.

claims for legitimacy by sexual minorities whose predilections had previously been illegal.

Also significantly, the '60s kids were the first television generation, and, as a result, the first social cohort whose view of reality was formed mainly by pictures rather than by words. Sixties kids thought more emotionally than did those of the Depression generation, and were largely uninterested in actual parliamentary politics, as distinct from utopian and romantic visions. Electoral turnouts began a long, slow, inexorable descent.

One striking thing about the '60s kids – perhaps their most noticeable characteristic from the perspective of Canadian history – was that they were not particularly Canadian. Their teachers had told them that political history mattered, but the consumer culture all around them told them it didn't. Less than their elders, the young inhabited the new "global village" identified by Canadian communications philosopher Marshall McLuhan – a "virtual" village which, like they themselves, had no history.

Raised in unprecedented security and material abundance, they were culturally disconnected from the pioneer and wartime ordeals and ideals that, until then, had formed the national character.

Above, a 1969 "digger house" on Spadina Avenue in Toronto, co-founded by proto-digger and feminist June Callwood. "Diggers" selflessly assisted questing youth to travel, avoid work and find themselves. A later generation would dub them as "homeless." Below, Toronto's finest haul a Yorkville youth protestor to a paddy wagon in 1967.

Yorkville in 1968 was the hub of youth culture in the 1960s. Most young people fell somewhat short of full-fledged hippiedom, but shared the laissez-faire hippie attitude towards drugs, sex and lifestyle choices.

Why Marchand believed it possible for Quebec to dominate Canada politically is difficult to say. Like most francophones, his early experience with Ottawa had been unfortunate. Back in the days of Mackenzie King, the young activist had been asked publicly to leave a federal labour conference because he couldn't speak English well enough; he was invited instead to confer with a "monsewer" elsewhere in the building – a junior functionary who could speak French.

Francophones were not oppressed in Ottawa; they were just not taken seriously. Even Prime Minister St. Laurent had been dismissed as a token. Legend has it that he had to struggle to add the words "Bureau du Premier Ministre" to his office door.

The Quiet Revolution claimed more from Ottawa than federal politicians like Lesage himself. Less visible but just as important was the exodus of a growing cadre of policy-level francophone federal civil servants. They were now involved in secularizing the school system, provincializing hydro, modernizing labour laws, and establishing provincial programs and services like those in other provinces.

The modernization of Quebec was only one-half of the Quiet Revolution, however. Its other great theme was expressed in its slogan "Maîtres chez nous" – masters in our own house. This was a direct appeal to many of the same nationalist voters who had earlier supported Maurice Duplessis's Union Nationale. By 1965, with modernization an established reality, nationalism was becoming the main theme. As the Quiet Revolution grew louder and more violent (see page 73), federalists such as Marchand were looking to Ottawa for answers, just as Ottawa was now looking to them.

The case for federalism in Quebec was being argued most forcefully by a Montreal law professor, Pierre Trudeau – a man still little known and little interested in anything outside Quebec. Liberated by a modest family fortune from the need to earn a living, Trudeau had spent the 1950s travelling the world, skiing, reading, having affairs and advocating for social democracy in Quebec (See page 102).

In 1962, as the Quiet Revolution moved towards nationalism, Trudeau wrote a blistering criticism of it entitled "New Treason of the Intellectuals," which he published in *Cité Libre*, a small but influential left-liberal commentary magazine he had helped found in 1950 to oppose Duplessis and the Union Nationale.

Trudeau was all for the modernization aspect of the Quiet Revolution, and he had helped bring it to pass. But he deplored the nationalist element. He maintained that Quebec's best future lay in playing a much larger role within the Canadian federal system.

By succumbing to the "self-deluding passion" of ethno-nationalism, he charged, Quebeckers were "throwing themselves headlong – intellectually and spiritually – into purely escapist pursuits." "A nationalistic movement," he warned, "is by nature intolerant, discriminatory, and, when all is said and done, totalitarian." In short, Quebeckers would simply be trading one crew of political oppressors for another. ("Rois nègres," Trudeau had once termed Quebec's rulers: cannibal kings, who ate their own people.)

If Quebeckers felt patronized and threatened by Ottawa, Trudeau told them to blame themselves: "Not only at Ottawa, but even at Quebec, [we see] a veritable charnel-house where half our rights have been wasted by decay and decrepitude, and the rest devoured by the maggots of political cynicism and the pestilence of corruption."

"If Canada as a state has had so little room for French Canadians," he insisted, "it is because we have failed to make ourselves indispensable to its future." Except for Wilfrid Laurier, not one French Canadian for three-quarters of a century had made himself crucial to any cabinet.

Not one francophone civil servant had matched the nation-shaping contributions of mandarins such as O.D. Skelton, Graham Towers and Norman Robertson. "The Anglo-Canadians have been strong by virtue only of our own weakness," challenged Trudeau. A single strong francophone equivalent to C.D. Howe in a federal cabinet would have gained more linguistic security for Quebec, he argued, than decades of posturing, pretension and obstructionism by Quebec premiers.

This essay drew the notice of more than the labour activists Trudeau had associated with for years, such as Gérard Pelletier and Jean Marchand. It also brought others into the discussion – social reformers such as Marc Lalonde, and observant Quebec anglophones such as Michael Pitfield. Both brought their own Quebec networks, and began introducing Trudeau's writing to federalists outside Quebec.

However, virtually nobody in Liberalism's upper echelons wanted Trudeau on board. In 1963, he had insulted their leader and ridiculed their Quebec caucus as a herd of trained donkeys. In 1962, he had campaigned in Montreal for the NDP. Quebec Liberals dismissed Trudeau as an opinionated dilettante in sandals and khaki shorts. Marchand, on the other hand, was a genuine player – a hard-headed organizer and motivator. In the summer of 1965, the party renewed earlier attempts to enlist him.

Marchand, heeding advice from René Lévesque that there was safety in numbers, insisted as a condition of running that the Liberals arrange for Pelletier and Trudeau to run too.

Only a growing sense of political urgency induced the Liberals to agree. And only a growing sense of his own mortality – he was now aged 45 – persuaded Trudeau it was time to move beyond critique to action. He had always despised the Liberals as opportunistic and power hungry, but he now concluded that they were the only federal party that would do what he wanted.

■ ■ ■ ■

Canada's sex-spy scandal

The Gerda Munsinger affair fires the nation's prurient imagination

by Craig Docksteader

The story of Gerda Munsinger would probably have never been known to the Canadian public were it not for a heated exchange on March 14, 1966, between former prime minister John Diefenbaker and Liberal Justice Minister Lucien Cardin.

The Liberals were back in power under Lester Pearson after defeating Diefenbaker's Conservative minority government in 1963 and again in 1965. For months, the Opposition had been hammering Pearson and his government over their mishandling of a case involving a Vancouver mail clerk caught spying for the Soviet Embassy.

Both Pearson and Cardin began making thinly veiled allusions to the Munsinger affair in the House of Commons, amounting to a cryptic warning to Diefenbaker that they were prepared to divulge what had happened. Days earlier, members of Diefenbaker's former cabinet had been threatened that if they didn't back off, their own misdeeds would be exposed.

Cardin would later claim that he had no prior knowledge of these threats, but after Diefenbaker called Cardin "a dwarf in giant's clothing" and accused the government of hiding the truth, Cardin lobbed his grenade.

"I can tell the Right Honourable Gentleman," retorted Cardin, "that of all the members of the House of Commons he…is the very last person who can afford to give advice on the handling of security cases in Canada. I want the Right Honourable Gentleman to tell the House about his participation in the 'Monsignor case' when he was Prime Minister of this country." Either the minister or Hansard got the name wrong.

Diefenbaker, seldom intimidated, shouted back, "None of these false threats mean anything. Go to it!"

Cardin snapped, "These are not false threats."

Bedlam ensued. Outside the Commons, a still-angry Cardin told reporters that the case was as serious as Britain's 1963 Profumo sex-spy scandal with London prostitute Christine Keeler, and if they wanted the story they should ask Diefenbaker. The media did, and soon rumours were piled on innuendoes.[1]

To douse the fevered accusations in the House of Commons, Pearson appointed Supreme Court Justice Wishart Flett Spence to head a royal commission of inquiry. By the time Spence released his report six months later, Gerda Munsinger was a household name, a former Tory defence minister was disgraced, and Diefenbaker's position as Conservative party leader was more precarious than ever.

The Munsinger story began in 1952, when her application for an immigration visa from East Germany to Canada under her maiden name, Gerda Heseler, was refused. She was suspected of being a prostitute and a Soviet spy. This put a red flag on her file that would surface some years later.

Nevertheless, Munsinger entered Canada in 1955, using her recently acquired married name. She settled in Montreal, where she met Diefenbaker's associate defence minister, Pierre Sévigny, in 1958. For the next three years, Munsinger had an affair with Sévigny, and claimed to have had at least one fling with another Conservative cabinet minister, "Gorgeous George" Hees.

The RCMP, however, were unaware of Munsinger's presence in Canada until June 28, 1960, when she applied for

Gerda Munsinger in 1966

citizenship and, routinely, her application was referred to the RCMP for security clearance. Because she had revealed that her maiden name was Gerda Heseler, the red flag went up, and the RCMP launched an investigation.

Munsinger was interviewed by police, and the phone in her Montreal apartment was tapped. It was then discovered that she was engaged in an active career of prostitution, worked at nightclubs operated by organized crime, and was having an affair with Pierre Sévigny.

Sévigny's defence portfolio, combined with lingering suspicions that Munsinger might be a Soviet spy, compelled the RCMP to report their findings to Diefenbaker's minister of justice, Davie Fulton.

One day after Fulton received the report, he and Diefenbaker confronted Sévigny.

Sévigny vehemently denied having any improper relations with Munsinger. (He later told the inquiry that he did not deny having had sexual relations with Munsinger, only that she had not been his "mistress," as the RCMP alleged.)

Diefenbaker told Sévigny that he was "not interested in explanations," only in whether a breach of security had occurred. Sévigny assured him that the relationship was over, that there had been no security breach, and that Munsinger was planning to leave the country shortly. Dief let it go at that.

The RCMP continued their surveillance of Munsinger until her final departure from Canada in 1961. They could find no evidence of any security breach, and, with that, the matter was forgotten.

Until Cardin's outburst, that is.

Pearson's independent inquiry lasted six months, capturing the attention and imagination of the country. Although the inquiry found that Sévigny – who had resigned from Cabinet over disagreements with Diefenbaker in 1963 – had not compromised national security, his reputation was ruined. Similarly, although the commission criticized Diefenbaker's leniency with his handling of Sévigny, it found no security breach. It just looked bad.

People felt that Diefenbaker should have fired Sévigny. Support to unseat Diefenbaker as party leader had been growing, and the inquiry report simply added fuel to the fire.

1. The Munsinger case was indeed a perfect copy of Britain's headline-rich Profumo scandal. The basic story was: "Tory associate defence minister has affair with beautiful high-class call girl; possible espionage; no evidence; political career destroyed."

Hapless former Conservative associate Defence minister Pierre Sévigny autographing a book for an admirer in 1965. Munsinger was not his "mistress," as the RCMP claimed, but just a prostitute whom he happened to visit very often.

On September 1, 1965, Pearson asked the Governor General to dissolve Parliament and call an election for November 8. He had several reasons. Parliamentary seats were to be redistributed in 1966, and 1967 would be reserved for Canada's centennial celebration. By 1968, Diefenbaker might well be deposed by his own rebellious party, and Liberals persisted in the unwise belief that Dief's continued leadership was one of their greatest assets. Pearson himself was reluctant to go back for a new mandate after only two years, but he was talked into it by Keith Davey and Walter Gordon.

On September 10, news media were invited to the Mount Royal Hotel in Montreal to hear why three star Quebec candidates – Marchand, Pelletier and Trudeau, in that order – would be running for the Liberals. Also on hand were Liberal MPs Guy Favreau, Maurice Lamontagne and Maurice Sauvé. Trudeau delivered a somewhat abstract explanation of their motives. What he didn't mention – and nobody else did either – was that he and Pelletier would not have been accepted as candidates except that they had called the press conference, all but

The Chief in the campaign of 1965 in Niagara Falls. Many Canadians, especially in the West, remained unenthused about the Liberals' new Canada, and stuck with the old warrior from Prince Albert.

Photo - Diefenbaker Centre

forcing the Quebec MPs courting Marchand to endorse them too.

Trudeau was severely criticized by prominent socialist allies for joining the Liberals – not least by the NDP candidate he had campaigned for in 1963, Charles Taylor.

Then, when no Liberal constituency organizations clamoured to have Trudeau and Pelletier – forcing the party to engage in backroom arm-twisting – the irony was not lost on Claude Ryan, editor of *Le Devoir*. These champions of grassroots democratic reform, Ryan noted acidly, were arranging fixed nominations in the vice-regal suite of the Windsor Hotel: "They are blessed from the top, and behave as if the mountain should come to them."

In the event, Trudeau won a nomination to represent Mount Royal fair and square, and with his two friends was elected to Parliament on November 8.

Nationwide, the Liberals were less successful. As they had in 1963, they went into the 1965 contest confident of winning a majority, but once again fell short – by two seats.

They had chosen to run on their achievements – the new flag, 4-percent unemployment, the new Canada Pension Plan and a recent tax cut. This time, they deliberately did not attack, or even mention, Diefenbaker.

It was a mistake on their part, because it left Diefenbaker free to attack them without reply, and he did so to good effect.

Across English Canada, Dief would fasten his riveting stare on campaign audiences and say, "It's unseasonably warm, is it not? I hope you won't mind if I remove my jacket." Then he would add in caustic reference to the Favreau scandal, "It was on a night as warm as this they sent out Lucien Rivard to flood the rink." His audience would roar with laughter, and Dief would launch into a jowl-shaking tirade about Liberal corruption, embellishing and inventing as he went along. A vote for the Liberals, Dief would thunder, was a vote for organized crime – indeed, the Liberal campaign slogan should be "Throw the rascals in."

Afterwards, Liberals were once again unhappily victorious. Davey resigned as national party organizer, Gordon did not return to Cabinet, and Pearson – now 68 years old and tired – began planning his exit.

They may have been disappointed, but the Liberal Party was far stronger now than they had found it. It had recruited new talent all across Canada, was better organized, and had adopted a policy direction that would serve it well for half a century.

The Progressive Conservatives, by contrast, were mired in quandaries. They had a failed leader who refused to leave, and whom half the party refused to follow. And they were hopelessly divided about Quebec and bilingualism.

Dief had faced a secret ballot vote on his leadership in 1964 and won, barely – some said because a youthful Alberta delegate and future leader named Joe Clark spoke enthusiastically in his favour, and persuaded other youth conventioneers to do the same. However, the same convention elected Dalton Camp president of the party. Camp, a Toronto advertising executive and transplanted Maritimer, was openly opposed to Diefenbaker, and it was in this divided state the party had gone into the 1965 election campaign.

"The papers say that Dalton Camp is revolting," quipped Diefenbaker privately. "I cannot disagree."

Robert Stanfield, with his wife Mary, enter the 1967 Conservative assembly that would elect him leader.

Dief confounded his critics by doing far better in the 1965 election than they expected, gaining two seats more than in 1963. "How many of you realize this fact," he would later demand of his rebellious party, "that in 1965, if, in 20 constituencies we had secured 11,300 votes more, we would be the government of Canada today?" However, this simply begged the question as to whether a new leader would have snagged those votes. Dief faced a second leadership review in 1966, and this time he lost. The party wanted him out, and they called a leadership convention for September of 1967.

Just ahead of it, in August, there was a Conservative "thinkers' conference" in Quebec.

It urged the party to accept that Canada was formed from "two distinct societies," rendering the phrase in French as "deux nations." Both phrases would in future prove fateful to the party. The thinkers also recommended a constitutional amendment to make French available in all Canadian legislatures and courts, and guaranteeing minority official-language schooling across the country where numbers warranted.

All this went forward to the party's policy committee at the September leadership convention, where it was overwhelmingly accepted. It was never presented to, nor accepted by, the party membership in a general meeting, and was vigorously opposed by many, especially in the West – and especially by John Diefenbaker, who had always denounced hyphenated identities, and whose "one Canada" absolutism had driven the last few francophones from his caucus.

Although the Conservatives had potential leadership candidates aplenty, half of them

September 1967, Diefenbaker packs his belongings and leaves the opposition leader's office he first occupied a decade earlier. He remained in Parliament until his death in 1979.

Photo - National Archives of Canada

were former federal ministers – Alvin Hamilton, Davie Fulton, Donald Fleming, Michael Starr and George Hees – who had been too long associated with Diefenbaker's stormy past. Dalton Camp wanted to run himself, but suffered the same problem. Greater interest fell on three provincial Conservative premiers: John Robarts of Ontario, Manitoba's Duff Roblin and Nova Scotia's Bob Stanfield.

All three denied having any federal interest, and Robarts soon made it clear he meant it. Of the other two, only Stanfield had remained attuned and attentive to the federal party over many years, and had commented occasionally on national matters as far back as 1964. Until now, however, he had remained dutifully and convincingly loyal to Diefenbaker, and had ignored Dalton Camp's insurrection.

In personality, Stanfield was a perfect opposite to the Chief. He was much more like Pearson – self-deprecating, conciliatory, quiet and hard-working.

Scion of a Truro textile-and-clothing manufacturing family, he had been an honours law student at Harvard. Not having had to work for a living, in 1948, at age 34, he had become leader of the Nova Scotia Conservatives – a party without one seat in the Legislature. A year later, the party won eight seats, and in 1956 Stanfield became premier. He had remained premier straight through to May of 1967, when his Conservatives won 40 of the province's 46 seats.

When he announced his leadership candidacy in July, Stanfield was introduced to the nation as "the man with the winning way." It was certainly his record.

Stanfield's entry into the race ended the leadership hopes of Dalton Camp, who quickly swallowed his personal disappointment and helped run Stanfield's campaign.

By the time the convention opened in September, there were 10 names on the ballot – not one of which was French.

The 11th and last person to enlist was Diefenbaker himself – doing so only 12 minutes before the convention deadline, and only because of the party's "deux nations" resolution in August.

The runoff in Toronto's Maple Leaf Gardens took many hours and five ballots, but yielded no surprises. Dief spoke well but fared badly, running a distant fifth in the opening round. Stanfield started and stayed in first place, with Manitoba Premier Duff Roblin holding position as a strong second. But when his fellow westerner Fulton chose to support Stanfield on the last ballot, Roblin lost, with 46 percent against Stanfield's 54 percent.

Diefenbaker, his support having melted away, marched dramatically out of the convention after the third ballot, though he later sent an emissary to publicly support Roblin. When Stanfield won, the Chief returned to the floor and strongly urged all Conservatives to support the new leader.

Diefenbaker remained in Parliament until his death in 1979, just short of his 85th birthday.

■ ■ ■ ■

Expo 67

Canada hosts the world

C anadians had never done anything like a world's fair. Expo 67, marking the 100th birthday of Confederation, became a source of conscious national pride that lingered long in memories.

Even Quebeckers loved Expo 67, because it was their idea and their triumph. Political resentments were temporarily set aside.

The idea for a centennial world's fair was initially floated by Canadian senator Mark Drouin in 1958, and later spearheaded by an anglophone/francophone duo.

There was skepticism from the beginning. Toronto didn't want the show. The international exposition committee awarded it first to the Soviet Union, to commemorate the 50th anniversary of the Russian Revolution. The Soviets then abandoned the idea for fear of polluting the socialist paradise with decadent bourgeois values. Even after Montreal's mayor, Sarto Fournier, seized hold and got funding from Quebec and Ottawa, there was widespread pessimism that the site could be built on time.

The theme, Man and His World, was chosen and developed

Despite politicians, unions and mercilessly tight deadlines, an army of Quebec volunteers achieved the miraculous.
Expo 67 opened on time on two islands specially created from subway-excavation waste.

With 61 national entries, Expo 67 became a launch pad for the multiculturalism of subsequent federal and provincial governments.

by a national brainstorming session of academics in Montebello, Quebec. The two kilometre-long islands on which Expo was built between Montreal and the south shore were created for the occasion from 28 million tons of earth and rock excavated from the new Montreal subway and dumped in the St. Lawrence River.

Only the fanatic commitment of an army of volunteers and enthusiasts saved the project from derailment by politicians, strikes and mercilessly tight deadlines. Overcoming all challenges, Expo opened in all its gleaming glory right on schedule, on April 27, and there is a settled consensus that it was the most impressive fair of the mid-20th century.

National pavilions ranged from the modest, colourful offer-

ings of poor African countries, to the more elaborate themed presentations of Canadian provinces, to the colossally expensive and futuristic competitive entries of the United States and the USSR.

Everything about the event massively exceeded expectations.

It was hoped as many as 45 countries would participate. In the end 61 did, along with 22 other organizations. Almost twice as many people came as expected, totalling 50 million day-visits over the six months of the fair. Expo 67 set the one-day all-time record for world fairs, with 569,000 visitors on its third day.

There really was a sense of blessing over the event. It was the "Summer of Love" in San Francisco, and, except for the escalating war in Vietnam, the world was enjoying a brief moment

The two most common comments about Expo were how crowded it was, and how friendly. Almost twice as many visitors arrived than expected, stretching services to their absolute limit and occasioning long lineups for everything. However, a mood of patience and goodwill pervaded the grounds, and the throngs were happy and well behaved.

Photos - Canadian Press Images (left)
National Archives of Canada (below)

of peace. The FLQ and foreign terror groups which made threats against Expo did not carry them out. The flower-bedecked Maharishi Mahesh Yogi, holding meditative court in the Youth Pavilion, pretty much set the tone.

The moment of tranquility was soon gone. The very next year marked the Six Day War that ruptured peace in the Middle East, civil strife returned to Northern Ireland after half a century of peace, Soviet tanks rolled in to suppress liberalism in Czechoslovakia, rioting and arson swept through the expanding inner-city slums of the U.S., the long post-war economic boom in Canada ended, the Parti Québécois formed, and the FLQ resumed its bombing.

In many ways, Expo 67 ushered in a new era – though not by any means an era that would reflect the optimistic goodwill of that unusual year.

In other ways, it marked the passing ideals of a vanishing age. The chosen theme, "Man and His World," would never have made it past feminists and environmentalists a generation later. Indeed, the whole idea that human purpose and progress are to be celebrated would soon be choked by newer, less cheerful doctrines that were already germinating in Canada and beyond.

Above, the massive Soviet pavilion, fully competitive in size and imagination to the competing American one at right. The U.S.S.R. initially wanted Expo 67 for itself, but then decided not to allow a free-world tourist horde to see behind the Iron Curtain.

Photos - Canadian Press Images

Coming as the convention did in the windup to Expo 67, the story of the Tory succession captured less attention than the party would have liked. Stanfield's laconic, low-key style didn't help. In November, he was elected to a Nova Scotia seat, and the party rose in the polls. But there was something lacking in Stanfield. He was just too reasonable to succeed in a party as fractious as the Tories, and in a Parliament run by Liberals.

An instance of this occurred in February of 1968.

Pearson had announced in late 1967 that he would resign in April of 1968. By February, the whole Liberal caucus had its eye on the leadership campaign, not on Parliament. Pearson was on holiday in the Caribbean, and his ministers were all over the country campaigning against each other.

Then, on February 19, 1968, the Commons voted 84 to 82 against a government tax bill. Pandemonium ensued.

Pearson hastily returned to Ottawa, and insisted that the tax-bill rejection had not been a "confidence vote," the loss of which requires an immediate election. Tradition and most Opposition members said otherwise. Besides, the combined Opposition outnumbered the Liberals (at that point, 131 seats to the Liberals' 128), and could have forced the Liberals, now effectively leaderless, into a devastating election.

Had Stanfield pushed the issue as hard as the hawks in his party were demanding, the subsequent history of Canada might have been quite different.

But he didn't. He was talked out of pressing the issue when the Liberals sent the governor of the Bank of Canada, Louis Rasminsky, to tell him that a national election would weaken the dollar and hurt the economy. On February 28, the Liberals put a motion before the House saying that the earlier lost vote did not reflect the confidence of the House, and it passed with 19 votes to spare, thanks mainly to Quebec Social Credit MPs supporting the Liberals.

Canadians celebrated Confederation's centennial with uncharacteristic exuberance, whether by simply planting a tree as this child did in Ottawa, or joining in a 100-man, 10-canoe race from western Alberta to Expo Island in Montreal. The gruelling 104-day historical re-enactment covered 3,300 miles over the fur trade routes of rivers and lakes that opened the country.

Photos - National Archives of Canada

Ushering in Centennial year at Queen's Park in Toronto, New Year's Eve, 1966. A mood of innocence and optimism swept the country.

By now, Pearson had achieved the main things he and/or the party had set out to do five years earlier. He announced on December 14, 1967, that he would resign in April, and soon thereafter he called a Liberal leadership convention for April 4, 1968.

Pearson had already set the theme for the leadership contest, with the release of the "By-and-By" Commission's preliminary report in 1965. It warned in dire terms that Canada was passing through the greatest political crisis in its history, and would break up unless Quebec's needs were satisfied.

Pearson later explained: "I wanted people to be shocked, and they were. Some Canadians realized for the first time that there were differences serious enough to destroy our country if no remedial action were taken."

Though the Liberals had chosen only four leaders since 1887, the more astute Liberals were conscious of two things. First, they had alternated the leadership between English and French: Laurier-King-St. Laurent-Pearson. Second, all leaders had been relative newcomers to Parliament.

Faces of the future. In announcing Cabinet changes in April 1967, a jovial Pearson showcased three rookie ministers, all from Quebec, who would all in turn become prime ministers: Pearson appointed Pierre Trudeau minister of Justice, John Turner became Registrar General (and later that year minister of Consumer and Corporate Affairs), and Jean Chrétien minister without portfolio.

Photo - National Archives of Canada

On these two laws had hung all their immense political success for the past eight decades.

This meant it was the francophones' turn; and as good luck and good management would have it, a suitably inexperienced francophone was available: Jean Marchand, one of the "three wise men" elected from Quebec in 1965. (In French Quebec, Marchand, Pelletier and Trudeau had been dubbed the "three doves.")

Marchand had certainly considered running, but now decided that neither his health nor his English was equal to the task. As an alternative, he suggested Trudeau.

Whether – or at what point – Pearson wanted Trudeau to be prime minister is a matter of speculation. Initially – and for obvious reasons – he preferred either Marchand or Guy

Favreau, whom he had tried to save from the disgrace of the Rivard scandal by appointing him to the purely honorary position of president of the Privy Council.

Pearson's experience of Trudeau must have left him skeptical. The "American lackey" insults Trudeau had furiously heaped on Pearson's head in 1963, though forgiven, had been forgotten by no one. He was not in any real sense a Liberal except from convenience. The larger, continuing problem, however, was Trudeau's whole unpredictable style and often flippant attitude. As seen by the anglophone caucus majority, Trudeau was a mid-40s bachelor, he dressed like a metrosexual, he talked about Mao and Plato, he womanized constantly and he avoided party alliances.

"After about 15 minutes," Keith Davey would later recall of their first meeting in 1966, "I figured he was nothing but an egghead. The snappiest thing about him seemed to be that he wore an ascot."

All the same, Pearson awarded Trudeau with such strategic assignments that it's hard not to conclude that he was grooming him.

Right at the outset, Pearson decided over Christmas of 1965 to make Trudeau his personal parliamentary secretary – a singular honour for a neophyte. Trudeau, who was in a London hotel on his way home from a lengthy ski holiday in Switzerland, told Pearson on the telephone that the job sounded interesting, and he'd think about it. Only a sharp, long-distance rebuke from Marchand (who had lobbied hard to get Trudeau the job), pointing out the obvious fact that this would put Trudeau at the centre of political power in Ottawa, caused Trudeau to accept.

Having accepted, however, Trudeau plunged in, and by all accounts worked hard, quietly and well without annoying people and showing off. Before long, he and Marc Lalonde were in the Prime Minister's Office and Privy Council Office respectively, collaborating on constitutional issues, which were a high priority to the Pearson ministry. Lalonde, a sombre Montreal lawyer who was already Trudeau's political guard dog, was at this point a civil servant; he did not enter Parliament until 1972.

In 1965, Pearson raised Marchand immediately to the post of minister of citizenship and immigration. Pelletier followed a year later as minister of external affairs.

An expanding caucus of new-guard Quebec federalists was soon meeting twice a week to discuss matters of concern. They were alarmed by growing nationalism within the Liberal government of Quebec. They were even more alarmed by the defeat, in June of 1966, of the Lesage government by the Union Nationale.

Liberals had, until now, assumed that Maurice Duplessis's party was as dead as its founder. Yet here it was, back in power, having won a new lease on life under a new leader,

Pierre Trudeau playing with a carnation in 1968. He was at first dismissed by the caucus – though not by Pearson, whom he had seriously insulted – as a sophomoric gadfly.

Photo - National Archives of Canada

Daniel Johnson, and a new slogan – "Equality or Independence." For a growing number in Quebec, including provincial Liberals such as René Lévesque, the new militancy was a logical progression from the 1962 victory slogan, "Masters in our own house!" But to federal Liberals, it was anathema.

Trudeau spoke often within this Quebec caucus group, but seldom outside it. Still, he was being watched. A year after his arrival in Ottawa, the English-language *Montreal Gazette* reported that "Trudeau is now regarded as one of the most brilliant constitutional minds in Ottawa."

His prospects were even more enhanced in April of 1967 when, at Marchand's urging, Pearson ushered Trudeau into Cabinet as minister of justice – one of the top portfolios. The English media now started to see him as a political force, and even as a possible leader – though most still assumed his odds of winning were slim.

All the same, about now a strange adulation began to set in that would soon sweep English Canada. Peter C. Newman, then Ottawa bureau chief for the *Toronto Star*, set the tone: "His intelligent, skull-formed face (which might have been carved in alabaster to commemorate some distant war of the crusades) is a pattern of tension, subtlety and audacity..."

Not all commentators were so impressed. Right-wing *Toronto Telegram* columnist Lubor Zink opined that in the "three wise men," "The New Democrats now have three French Canadians in the Pearson ministry. Not bad for a party which has so far failed to elect a single MP in Quebec..."

Trudeau did not hide his left-wing, progressive views. "Justice should be regarded more and more as a department for planning the society of tomorrow," he told the *Star*, "not merely the government's legal adviser...If possible, we have to move the framework of society slightly ahead of the times..."

Pearson at Expo 67, accompanied by Governor General Roland Michener, Quebec premier Daniel Johnson and Montreal mayor Jean Drapeau.

Trudeau's early years

Portrait of an angry young French-Catholic reactionary

He was born Joseph Philippe Pierre Yves Elliott Trudeau on October 18, 1919, one year after the end of the First World War.

Nothing in his early years marked him out for greatness. Even the nonconformity for which he was later so famous was not at first apparent. As a young man, he was a conventional thinker, believing and accepting what he was taught.

In 2006, six years after his death, Canadians were shocked to learn that, in his youth, Trudeau – whom they had always assumed was a lifelong champion of national unity and secular liberal values – was plotting to separate Quebec from Canada by armed insurrection to establish a right-wing French-Catholic dictatorship.

In learning this, many became uncomfortably aware of something about Quebec they probably didn't want to know. Trudeau was simply reflecting popular wartime Quebec support for Latin strongmen in Europe – a tendency towards fascism that, by mutual unwritten consent of Canada's French and English elites in the 1960s, was quietly forgotten.

Trudeau was born and raised in Montreal, on a working-class street in the suburb of Outremont, the son of a francophone father named Charles and a Montreal anglophone mother, Grace Elliott. Pierre had a sister, Suzette, who was one year older, and a brother, Charles (nicknamed Tip), three years younger.

Charlie Trudeau, a cheerful, self-made extrovert who died when Pierre was 15, was a pure-wool Quebec Catholic, a descendant of New France. Pierre retained fond childhood memories of holidays at the ancestral Trudeau farm at Napierville, south of Montreal, where he was fascinated by large pigs and small hen houses, could run through the hay meadows, and play hockey with numerous robust country cousins.

Grace Elliott was the child of a racially and religiously mixed marriage. She was raised a Catholic by her francophone mother, but always (some said) spoke French with an accent inherited from her Scottish Protestant father. Regardless, according to Trudeau and his sister Suzette Rouleau, the household was as bilingual as any home could be. Language was never an issue.

Trudeau remembered his father as a hard worker, often away building a chain of service stations. In his 1993 *Memoirs*, he described the street on which he grew up as a rough-and-tumble mixture of Jews, Irish, Scots, English and French. He spent his first three years of school with Irish Catholics on the English side of a Catholic bilingual elementary school. Small for his age, he learned to box early on, and by his own admission worked as little as possible. Only later, at the francophone Collège Jean-de-Brébeuf, did he become studious.

Just at the time the Depression descended on North America in 1930, Charlie Trudeau sold his gas stations and moved his family to the affluent end of Outremont. While the rest of Quebec struggled through a decade of low wages and high unemployment, the Trudeau family was touring Europe and summering in the Laurentians at Lac Tremblant, which was then mostly wilderness.

By all accounts – not just his own – Trudeau's childhood was a happy one. He was a gregarious, energetic, somewhat smart-aleck boy who was developing self-discipline, who took his faith personally and his church seriously, who adored his mother and greatly admired his father.

All of this bears on something that was said of Trudeau by Quebec's nationalist elite later on: that he was an Outremont *arriviste* who despised his own people. Even his anglophone biographers such as Christina McCall felt there was some truth to this.

However, the evidence of his early years is quite the opposite. He loved Montreal, he loved the province's history and its bucolic countryside and rural culture, he loved its wilderness, he loved the Catholic faith, and he loved the French language, which remained his preferred language for writing.

He did not despise the ordinary people of Quebec, nor they him. As long as he was federal leader, Quebec voted overwhelmingly Liberal; and as soon as he was gone, they opted first for the Conservatives and then the separatist Bloc Québécois. By the early 21st century, federal Liberals were unelectable in most of Quebec, even under Quebec leaders. It was Trudeau himself they had respected.

Still, there was clearly something about Quebec Trudeau did despise, and he despised it so strongly that it that impelled him into national politics and the Prime Minister's Office. He hated Quebec's cultural and political insularity. He scorned its nationalist intellectuals, and they returned the sentiment.

This much was obvious all along. What was not obvious was why he felt the contempt so deeply and personally.

Only after his death in 2000 did the answer become clear: he hated Quebec's introspective nationalism because as a young man – until the age of 25 – he shared it. He believed in it to the core of his being. And, like a reformed smoker, once he had kicked the habit, he despised it.

Trudeau's adolescent separatism was revealed in 2006 by sympathetic biographers Max and Monique Nemni, in their book *Young Trudeau: Son of Quebec, Father of Canada, 1919-1944*. Their idea had been to chronicle Trudeau's early intellectual development – that part of his life which had hitherto been little explored. Trudeau himself had given them several interviews and access to voluminous childhood and adolescent essays, journals, school reports and letters.

When Trudeau was growing up and forming his ideas in the 1930s and '40s, collectivist ideologies were the order of the day. Collectivism can take several forms. In English Canada, it became the socialism of the CCF party, a mixing of Marxist materialism and social-gospel Protestant Christianity, among other things.

But Quebec's was quite different. It was right-wing collectivism, resulting from an increasing French nationalism within the Catholic Church in Quebec, and the Depression appeal of Latin dictators in several European countries before and during the Second World War. There were four of these dictators: Marshal Philippe Pétain in Vichy France, Prime Minister António Salazar in Portugal, General Francisco Franco in Spain and Benito Mussolini in Italy.

Hitler and Naziism, because they were anti-Catholic, were never much admired in French Quebec – although most of what was said against them in the English press was widely dismissed as British (i.e., Protestant) fabrication and propa-

Pierre Elliott Trudeau as a Collège Jean-de-Brébeuf high-school student in 1938. He absorbed and wholly embraced the Catholic French nationalism promoted by his Jesuit teachers.

Photo - National Archives of Canada

ganda. Still, the man most appealing to Quebec's political intellectuals during the war was Marshal Pétain. He was French, pro-church and pro-family, and had saved what was left of France from Nazi aggression by negotiating a truce with Hitler.

In fact, there were three dark intellectual currents in Quebec at the time. One was anti-British, anti-conscription ethnic nationalism, another was anti-democratic fascism, and the third was anti-Semitism. Trudeau, according to the material he gave the Nemnis, was immersed in all three.

When he had attended the Collège Jean-de-Brébeuf – the premier French-language high school in the province of Quebec – Trudeau had authored a play he entitled *Suckers*, urging French Canadians not to buy from Jews instead of their own people. This was a common Quebec prejudice at the time. The play was performed ("with great success," according to its proud young author) for the students' parents.

Diligently and painfully, the Nemnis reconstructed the emergence of a young Quebec fascist – or something so close to one as to be indistinguishable. In 1936, when he was 17, Trudeau wrote a tongue-in-cheek essay on how he would one day lead a revolution which would take Quebec out of Canada and establish a French Catholic state.

A year later, he became passionately interested in the ideas of a European fascist, Alexis Carrel, who believed that political and sexual equality was a delusion, democracy bred moral degeneracy, the only worthwhile Christianity was Catholicism, and habitual criminals should be killed. Carrel held that a new, self-disciplined, ascetic elite must capture and command the governments of nations.

Many of the writers Trudeau read and admired were cut

After a year in Ottawa as a constitutional intern, Trudeau took off on a vagabond's journey around the world. He is pictured here in Arab headdress in 1949. Political tensions were dangerously high, and he was briefly detained as a suspected Israeli spy.

It was pure revisionist fantasy. The Jesuits in 1930s Quebec – including Bernier – were as anti-democracy, anti-capitalism and anti-pluralism as they were anti-communist. Most Jesuits believed in right-wing Catholic "corporatism" and autocracy, and they had found a heart-and-soul disciple in the young Trudeau.

Even in his 1993 memoirs, Trudeau chose not to revisit this unappealing aspect of his own past, and that of his province. But it was otherwise with the Nemnis. He told them frankly in 1998: "You who read the history books, what do they say about this period? I know very well what people were saying then. They said that Pétain was a hero and de Gaulle was a traitor. They said that Mussolini, Salazar and Franco were admirable corporatist leaders. They said that the democratic leaders were sellouts. That is the atmosphere in which I was brought up."

Before he died, Trudeau decided to set the record straight, even if it meant acknowledging Quebec's shame and revealing his own youthful foolishness; and this the Nemnis faithfully did.

Their book makes clear that most Quebeckers were not faintly interested in fighting Naziism – not because they were unaware of its evils, as was later claimed, but because they didn't care. Any sense of obligation to godless mother France was long gone. There was a deep, ugly, open anti-Semitic streak in Quebecois culture, and they felt as little love for the English as they did for the Germans.

Therefore, when the centennial of Quebec's Patriote uprising against the British came along in 1937 and 1938, the evidence makes it almost certain that Trudeau was among the youths fighting with police.

When Canadian volunteers were serving overseas, Trudeau went canoeing in the north, wrote sarcastic plays about Quebec "vendus" who supported the war effort, annoyed the coastal civil patrols guarding the St. Lawrence shoreline against spies being landed by German U-boats, and rode around on a Harley-Davidson motorcycle wearing a borrowed German army uniform and spiked helmet from the Franco-Prussian War.

from similar cloth. What enabled the Nemnis to know why Trudeau thought so highly of these writers was his habit of making profuse notations. At one point, he actually addressed the Nemnis from 60 years earlier – that is, he addressed a thought about Blaise Pascal to those who would be reading his voluminous personal notes at a later time.

Though the Nemnis intended to interview Trudeau as they progressed, they had barely begun their research when he died. But he did say something in a preliminary interview which they thought was significant.

In 1969, during the time of Trudeaumania, the Jesuit Father Robert Bernier, Trudeau's most influential teacher, told *The New Yorker* magazine, "I insisted not only on facts and dates but on thoughts: the importance of the democratic spirit, and the idea of federalism as a way of having political unity and cultural difference in the same country – a pluralistic society...We could easily enter into the mind of [the great liberal democrats] Locke, de Tocqueville, Acton, Jefferson. Our little life gave the boys respect for the rational, an instinctive repulsion against the rising Fascism and Naziism..."

This became the authorized version, repeated at face value in subsequent biographies.

When conscription was imposed on Quebec, Trudeau was in the mass protest – and perhaps the subsequent riot – shouting "Down with the *Gazette*! Down with the Jews!"

But the most interesting of Trudeau's youthful indiscretions was his leading role in a separatist secret society called "Les X."

It began with several of his Brébeuf classmates, and seems to have included a teacher or two as well. How large the organization got is difficult to say – some guess it might have included a hundred or more, but, being secret, it left no membership records.

The aim was to establish – by force, apparently, although military preparations for the insurgency seem not to have become far developed – a French Catholic homeland in Quebec under the new name of "La Laurentie." It was to be governed by a philosopher king appointed for life instead of by a parliament, and run on corporatist principles administered by an elite meritocracy.

"La Patrie," wrote Trudeau of his envisioned Utopia, "...is a living framework, created by God, where men pursue Happiness in a community of faith, of mentality, of blood, of language." The Laurentie project was a textbook case of the intellectual inbreeding that characterized Quebec political thought at the time, and some would say still does.

The imperative of racial purity was big in Quebec. In a 1942 speech supporting the nationalist, anti-conscription candidacy of Jean Drapeau, Trudeau called for pro-conscription "traitors" to be "impaled," and for the "damned bourgeois of Outremont" to be "eviscerated."

Trudeau began plotting "Les X" in the summer of 1942, but seems to have dropped it in the following year. Much was changing by 1943 – for Trudeau, and for the world.

The turning point in the war had come, and the Allies were plainly going to win. This moved Trudeau's friend and co-conspirator, Jean-Baptiste Boulanger, to lament, "The peace will be made without us, and against us." Morally depraved democratic capitalism had proven stronger than they had thought, and fascist corporatism in Europe was on the wane.

Besides that, Trudeau, having graduated in law from the Université de Montréal, was now applying to study economics and political science at Harvard University.

Trudeau continued reading fascist political writers sporadically until the autumn of 1944, when he was granted a military exemption from the Canadian draft and was accepted to begin studies at Harvard.

In his 1993 memoirs, Trudeau said Harvard had a life-changing impact. The campus had attracted some of the world's best and brightest. For the first time in his life, Trudeau found himself surrounded by people who were smarter than he was, and by ideas far removed from the narrow religious obsessions and racial paranoia of Quebec.

He wrote that year that he had to "relearn how to think."

Trudeau in 1957, a young intellectual of the left. Although academically qualified to teach law, he had been blacklisted by the Duplessis regime he so scathingly criticized in the magazine *Cité Libre*.

Photos - National Archives of Canada

It was at Harvard that he proclaimed himself "Pierre Trudeau, Citizen of the World." After the war, he went to study in Paris and London, took a vagabond tour around the globe and became a left-wing founder of the small magazine *Cité Libre*. He was collectivist still, but now of the left, not the right.

He became, in fact, so different a man that it would have been hard for those who grew up with him to recognize him – just as it was hard for those who did not grow up with him to believe he started as a fascist street tough.

PART TWO

1968-1979

The idyllic suburban ideal of the 1950s continued through the 1960s, as in this Canada Mortgage and Housing Corporation archive photograph of an unidentified Toronto street. Beneath the surface, however, social and economic forces were gathering that would radically redefine the nation.

Photo - Provincial Archives of Alberta

In 1968, Trudeaumania swept the nation, especially among those for whom "Beatlemania" had been a passion six years earlier. Here Pierre Trudeau lands on a campaign stop at the Calgary airport. Between star appearances he was a moody and often peevish leader who almost cancelled his western tour because he could win anyway.

Great expectations

The rise and fall of Pierre Trudeau

The political pace now quickened.

Pierre Trudeau's six-month transition from dressy playboy to prime minister is one of the most remarkable stories in Canadian political history. It was, in the phrase of that era, a "happening."[1]

It began behind the scenes, during the triumphal tour of Quebec on July 23, 1967, by Charles de Gaulle, president of France. Invited by the Premier of Quebec, Daniel Johnson, the aging European war hero was greeted with wild devotion – a devotion singularly lacking in Quebec during France's hour of need a generation earlier.

De Gaulle arrived on a French navy cruiser, and he entered Quebec City, as René Lévesque would later recall, like he had entered Paris in 1944: as a liberator. He continued to Montreal in a triumphal motorcade, passing through dozens of ancient small towns named for forgotten saints and lined with people waving blue-and-white Quebec flags. Stopping in Deschambault, he invited the crowd to sing the national anthem. De Gaulle began singing "O Canada," the crowd drowned him out with the anthem of the French Revolution, "La Marseillaise": "Come, children of the fatherland, the day of glory has arrived. To arms, citizens!"

The next day, when he greeted a huge and happy throng from a balustrade at Montreal's city hall, he shouted , "Vive Montréal!" And then, "Vive le Québec!" And then, with emphasis on the last word, "Vive le Québec *libre*!" The last part was not in his prepared text;

---

1. Of many biographies of Trudeau, the best-known is the two-volume *Trudeau and Our Times*, co-authored by Christina McCall and Stephen Clarkson, and published in 1990; McCall's 1982 book *Grits: An Intimate Portrait of the Liberal Party* is also considered a seminal work. The most complete, even-handed and factual account of Trudeau's first government is *Paradox: Trudeau as Prime Minister* by Anthony Westell (1972). A very thorough main source of the first three Trudeau ministries is *The Northern Magus: Pierre Trudeau and Canadians* by Richard Gwyn (1980), who was *Toronto Star* parliamentary columnist for the Trudeau period after 1973, and before that executive assistant to Trudeau cabinet minister Eric Kierans.

it just came out in the exhilaration of the moment. Quebec went wild.

English media were outraged. Pearson, trained in diplomacy and warned by his officials well in advance that de Gaulle was planning to make trouble, was inclined to follow the advice of his external affairs minister to let the incident pass. Why amplify a remark that had already boosted the separatist cause? Why explode the same grenade twice?

But francophone federalists were even more furious than the English. Montreal Mayor Jean Drapeau gave the president a thorough dressing down at a banquet that evening, though he later admitted de Gaulle probably never really understood how much damage he had done.

Back in Ottawa, Trudeau and Marc Lalonde pushed Pearson hard to respond. Had they not, the world's impression of the Quebec situation – the impression that French Quebeckers were genuine victims of oppression – might well have been established by the French president. In the end, Pearson agreed with Trudeau. Quebeckers did not need liberation, he rebutted archly on television – they were already free. He called de Gaulle's comment "unacceptable" – the diplomatic way of telling the French president to go home, which he did.[2]

This was the first instance of Trudeau pushing back against Quebec.

One incident that brought Trudeau to the fore was the 1967 grand tour of French president Charles de Gaulle from Quebec City to Expo 67, where he is pictured above (inset above) with premier Daniel Johnson. His impromptu cry of "Vive le Québec libre!" from a balcony at Montreal's city hall, above, goaded the Quebec federalists in Pearson's Cabinet into a counterattack.

While de Gaulle was later being upbraided by Montreal mayor Jean Drapeau, Ottawa was preparing a rebuke that would unceremoniously send him home.

On September 4, 1967, Trudeau spoke to the Canadian Bar Association's annual convention in Quebec City. The solution to Quebec separatism, he suggested, was to patriate the Canadian Constitution from Britain, and include within it a new Charter of Rights securing French-language rights and the basic freedoms of all citizens.

None of this was new thinking for Trudeau, but it was new for the media, who questioned him skeptically about it afterward. Annoyed by their apparent disbelief, Trudeau told them that the only alternative – granting Quebec special federal status – was just "une connerie," which was a gross French vulgarity meaning "messing around." Pearson was appalled, but it got reporters' attention.

The next day, Pearson announced there would be a February first ministers' conference on the Constitution. As justice minister, Trudeau would take part.

In October, Trudeau published in French a book of his own essays entitled *Federalism and the French Canadians*, and began work on an English translation. Sales, though initially slow, picked up as his profile rose. It consisted mainly of *Cité Libre* articles from the past decade-and-a-half, arguing for socialism and federalism. (Except for his mainly anecdotal 1993 *Memoirs*, Trudeau never actually authored a book; he was always an essayist and contributor.)

On October 14, 1967, René Lévesque quit/got fired from the Quebec provincial Liberals for conceiving and advancing the idea of "sovereignty association." It meant a new arrangement between Quebec and Canada less complete than "independence," but a lot more than the special status being sought by both the Union Nationale and, now, the provincial Liberals. No senior Liberals left the party with him, but a throng of young people followed him out the door. A year later, they would found the Parti Québécois.

In November, across the Atlantic Ocean, General de Gaulle returned to the subject of Quebec, saying France would recognize and support the province if it chose to separate.

In December of 1967, just before the Christmas break, Trudeau startled the nation by bringing into Parliament liberalization amendments to the federal Divorce Act and to the Criminal Code sections banning abortion and homosexual acts. The legislation had long been in preparation, but earlier justice ministers had avoided introducing it. Trudeau took the risk and reaped the credit.

His most memorable line, "the state has no business in the bedrooms of the nation," which cemented in place for all time his reputation for original liberal thought, actually came from a *Globe and Mail* editorial headline a few days before.

---

2. In de Gaulle's absence, Pearson and Governor General Roland Michener and their wives ate the meal that had been prepared for the official reception at Rideau Hall, seated at the table of honour in a large empty dining room, drinking the fine wines chosen for the occasion and addressing salacious impromptu speeches to de Gaulle as if he were present.

On December 14, midway between introductions of the divorce and Criminal Code bills, Pearson announced that he was resigning, and that the party would assemble from April 4 to April 6 of 1968 to choose his successor. This allowed a wide array of ministers who had been discreetly jockeying for position to start pursuing their ambitions openly.

Trudeau remained silent on the leadership, and went to Tahiti for Christmas. Nonetheless, the media paid more attention to his diving exploits there than it did back home to all the starting-gate jostling of all other potential candidates combined. It was in Tahiti where Trudeau first met a university undergraduate named Margaret Sinclair who was vacationing with her parents.

By mid-January he was back in Canada, and back at work, travelling the country and conferring with provincial premiers and ministers in advance of Pearson's February constitutional conference. With Pearson's blessing, Trudeau spoke to media and audiences everywhere about the need for national unity, and his plan to "take the fuse out of explosive Quebec nationalism" by means of a constitutional charter. Other leadership hopefuls had no such opportunity for publicity, and no such encouragement from the prime minister.

About his increasingly obvious leadership bid, Trudeau alternated between coy and glib. However, he remained deadly earnest about the need for "one Canada." At moments, he sounded almost like Diefenbaker on the subject, except that, unlike Dief, Trudeau was consumed with the need for bilingualism "so that Quebec is not a ghetto for French Canadians."

This led to Trudeau's address to a federal Liberal conference in Quebec on January 26, where he delivered, once again, a resolute defence of federalism under a more centralized bilingual government. One thousand delegates gave him a standing ovation, a chant in French ("He's won his epaulettes") and even a song.

Parliamentary news media had never encountered a politician quite as mercurial as Trudeau, who alternated between gravely sanctimonious one minute to unapologetically juvenile the next. But his playfulness and unpredictability suited the times. Here he is dodging inquisitive newsmen in February 1968, a few days before confirming that he would seek the Liberal leadership (below left). Trudeau found the news media both necessary and annoying. At one point in 1968 he turned the tables by snatching a camera from the pre-eminent national news photographer of the era, Duncan Cameron, and taking a picture of him (below right).

Photos - Canadian Press Images (below left), National Archives of Canada (below right)

Pearson, Justice minister Trudeau and Quebec premier Daniel Johnson at the 1968 constitutional conference. Pearson urged conciliation. Trudeau attacked Johnson. English Canada cheered.

Photo - National Archives of Canada

Pearson's constitutional conference opened in Ottawa on national television on February 5, 1968, and once again Trudeau made himself the star of the show. The prime minister cautioned everyone to speak carefully, given the fragile condition of the federation. On day two, however, it descended into a personal grudge match between Quebec Premier Daniel Johnson and federal Justice Minister Pierre Trudeau.

Johnson mocked Trudeau's vaunted Charter as a transparent ploy for his undeclared leadership campaign, and intimated that he spoke only for his riding of Mount Royal, an ancient bastion of Anglo-Quebec wealth and privilege. With Trudeau's attitude, said Johnson, why have provinces at all?

Trudeau retorted that Johnson (who was culturally francophone) was an Irishman set on destroying French power in Ottawa. Point for point and insult for insult, it continued until Pearson called a coffee break for tempers to cool. Opinion was divided at the time as to which man won the exchange, but regardless, Trudeau made his pro-Ottawa message known to the nation.

To many Canadians growing weary of separatist threats from Quebec, Trudeau was an instant hero.

■ ■ ■ ■

By now, the Toronto media were pegging Trudeau as front-runner for April, even though he had still not declared his candidacy. A draft movement began in Toronto, chaired by senior MPs Donald Macdonald and Robert Stanbury. Among academics, a petition asking him to run soon had 150 significant names on it from English universities.

On February 16, Trudeau announced his leadership bid. His rising popularity no doubt weighed upon Robert Stanfield's decision to capitulate in the February 19 non-confidence crisis: why be seen as sabotaging Canada's last best hope for unity?

If so, it amounted to surrender. A little later, on the eve of the April Liberal convention, Dalton Camp consulted with Stanfield in Ottawa, and they agreed privately that Trudeau was going to win the leadership and would win the next election.

At about this time, René Lévesque published a short book called *Option-Québec* arguing the need for a new sovereign relationship between Quebec and Canada. Almost as though in response in early March of 1968, Trudeau's book of essays, *Federalism and the French Canadians*, appeared in English, and sold briskly.

Endorsements for his leadership bid now poured in, as the phenomenon of "Trudeaumania" swept the country. People – especially females – with no previous interest in politics suddenly discovered one. Wherever he went, Trudeau was mobbed by crowds demanding autographs,

The people's fascination with Trudeau, especially in central Canada, lasted longer than his did with them. It was still going strong at this unidentified location in the June 1968 election campaign.

Photo - National Archives of Canada

women demanding kisses and reporters demanding interviews.

To Quebec's political media, it was a bit puzzling. To them, Trudeau was old hat – a respectable amateur and Outremont snob who had been theorizing forever about socialism and federalism, but who had sold out, as most people did in the end, to the odious national Liberals.

To the English media, however, Trudeau was new and fascinating.

They said he could box, and held a brown belt in judo (apparently true).

He was said to be fabulously rich. (He wasn't, but he was affluent enough to drive a Mercedes convertible without having to work.)

Having a French father and an English mother, he was said to be that rare phenomenon – the perfectly bilingual Canadian (true).

He had been a bearded vagabond with a packsack wandering the globe 20 years before it was fashionable (true).

He had been progressive, internationalist and socialist during the dark and oppressive era of Maurice Duplessis (partly true; see page 105).

He had visited both the USSR and China at the height of the Red Scare (true). In fact, he was a Communist plant. (Well…anyone might have been a Communist plant.)

He favoured nuclear disarmament (true).

The intensity of the Trudeau phenomenon, though by no means universal, convinced Liberal competitors and Conservative opponents he was un-stoppable. Here a young woman at the April 1968 Liberal convention kneels to kiss his image. Below, Trudeau pretending to do with a complementary press club tie what many others longed to do themselves.

Photos - Canadian Press Images

Educated at Harvard and the London School of Economics, he was a profound, original thinker (debatable).

He was a never-married playboy at 49 (true). It was also whispered – and later stated by the FLQ – that he was a homosexual (for which there was never a shred of evidence, and not for lack of seekers).

Trudeau played it for all it was worth. According to his mood, he might say he didn't really want to be prime minister, or that it was all a monstrous practical joke on the Liberal Party. He said he stood by all his earlier criticisms of the party, but indicated, in airy and often glib generalities, that under him the party would change, and the whole country with it. It became a political strip tease.

What did Trudeau think of the monarchy? Oh…he personally was not against the monarchy, but ranked it in importance below skiing.

Would he run a socialist government? Maybe, said Trudeau, and maybe not. "I'm not a believer in doctrines."

On the eve of the Liberal convention that elected him leader, Trudeau spent an evening at a huge dance-party in Aylmer, Quebec. Whatever their merits, rival candidates Robert Winters, Paul Martin Sr. and Paul Hellyer were fatally uncool.

Photo - Canadian Press Images

Typical representatives of the Sixties Generation hanging out and being captured on film by Toronto art photographer Michael Lambeth. Trudeau's appeal lay in slogans rather than policy. He spoke of "Bringing in new guys with new ideas," of the "just society" and of "participatory democracy." To people with no experience, it sounded hip and well thought out.

Photo - National Archives of Canada

How could he change Canada? He would bring in "new guys with new ideas."

Such as what? Reform Parliament. Reform government. Withdraw troops from NATO. Recognize Communist China.

But what would the Americans say? Who cares? They had blacklisted him in the past for visiting Communist countries, said Trudeau. (In fact, they had not.) Besides, "we know darn well the United States will defend us."

With the U.S. now fighting Communism in Vietnam, with U.S. draft dodgers fleeing into Canada, and with radicalism sweeping through campuses and news media, nothing Trudeau's opponents dredged up against him from earlier days damaged him. In fact, it helped him.

At this point, it hardly mattered what he said, as long as it was mildly outrageous.

■ ■ ■ ■

Little actual policy had been discussed, by Trudeau or anyone else, when 2,500 eager Liberal delegates transformed the Ottawa Civic Centre into a surging and sweltering human sea of noise and colour. Balloting on April 5 took a gruelling seven hours. The food services gave out and the fancy new IBM punch-card voting system malfunctioned.

With eight candidates – old-guard, new-guard, and Trudeau – alliances were diverse, even bizarre.

Favoured to win, at least before Trudeau came on the scene, had been two Toronto ministers from the St. Laurent era, both seen as pro-business and moderately right-wing: Transport Minister Paul Hellyer and Trade Minister Robert Winters. A third veteran of bygone days was Paul Martin, father of the Paul Martin who would briefly serve as prime minister a generation later. Standing for the anglophone new guard was John Turner.

Of several also-ran candidates, the most noteworthy was an immigrant named Ernst

Three Trudeau delegates in 1968, one voting and two non-voting. Trudeau had the momentum but not the numbers for a swift victory.

Photo - Canadian Press Images

Zundel, who many years later would be deported to Germany for hate-mongering and Holocaust-denial; he addressed the convention, but withdrew his name from the ballot.

Up in the bleachers under his orange-and-white colours, Trudeau was at his insouciant best, laughing, blowing kisses and catching grapes in his mouth. Key to his success was the support he had received only days before from Finance Minister Mitchell Sharp, who had initially been expected to run himself.

Hellyer had killed his own momentum the day before with a poor speech. On the first ballot, he came in only slightly ahead of Winters, and their combined vote fell 6 percent short of Trudeau's 31.5 percent. "Go to Winters!" yelled cabinet minister Judy LaMarsh to Hellyer, within range of a CBC microphone. "Don't let that bastard [Trudeau] win – he isn't even a Liberal!"

As the English vote dispersed during subsequent ballots, it did not surge towards Pierre Trudeau, but rather it split evenly. On the fourth and final count, Trudeau crossed the finish line with 51 percent, compared to 40 percent for Winters, and John Turner's 8 percent.

Turner, an intense and handsome individual dismissed by many as superficial, was nonplussed by Trudeau's strength, blurting out at one point, "What's this guy got, anyway?" Still, he refused to support either the old guard's Winters or Trudeau, preferring to keep his name on the ballot, his cabinet options open, and not to leave the impression of an English-French division.

The answer to Turner's question was surely self-evident. Trudeau was winning because he was the sole francophone in the race, and under the Liberals' established pattern it was the French turn for the leadership. Moreover, like King, St. Laurent and Pearson when they took the leadership he was relatively new to Parliament, added to which he was an articulate and proven national-unity francophone from Quebec, where they were becoming all too rare. And last but by no means least, he was a bachelor with remarkable panache who appealed especially to women.

All that he was lacking was anything resembling a program.

As it would soon become clear, Trudeau won office with no plan at all. He had phrases and concepts, he had several priorities, and he had instincts and attitudes. But, given the speed of his ascent, there had been neither time nor need for anything more complete. The Liberals had not held a policy convention since 1966, and had deliberately avoided policy formation in 1968 to avoid a clash of priorities between the grassroots members and their new leader, whoever it might be.

Despite the even split at the convention, the Liberals quickly united behind Trudeau. Having no real sense of what he intended to do, it was easy for everyone to hope for the best.

So it happened that 30 months after joining the Liberal Party, Trudeau was its leader.

John Turner famously stayed on the ballot to the bitter end, denying Winters his last chance at victory, and reducing the appearance of a French-English division.

Photo - Canadian Press Images

■ ■ ■ ■

Three days after he was sworn in as prime minister on April 20, he asked Governor General Roland Michener to call an election.

In his haste, Trudeau denied Pearson his farewell speech to Parliament, and the opportunity for members to offer witty tributes. Trudeau never did apologize, and Pearson later commented that he was personally hurt by it. But Trudeau's people sensed, correctly, that they had momentum, and, more than anything, they wanted a majority.

Lasting 63 days, it was the fourth-longest campaign in Canadian history, and in many ways its most memorable.

"It was not an election campaign at all," Keith Davey recalled later, "it was a coronation. It didn't teach Pierre Trudeau anything about politics or about the Liberal party. All he had to do was show his face and make his speech about the 'just society' and 'participatory democracy' and all that jazz."

With the crucial last-minute support of Liberal establishment stalwart Mitchell Sharp, Trudeau started in first place and held his lead from one ballot to the next.

Photo - Canadian Press Images

Almost everywhere he went, Trudeau was mobbed by fans – on airport runways, on downtown streets, in hotel lobbies.

He didn't make promises, he made pronouncements. If anything, he promised cutbacks – "no more free stuff" and "no new medicares."

Instead, he talked about the "just society" and "participatory democracy." He never said what they meant, because he didn't know, and neither did anyone else. "Come work with me," he urged Canadians on his campaign poster – let's find out together.

When he did speak about something specific – as he did at an open-air rally in downtown Toronto on the future of cities – what he said was just as dull as anything Robert Stanfield might have uttered. But all party president John Nichol remembered later of that particular event was the chanting of 10,000 Toronto office workers echoing eerily upward – "Tru-deau! Tru-deau! Tru-deau!"

According to Christina McCall's account in *Grits*, Nichol found Trudeau a strain during their two months together. What the public saw was Trudeau bounding up on stage and performing like a rock star. What Nichol saw was a difficult political amateur demanding privacy between performances and refusing to hobnob with local party bosses and workers.

At one point, only Nichol's threat to resign induced Trudeau to follow through with a planned campaign swing through the West.

Why go, argued Trudeau, when he was tired, and they were already ahead in the polls? It either didn't matter to him or didn't occur to him that hundreds of Liberal volunteers in the four western provinces had spent weeks organizing it.

McCall mentioned a similar episode when Trudeau almost ducked a large national campaign strategy-team reception in Ottawa. Why go in, Trudeau asked Nichol at the door of the hotel suite? People were obviously enjoying themselves without him. Because, said Nichol patiently, they are waiting to meet you so they can go home and say they gave you essential advice.

Trudeau commented on campaigning in his 1993 book, *Memoirs*. "I did enjoy campaigning up to a point," he recalled. "I didn't like to kiss babies, though I didn't mind kissing their mothers. And I really enjoyed mingling with crowds, as long as there wasn't too much of it...if they [his handlers] didn't want me to start making faces and so on, they had to limit the time."

Against this rampant "Trudeaumania," poor, dull, stammering Bob Stanfield didn't stand a chance, and he knew it.[3]

Both leaders could be discursive bores on occasion, but Trudeau, when his adrenalin was pumping, was a master of the 10-second TV sound bite.

Not Stanfield. He seemed to have no adrenalin at all, and no talent for one-liners. He was

Victoriously ensconced in the Prime Minister's Office, Trudeau was on top of the world. But instead of resting, he plunged headlong into an election campaign.

Photo - Canadian Press Images

---

3. Few books about Stanfield have been published. A very readable one – *Stanfield*, covering his career up to 1972 – was written by *Globe and Mail* columnist Geoffrey Stevens.

everything the age did not want: polite, not flippant; traditional, not hip. He was five years older than Trudeau, and seemed ten years older, in an age that valued youth. He was cautious and conciliatory in an era that was impatient and confrontational. He was English, provincial and dull, when the country wanted someone French, entertaining and cosmopolitan.

On the Tory policy front, things were just as bad – especially the party's confusion on Quebec, the key issue of the day, and indeed of the new era. Was "deux nations" – meaning, presumably, some sort of special status for Quebec – Tory policy or not? Yes, said Diefenbaker angrily, but it shouldn't be. Many unhappy western Conservatives agreed with him. No, said Stanfield; the party membership had never approved "deux nations," and neither had he. Well, said Marcel Faribault, the key francophone candidate in Quebec, maybe it was party policy and maybe it wasn't – but perhaps it should be.

When his campaign bus broke down in Montreal, Trudeau passed the time dancing with onlookers. In the language of the time, Trudeau was "in" and everyone else, by definition, was "out."

Photo - Canadian Press Images

The Liberals struck hard on this chord again and again, and the Conservatives suffered.

On top of which, Stanfield's campaign tour was a disorganized disaster of speeches too long, crowds too small, planes too slow and problems not anticipated.

While Stanfield spoke one evening to a paltry 4,000 party faithful in vast Toronto in an indoor arena smelling of cows, Trudeau was in little Victoria speaking to 10,000 on a pristine outdoor slope overlooking the ocean. When Stanfield mumbled confusingly about implementing a guaranteed annual income, Trudeau said with a dismissive insult, "I would not buy a set of long underwear if I didn't know how much it cost."

The fact that Stanfield's family manufactured underwear was derided far and wide. It wasn't fair, but the country was not in a reasonable mood.

The media, which had been so impressed a year earlier with the Tory leadership process and the way Stanfield had won it, now mocked him.

But perhaps Stanfield's worst fault was that he was just plain unlucky. On the evening before the vote on June 25, Trudeau had the immense good fortune to be attacked in Montreal at the annual St.-Jean-Baptiste parade honouring the province's patron saint.

Trudeau was on the dignitaries' stand in front of the library on Sherbrooke Street. Threats of violence by separatists had prompted Mayor Jean Drapeau to reconsider his in-

In addition to being "out," Stanfield's Conservatives had the disadvantage of a terribly mismanaged campaign – one which stood in odd contrast to his well-run campaign for the leadership the previous year.

Photo - Canadian Press Images

vitation, but Trudeau arrived anyway, declaring, "The Prime Minister of Canada can watch the festival of St. Jean in his own home town!"

Sure enough, a noisy crowd of separatist agitators had stationed itself across the street, and on cue moved through the parade in the dark to throw rocks and glass bottles at Trudeau. After a short volley, the premier of Quebec and the archbishop of Montreal dove for cover. Trudeau, after ducking briefly, resumed his seat, smiling contemptuously at his assailants as police moved against them. Television cameras caught it and the next day it was heading Canadian newscasts as voters went to the polls.

Nobody considered Stanfield worth throwing Coke bottles at. The Liberals won a solid 154-seat majority.

■ ■ ■ ■

Trudeau seated amid dignitaries on the reviewing stand of Montreal's St.-Jean-Baptiste Parade the evening before the June 1968 election. Shortly after this was taken, separatist demonstrators from across the street started hurling rocks and bottles. Television news cameras captured Trudeau, after other notables had fled, returning to his seat and looking nonchalantly down while police moved in to restore order. That footage played nationwide the next day as Canadians went to the polls.

Photo - Canadian Press Images

espite fate and talent so heavily favouring Trudeau, and despite all the media hype, the Liberals fell short of the objective Trudeau had set them – a majority in all regions.

In fact, Trudeaumania brought with it no overwhelming or lasting shift in the country's regional voting pattern: it simply extended the existing one.

Ontario, Liberal since 1963, was more so: of its 88 seats, 63 went to the Liberals this time, compared to 51 before.

Quebec remained mostly Liberal, holding even at 56 Liberal seats of 74; most of the rest went Créditiste.

The Atlantic, loyal to Stanfield, was less Liberal than before, falling from 15 to seven Liberal seats out of 32.

The West responded better to Trudeau than it had to Pearson, giving the Liberals 27 seats out of 68, compared to a paltry eight seats three years earlier; but the NDP and Conservatives together still outnumbered western Liberals.

In some ways, the real loser in 1968 was the NDP. Having won a meagre 22 seats, founding leader Tommy Douglas had to accept that the major breakthrough the party had hoped for since its formation in 1961 was not going to occur. Popular support seemed to be frozen at 17 percent. Canada was undoubtedly more left wing than before, but the benefit appeared to have fallen to the Liberals.

Stanfield, for his part, could draw solace from the fact that, with 31 percent of the popular vote, he had almost matched Diefenbaker's last loss (32 percent). Unfortunately for him, Tory support was now more heavily concentrated in the West and the Atlantic provinces, and the party lost 25 seats, most of them in Ontario.

Worse for Stanfield was that the Tory MPs returning to Parliament, especially from the West, were mainly the irascible anti-Quebec hard-liners with whom he least agreed (Diefenbaker, Jack Horner and many others), while the "progressive" candidates in the East who most strongly supported him (Faribault and Camp, for instance) went down to defeat.

"All the bonks got elected" Stanfield ruefully told a friend, "and all the good members were defeated."

To the Liberals, of course, it mattered far less where their majority came from than the fact that they had it. They had gained the crucial 5-percent increase in popular vote they had needed for the past decade, and they had Trudeau to thank.

■ ■ ■ ■

The bigger losers in 1968 were the NDP, not the Conservatives. Their national support seemed to be frozen below one voter in five. After four attempts, Tommy Douglas (right) stepped down as leader, and David Lewis, a labour lawyer, staunch anti-Communist and lifelong party man, took over.

Photo - National Archives of Canada

At the same time Trudeau was going for a tour in this Canadian Forces fighter jet, he was cutting the Defence budget and angering allies by halving Canada's NATO commitment.

Photo - Canadian Press Images

Dalton Camp, for one, saw what was coming. Trudeau had attracted support from people with contradictory expectations, and was bound to disappoint many. As did Diefenbaker in 1958 (and as Mulroney would later in 1984), he had roused impossibly high hopes. And Dief at least had made specific promises, which people later could forgive him for breaking in a deteriorating economy.

Trudeau, by contrast, had promised an undefined "participatory democracy," and an equally undefined "just society." Voters took them to mean "power to the people" and "prosperity for all." But the first was meaningless, and the second impossible.

Third – and perhaps most importantly – Trudeau had raised high hopes of peace with Quebec.

The drive for autonomy in Quebec was continuing to gain momentum. Two years earlier, the Union Nationale had returned to power under the slogan "Equality or Independence," and the provincial Liberals had chosen to echo them.

The provincial Liberals had issued an Opposition demand of their own that Ottawa

Keith Spicer – journalist, academic and policy-level bureaucrat. From 1970 to 1977 he was Canada's first Commissioner of Official Languages. A review by the end of that term concluded that the policy wasn't working.

Photo - Canadian Press Images

grant Quebec a "particular status," making it entirely sovereign in matters of social juris-diction (as indeed the Constitution indicates every province is), and paramount over Ottawa in shared responsibilities.

A growing number of national politicians saw some sort of special accommodation for Quebec as the only workable course. No two proposals were the same, but the general di-rection was clear and increasingly accepted. The federal Conservatives and the NDP had, in varying and uncertain degrees, both bought in, if only because it seemed the only way they could win support in Quebec.

But not so Trudeau, and he had become by far the most popular politician in the province. To him, any unique recognition of Quebec was unacceptable, whether it was called "special status," "compact federalism," "deux nations" or anything else. During his mete-oric rise to power, he had described Quebec's ever-growing demands as a "time bomb," and his first major act as prime minister was an attempt to defuse it.

When Parliament opened in the fall of 1968, the government introduced as its centrepiece legislation the Official Languages Act. The aim, explained Trudeau, was to make French speakers feel at home in all parts of Canada by thoroughly bilingualizing all federal services and operations.

The OLA, as it has been known ever since, was Trudeau's landmark attempt to estab-lish the complete equality of English and French. He told the House of Commons: "We want to live in a country in which French Canadians can choose to live among English Canadi-ans, and English Canadians can choose to be among French Canadians, without abandon-ing their cultural heritage."

Following many recommendations of the By-and-By commission, the OLA was to give Canadians everywhere the right to communicate in French with the federal government – in-cluding crown corporations such as Air Canada and Canadian National Railways – and to read all official documents in both languages. The Act called for French-language federal staffing in areas where the minority population comprised 10 percent or more. It made both

Opposition to the Official Languages Act was centred in Alberta, where MP Jack Horner led a "prairie cavalry" which was as hostile to Stanfield as to Trudeau. Their best efforts, however, fell far short of stopping federal bilingualization.

Photo - National Archives of Canada

The Official Languages Act was predicated on the dual idea that French-speakers should feel at home across the country, and that eventually more people would become bilingual. However, over the next several decades, it did not stop the growth of a powerful separatist movement in Quebec, and the proportion of Canadians capable of speaking both languages hardly budged, never rising above one-in-five.

Photo - National Archives of Canada

languages available in federal courts and agencies, bilingualized the federal presence in the national capital, and expanded language training for the civil service.

To supervise all this and report annually to Parliament, the Act provided for an Official Languages Commissioner. First named to the task was Keith Spicer, a lively anglophone journalist and academic from Ontario who was married to a francophone; he declared that the best place to learn French was in bed.[4]

In some circles, the OLA was strongly resented and resisted. Senior civil servants saw it closing their career paths; a significant, silent exodus of senior anglophones began, enabling the government to promote francophone replacements. Non-official ethnic minorities saw their own cultural status as diminished by the elevation of French. Three western premiers forced some modifications to the OLA by threatening to challenge its constitutionality in court.

As the debate dragged into the 1969 spring sitting of the House of Commons, parliamentary resistance became centred in a shrinking band of Conservative MPs from the West – a self-described "prairie cavalry" led by ranching MP Jack Horner of Alberta.

Though Horner's leader Stanfield supported Trudeau's legislation – as did most of the Conservative caucus – plenty of Canadian voters did not. Despite high approval in Quebec, support for the OLA across Canada in a Gallup poll was only 56 percent. In the West, 70 percent were opposed to it.

---

4. Contrary to common assumption, the OLA did not require "French on cornflakes boxes." French had begun appearing voluntarily on Canadian consumer packaging earlier in the 1960s, encouraged by federal examples such as the Diefenbaker government's introduction of bilingual government cheques in 1962. Mandatory bilingual packaging came later, with the Consumer Packaging and Labelling Act of 1974.

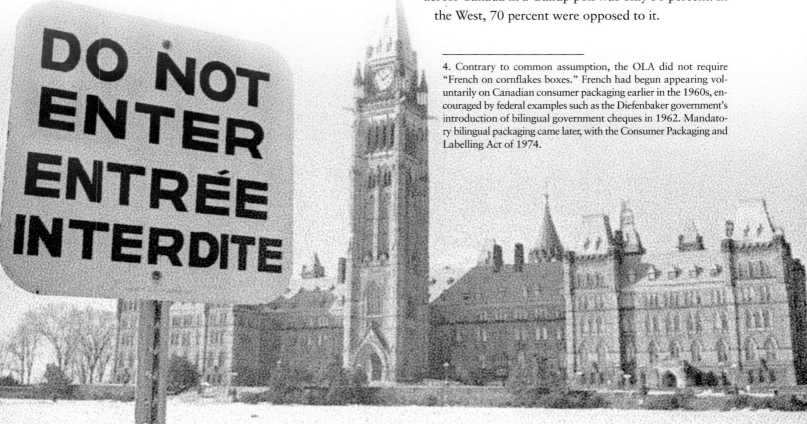

DO NOT ENTER
ENTRÉE INTERDITE

Horner saw Stanfield's support for the OLA as the last straw and a good reason to push him out as leader. He and his cavalry were not very secretive about it. They wanted a stronger, more dynamic, more conservative replacement. Riding in a car with Stanfield across the Alberta prairie one night, Horner bluntly told Stanfield he considered him a socialist.

Some of the western criticisms of the OLA were manifest nonsense; others would be proven true in time, but only long after anything could be done about it.

At bottom, the argument centred on opposing cultural fundamentals. "Their cry [in Quebec] is 'Masters in our own House'," objected Alberta MP Harry Moore. "It could now be 'Masters in yours, too.'"

Trudeau's rebuttal was to ask how Albertans would like it if the only language spoken in their national capital was French. Little as they wanted the OLA, most Canadians had come to accept it as necessary to placate Quebec.

Stanfield, as always, tried to convert his caucus dissenters with suasion rather than head-on confrontation, and succeeded with some. The legislation easily passed second reading by a voice vote. At that point, Horner and four allies stood and demanded a recorded vote, as was their right. The count was 191 in favour of the OLA, to 17 opposed – all of whom were Conservatives, including Diefenbaker, and all but one from the West.

The following day, Stanfield lit into his caucus dissenters so furiously that he forced them to back down, and in the process probably saved his leadership. MPs had never seen him enraged before.

It didn't matter, he remonstrated, that they had opposed the caucus majority – it was their right; but they had betrayed the party by demanding a recorded vote, knowing they had lost. The sole point of the count was to embarrass fellow Tory MPs who had voted in favour of the bill, but who came from constituencies where most people were against it. "There are some things in a political party one doesn't do to one's colleagues," scolded Stanfield. Were they too hidebound to recognize the party's need to regain seats in Quebec? He concluded menacingly that whether the westerners liked it or not, he was leading them in the next election.

■ ■ ■ ■

Conservative leader Stanfield was never well accepted in the West, especially Alberta. He lacked the force of personality and bloody-minded ruthlessness necessary to impose unity on his fractious caucus.

Photo - Canadian Press Images

Trudeau, meanwhile, had challenges of his own, and not just with official languages. The country was impatiently awaiting political miracles. For Canada's huge unilingual majority, official bilingualism was at best a nice gesture, and at worst an annoyance. What about power to the people, and prosperity for all? Where were they?

The more acute members of the media corps were figuring out by now that behind the Trudeaumania myth – a myth they themselves were 50-percent responsible for creating – in reality there were three Pierre Trudeaus.

There was Flamboyant Pierre, pirouetting behind the Queen's back, high-diving, sliding down banisters, dating movie stars, mouthing profanities in Parliament, chumming with Castro and quoting Plato. There was Socialist Pierre, who believed that with enough federal funding Canadians would be happy and united. And there was Pierre the Strongman – a cold, proud, shrewd, inflexible and courageous autocrat driven by a sense of personal destiny.

Trudeaumania lingered longer with the public than the news media. The real Trudeau was proving harder to cover than the fantasy version, partly because the man was so complex and unpredictable, and partly because he held journalists in contempt.

The same process of discovery was taking place within the Liberal Party; for except for a few ministers and personal friends, Liberals knew no more about Pierre Trudeau than anyone else did.

"Participatory democracy" died a swift death. In the fall of 1968, senior members of Cabinet, caucus and the Prime Minister's Office held a seminar on the subject under the tutelage of Canada's new global communications guru, Marshall McLuhan.

Though McLuhan was by any measure a brilliant theorist, this was not one of his more insightful moments. He saw Trudeau as having a natural affinity with the young, and "a delicate, sensitive, responsive personality which is not in any sense overbearing." He strongly advised the Liberals not to let their leader "waste his time being plugged into the bureaucracy...His job is to work in close relationship with the people, probing and working towards solutions to specific problems."

In reality, as the Liberals present already knew, Trudeau had no natural rapport with the young, nor they with him when they got to know him. In general he considered them ill-educated and bad-mannered. As for the workaday problems of "the people," he had no personal experience and little interest.

To the relief of all, the McLuhan seminars were discontinued, ostensibly because the guru wanted too much money.

Not that money was felt to be scarce. The problem was that "participatory democracy" was a meaningless phrase. After a hugely attended, massively expensive 1969 party "teach-in" at luxurious Harrison Hot Springs in British Columbia to consider the plight of the disenfranchised poor, "participatory democracy" subsided into "Liberal party reform" – a subject in which almost everyone lost interest as soon as the challenges of governing crowded out all else.

Trudeau commented with his trademark shrug in 1971: "To participate doesn't mean you're going to make the decision."

Communications deep thinker Marshall McLuhan, an international academic star, was called in to advise the new government. The Liberals didn't listen long.

Photo - Canadian Press Images

Love and hate for Henry Morgentaler

One Canadian prominent in the news of the 1970s and 1980s was abortionist Henry Morgentaler of Montreal, and later of Toronto.

Morgentaler was a Polish Jew who had survived the Auschwitz death camp in 1944-45. After release he studied medicine in Germany. He immigrated in 1950, finished his medical training here, and established a general practice in Montreal in 1953.

Responding to significant demand, he spent the next two decades secretly specializing in illegal surgical abortion. Canadian criminal law had always allowed abortion, but only to save the life of the mother — a rare occurrence even then.

Morgentaler never pretended that he was providing essential medicine. He told a radio interviewer in 1988 that fewer than one-tenth of one percent of the thousands of abortions he himself had performed were done for reasons of serious health emergencies.

Convinced that individual women should have sole legal right to decide if they were carrying a new human being or a "clump of cells," Morgentaler began practising abortion in the open in 1969, and soon ended up criminally charged. The 1969 Trudeau/Turner amendment to the Criminal Code did not help him, because it required abortions to be approved and done in a hospital.

Morgentaler was charged in Quebec with illegally providing abortions, and acquitted by sympathetic juries in 1973. He was charged again in Ontario in 1983 and acquitted in a landmark Supreme Court 1988 decision that struck down the 1969 law as unconstitutional because it was unevenly applied across Canada. The court fell short, however, of giving women a constitutional right to abortion.

Meanwhile Morgentaler opened a chain of private abortion clinics across the country, and became very wealthy. Though a hero to feminists and the left, he was despised by moral conservatives and scorned by the medical profession. A 1976 Quebec medical college investigation into a botched abortion concluded that he was far more concerned about "protecting his fees" than in providing good care; he was forbidden to practice for a year. He was also convicted of cheating on taxes.

Even his eventual admission to the Order of Canada caused six other recipients to leave in protest. He was, as biographer Catherine Dunphy conceded in the title of her book, "a difficult hero."

Photo - Canadian Press Images

Revolt of the sisterhood

Feminism turns Canada's economy and society inside out

One of the many exotic and quixotic ideologies which propelled Canadians into street demonstrations in the 1960s was feminism – or, in the phrase of that decade, "Women's Lib."

The movement had a predecessor of sorts – the women's crusade for suffrage and against alcohol half a century earlier. This "first-wave" feminism had won women the vote but failed to rid society of liquor. It then vanished as a political force with the Depression, only to reappear in a new form in the late 1950s.

The original feminism had been strongly pro-marriage and pro-family. It was also noticeably racist, opposed to equal rights for Africans and Asians – still a common attitude among white people in the early 20th century.

If given a greater political say, the early feminists argued, women could strengthen the family, and with it the existing social order. By contrast, the second-stage feminism of the 1960s wanted to replace the social order with something quite new – the absolute equality of women and men, leaving children as a lifestyle choice rather than an imperative.

Probably the most effective Canadian champion of the "equality feminism" of the 1960s was the Toronto magazine *Chatelaine*, edited in the crucial years 1959 to 1971 by Calgary native Doris Anderson. Month in and month out, while the advertisers promised women happiness from bras and appliances, editor Anderson sold them on the merits of getting jobs, abortion and easy divorce.

Doris Anderson, editor of Chatelaine magazine and a leading Canadian feminist in the 1960s, was later president of the National Action Committee on the Status of Women. Here she is upbraiding solicitor general Robert Kaplan in 1982 for saying that feminists should be more grateful for Liberal policy changes.

Photo - Canadian Press Images

Women suffered, said *Chatelaine*, from "'housewife-itis', a compound of "frustration, fatigue and freneticness." To American activist Betty Friedan, author of the revolutionary 1963 book *The Feminine Mystique*, women's unhappiness was "the problem with no name." She blamed it on the mindless, soul-destroying tedium of housekeeping, pregnancy and raising children, and likened the plight of North American women in suburbia to Jews in Nazi concentration camps.

If "housewife-itis" was hard to name and harder to define, perhaps it didn't really exist. In 1961 *Chatelaine* surveyed a representative selection of its two million female readers and found 90 percent were pleased with their domestic role, describing it as "the best job in the world." This it took as evidence that women had been brainwashed, and the barrage of magazine articles about female discontent, futility and despair intensified, relieved by articles proclaiming the satisfactions of a paid career and sexual freedom.

As the equality movement attained critical mass by mid-decade, the main agenda was to legalize abortion, establish daycare, equalize jobs, equalize pay, and equalize rights in marriage and divorce.

Most of these were soon delivered. Daycares soon opened. Wage discrimination (paying women less than men for the same job) was soon outlawed in most provinces, job opportunities for women soon broadened, and Trudeau introduced no-fault divorce in

1968, along with what soon became abortion on demand in most parts of Canada.

Only by the end of the decade, however, did it become clear that the goals of the feminist movement went much further. As equality became more the norm, new demands arose that were harder to satisfy – or even to understand.

Adapting Marx, feminist leaders (for example, Kate Millet and Shulamith Firestone) said the enemy was "patriarchy," or rule by males. Men, it was asserted, enslave women by marriage and childbirth.

The rhetoric grew more extreme as the 1970s wore on. Homemakers found themselves reviled and derided by other women as "parasites" and "house slugs," and treated as an anachronism by media and professions. The number of working women swelled throughout the decade, reaching just over one-third of the workforce by 1970. How many chose to work, and how many were forced to by the squeeze on family income exerted by rising taxes and a shrinking dollar-value, has been argued about ever since.

Inevitably, governments were dragooned into the cause. After long resistance, Prime Minister Pearson in 1967 acceded to the demands of editor Anderson, cabinet minister Judy LaMarsh, Ontario activist Laura Sabia, and many others for a Royal Commission on the Status of Women.

By 1970, the movement was starting to divide on the question of whether men and women are biologically different in mind, not just in body, or whether they would behave the same if raised the same. It's an issue that feminists were still debating by the turn of the century thirty years later.

After 1970, equality feminism began to fragment, though

A 1969 experiment with "bus bunnies" to increase Toronto Transit ridership did not last long, but provided a textbook case of the sin of "sexism." Looking at the expressions, it's hard to say who is more bored with whom.

feminism continued to grow. Many feminists were content with their early gains, and went on to pursue ordinary working careers. A few others followed the path of Australian PhD and pornographer Germaine Greer into sexual libertarianism.

A larger number – especially lesbians and academic Marxists – progressed to the more rage-driven anti-male political agenda of "third-wave" feminism, by founding feminist publishing co-operatives, taking control of university faculties, and running government-funded advocacy programs like LEAF (the Legal Education Action Fund). All of these aimed at deconstructing what they saw as patriarchal law and social thought, and remoulding it to fit a feminist paradigm.

What united all second- and third-wave feminists (though not their first-wave foremothers) was the demand for abortion, invariably described as control of their bodies. They might disagree on everything else, but not that.

Most social commentators identify feminism as the Sixties revolution that changed society more than any other. It coincided with a collapse in the Canadian fertility rate from an average of almost four children per woman in the 1950s to under 1.5 from the 1970s to the end of the century – far below the replacement level of 2.1 children per woman.

This in turn drove many other changes, from higher immigration to the viability of social programs such as the Canada Pension Plan.

Feminists protested the 1968 Miss America Pageant in Atlantic City, New Jersey. An unidentified participant chose this occasion to jettison her bra, a common political statement of that era.

The most frequent cause of feminist marching in Canada was abortion, as in this 1972 Edmonton event.

Photos - Canadian Press Images

In the matter of democracy, the real legacy of the Trudeau era, by all informed accounts, was the movement of power upward to the prime minister, not downward to the voter.

The members of Trudeau's new power elite, with all due respect to Marshall McLuhan, were only too happy to have him "plugged in to the bureaucracy," because they themselves ran it, and Trudeau was content to let them. Though still fairly new to Ottawa, Trudeau had strong ideas about Cabinet and the parliamentary process.

The results were invisible to the public, but his efforts permanently reshaped Canadian government.

"When I became a Cabinet minister myself [under Pearson in 1967]," Trudeau recalled in his memoirs, "Cabinet agendas were hastily slapped together and followed only sporadically, if at all. As a result, the Cabinet wasted an inordinate amount of time discussing insignificant topics."

In Trudeau's view, government policy was formed too much by bureaucrats and not enough by elected politicians in Cabinet who were (at least in theory) accountable to Parliament.

For Cabinet to be more accountable to Parliament, Trudeau reasoned, individual ministers must become more accountable to Cabinet collectively. It was time to leave behind the old days of King and St. Laurent, when powerhouse ministers such as C.D. Howe ran their own departments by unilateral fiat, and less assertive ministers left everything to their permanent deputies.

Even worse, in Trudeau's view, was the haphazard, crisis-driven Cabinet system of affable Lester Pearson.

Trudeau wanted "coordination." But that presupposes a coordinator, and it soon became clear who the coordinator would be. Trudeau later told chronicler George Radwanski: "If a minister is proposing something and I think it's dead wrong, I won't let him put

Bemused Calgary Stampeder fans watch in November 1970 as a bizarrely attired Trudeau makes his way down to the field to present the Grey Cup to the winning Montreal Alouettes. The get-up was dubbed his "Mandrake the Magician" costume. Trudeau was the first and last prime minister to dress eccentrically.

Photo - Canadian Press Images

the thing to Cabinet. If I think [a Cabinet discussion] is going in a way that I approve, fine, I'm happy to let the consensus develop."

Under Trudeau, "Cabinet consensus" became whatever the prime minister decided, which was then duly impressed on government MPs in Parliament.

Over the ensuing months and years, Trudeau's wide-ranging reorganizations led to an ironic, though predictable, result. Power did not shift from the bureaucracy to the Cabinet collectively, as he said it should, and certainly not back to Parliament, and least of all to "the people." It gravitated upward to the Prime Minister's Office and the Privy Council Office, both of them under the direction of the prime minister himself.

The PMO handles the leader's political affairs, and the PCO handles the federal civil service.

Only 30 years earlier, Mackenzie King had run the entire federal government with three boxes in his office for Cabinet memoranda: one marked "Yes," one "No" and the third "Pending." The Privy Council Office consisted of one clerk supported by one assistant, who took notes of what Cabinet decided.

Then came the Second World War, bringing with it federal management of the economy, national rationing, homeland security, military conscription, and campaign theatres on three continents and two oceans. This produced a flood of 60,000 Cabinet orders and another 60,000 Treasury minutes, overwhelming King's three-box system. It also far surpassed the capacity of Parliament to scrutinize or Cabinet to control.

King's solution was to appoint a Montreal lawyer named Arnold Heeney to fill the traditional role of Clerk of the Privy Council, as well as a brand new role, Secretary to the Cabinet – the first sign of bigger things to come.

By the time peace returned in 1945, the number of PCO senior staff helping King steer the Cabinet had grown to 10, while his total staff numbered about 30. Long-time King minister

Prototype mandarin Arnold Heeney in the 1950s, founder of the modern federal bureaucracy. Until he arrived, Mackenzie King made do with three boxes, labeled "Yes", "No" and "Pending."

Photo: National Archives of Canada

Charles ("Chubby") Power said the PCO had become a virtual super-Cabinet of civil servants who operated above the ministers and deputies in the line departments of government, and who accounted only to the prime minister.

As post-war Ottawa shifted from military to social priorities, this PCO super-Cabinet went on getting gradually bigger. The PMO developed as a natural and necessary adjunct in the 1960s. Due to its political purpose, the PMO was staffed by temporary party personnel loyal to the leader, not as the PCO was by permanent officials loyal to the civil service.

Under Trudeau, both offices reached a size and scope that would have astonished King, or even Pearson. But there were reasons. In the transition from Pearson to Trudeau, prime-ministerial mail had doubled in volume, and speeches, conferences and official travel, both domestic and foreign, were much more frequent.

Michael Pitfield, finisher and perfecter of prime ministerial supremacy. His studies of the empire of Byzantium convinced him that power falls to him who controls the flow of information to the chief executive.

Photo - Canadian Press Images

Something had changed which, until now, nobody had thought much about. Most Canadians now got their news and views from television and opinion polls. They expected to see their prime minister regularly, and to hear what he had to say about everything, from capital punishment to eels in the Great Lakes.

This took far more political finesse and central-office organization than in the old days of newspaper interviews and train travel. To avoid political embarrassment and wasted time, it required detailed, minute-to-minute management of itineraries, wardrobe, backdrop, media monitoring and scripting. It was also essential for PCO officials to know at all times what all departments of an expanding civil service were doing, to anticipate political problems, and, when things got tense, to step in and manage problem files directly.

Upon taking power, Trudeau doubled the size of the PMO to a staff of 85, and tripled its budget – and, even then, personnel were overworked and turnover was high. He entrusted the PMO to his fiercely loyal Montreal friend and ally, the austere Marc Lalonde, to whom Trudeau was not merely a friend but something close to a religious cause. Between them, they established the modern PMO that helps make Canada's prime minister arguably the most unchecked chief executive in the democratic world.

To run the much larger and more complex Privy Council Office, Trudeau left in place Pearson appointee Gordon Robertson. Trudeau knew Robertson personally, having worked with him during a brief constitutional apprenticeship in Ottawa in 1948, and more recently as Pearson's parliamentary secretary.

Robertson, as did all his predecessors, rejected any suggestion that his job as PCO Clerk was to serve as the prime minister's deputy minister. He preserved the vanishing principle that both the Cabinet and the civil service are authorities in their own right, and not mere instruments of the prime ministerial will.

Trudeau thought otherwise, and when Robertson retired in 1975, Trudeau replaced him with a long-time political associate from Montreal, the owlish and bookish Michael Pitfield, then aged 37.

Pitfield had concluded from his scholarly study of the Byzantine imperial court that power lies in controlling the knowledge of the emperor. It was Pitfield who established the principle that the Clerk of the Privy Council is accountable to the prime minister, not independently to Cabinet – and that has been the assumption ever since.

Trudeau was often accused of holding Parliament in contempt. He once famously quipped that MPs were "nobodies fifty yards from Parliament Hill." Nonetheless, he devoted considerable effort to reorganizing and streamlining Cabinet and parliamentary committees to give ministers and MPs a greater role. He also inaugurated government funding of opposition party research, and he rarely missed a Liberal caucus meeting, the one chance backbench MPs get to speak directly to the leader.

None of which changes the fact that Trudeau centralized power in his own hands more than any prime minister before him, the significance of which outweighed and outlasted all the rest.

■ ■ ■ ■

Meanwhile, the situation in Quebec continued to disintegrate.

A constitutional meeting with the provinces, scheduled by Pearson for December 1968, was fast approaching. It had to be postponed when Quebec Premier Daniel Johnson died in September.

When the conference opened in Ottawa in February of 1969, any federal hopes for a more conciliatory approach from the new Union Nationale premier, mild-mannered Jean-Jacques Bertrand, vanished the moment he opened his mouth.

The problem, declared Bertrand to his fellow first ministers, was not – as Trudeau assumed – that Canada was home to two main languages. The problem was geographic. Canada contained two very separate national communities in need of a more harmonious relationship.

"The important thing for French Canadians from Quebec," he went on, "is not that they be allowed, as individuals, to speak their mother tongue in regions of the country where it has little chance of being understood. What they want is the opportunity to live together in French, to work in French, to build a society in their image, and to be able to organize their community life so that it will reflect their culture. And this cannot be achieved unless the government of Quebec has powers proportionate to the responsibilities it is expected by its population to shoulder."

Probably the last "hip" act of Pierre Trudeau was his meeting with Beatle John Lennon and his wife Yoko Ono on December 23, 1969. Scheduled two weeks earlier at the Beatle's initiative, the interview was slotted into the PM's agenda as a five-minute greeting but lasted almost an hour. Afterward Lennon agreed that Trudeau was a "beautiful person" and "a man of peace," and the PM referred to his visitors as "ambassadors." Lennon acknowledged himself as an ambassador for "youth," and said the world needed leaders like Trudeau. "Smile, clap hands and hope, and the world will find peace," Lennon advised. He imparted the added thought, "Talk, old-fashioned as it is, is still the great means of communication." Eight days later the '60s were over, ending both the decade of love and of Trudeaumania.

Photo: Canadian Press Images

Urban life by the 1970s, as evidenced by the new Coffee Mill Café in Toronto's Yorkville district, reflected a new sophistication, culturally and politically. Among parties, the Liberals expressed that mood and style better than anyone else.

Photo: National Archives of Canada

He concluded with a key point. "Without Quebec," he said, "there might still be French minorities; but French Canada would no longer exist."

The conference got nowhere because Ottawa would not forgo the power it had assumed to spend federal money in provincial social jurisdictions, and the provinces could not agree among themselves on a better federal alternative.

The so-called "have-not" provinces, especially in the Atlantic region, wanted more federal social spending because it shifted money their way from the more prosperous regions. Quebec, which was at this time only a moderate net-recipient of federal funds, still wanted Ottawa to vacate social-spending fields entirely, and leave corresponding tax room to the provinces.

However, problems in Quebec went far beyond funding disputes and constitutional abstractions. The year 1969 would prove to be the worst so far for labour strife, student protests and political violence.

■ ■ ■ ■

B eatles pop star John Lennon and new bride Yoko Ono at a famous week-long May 1969 Montreal "bed-in" to protest the war in Vietnam. Lennon was the only political activist among the Fab Four. Having staged an earlier "bed-in" in Amsterdam that year after their wedding, generating a surge of free-world media coverage, John and Yoko attempted a second in New York, but Lennon was barred from entering the U.S. because of a 1968 British conviction for possessing marijuana. The couple then chose Montreal's Queen Elizabeth Hotel instead. There they gave news interviews and hosted a raft of celebrity visitors, ranging from right-wing U.S. cartoonist Al Capp to Timothy Leary, the world's first LSD "acid head." At the end of the event they broadcast their newly penned song, "Give peace a chance," possibly the most incoherent song ever to hit the pop charts:

'Ev'rybody's talking about
Bagism, Shagism, Dragism, Madism,
Ragism, Tagism
This-ism, That-ism, is-m, is-m, is-m

All we are saying is give peace a chance,
All we are saying is give peace a chance

Ev'rybody's talking about Ministers,
Sinisters, Banisters
And canisters, Bishops, and Fishops,
And Rabbis, and Pop eyes, Bye, bye, bye byes'

Two equally meaningless verses followed, after which the refrain was sung 14 times.

Two years later, after the Beatles had disbanded, Lennon wrote and recorded the song "Imagine," his only solo creation that would stand the test of time. The pleasantly wistful lament perfectly expressed the yearning and agnostic spirit of his generation.

'Imagine there's no Heaven
It's easy if you try
No hell below us
Above us only sky
Imagine all the people
Living for today

Imagine there's no countries
It isn't hard to do
Nothing to kill or die for
And no religion too
Imagine all the people
Living life in peace

Imagine no possessions
I wonder if you can
No need for greed or hunger
A brotherhood of man
Imagine all the people
Sharing all the world

You may say that I'm a dreamer
But I'm not the only one
I hope someday you'll join us
And the world will live as one'

A decade later, in September 1980, Lennon, told *Playboy* Magazine that he had at one point been worth $150 million, but had lost and given most of it away. Three months later he was fatally shot, four times in the back, by a fan/stalker outside his apartment in New York, only a few hours after telling a radio host he felt perfectly safe anywhere in the city.

It had begun six years earlier, when, on the night of March 7, 1963, a handful of young men painted the letters "FLQ" on three Canadian army facilities in Montreal, and then threw Molotov cocktails at them.

This harmless initial sally of Le Front de libération du Québec was just the overture to a long and violent opera. The Montreal subway, then under construction, proved to be a good place to steal dynamite from, and the liberationists learned to use it. In April, they blew up the CN main line only hours before John Diefenbaker came through on his campaign train. Another explosion ripped through the federal revenue building in Montreal. And police found 24 sticks lashed to a television broadcasting tower on Mount Royal.

The police responded with raids and arrests, but these didn't prevent the FLQ from carrying out their first murder. On April 20, 1963, an elderly night watchman putting trash in a garbage can at a Montreal army recruiting centre was inadvertently blown up. Provincial politicians – including leaders of the separatist party RIN (Rassemblement pour l'indépendance nationale) – denounced these atrocities, but to no avail.

Within the FLQ band of brothers, any misgivings about killing the innocent were consoled with the thought that the victim, Wilfred O'Neill, was English. The violence escalated.

Quebec's revolutionaries were driven as much by Marxism as by ethnic nationalism, and they loudly declared common cause with Communist insurgency movements elsewhere – Cuba, Vietnam, Palestine and the urban U.S. They denounced equally bourgeois capitalism and anglo imperialism, and were prone to compiling lists of the Quebec "vendus" (sellouts) they would slaughter after "the people" had risen up and thrown off their anglo capitalist slave-masters.

One founder of the FLQ, Georges Schoeters, had fought against the Nazis as a young teenager in the Belgian underground. The rest, mostly students and mostly male, were standard middle-class campus radicals or working-class union agitators.

Signs of worse times to come. In 1963 political vandals decapitated a Quebec City statue of Queen Victoria.

In 1963 members of Montreal's bomb squad were called to defuse a mailbox bomb planted in Westmount by the new FLQ organization.

Photos: Canadian Press Images

A few were drawn simply by the excitement of blowing things up. One of O'Neill's killers, 18-year-old Yves Labonté, explained that he did it for "les kicks." He and his comrade Jacques Giroux had dumped their bomb in the recruiting-office trash bin only because they had encountered too many police in the vicinity of their real target, the John A. Macdonald monument in Dominion Square.

The murder of O'Neill led to jail sentences for all the FLQ's founders, but more volunteers enlisted. The FLQ was never really a single organization, but a series of small groups adopting the name as they pursued left-wing nationalist sedition. Their relationship with the RIN, and later the fledgling Parti Québécois, ranged from cool to hostile. René Lévesque despised them.

In 1964, an FLQ spinoff calling itself the ALQ (L'Armée de libération de Québec) robbed four banks and stole a considerable arsenal of small arms and ammunition from two federal armouries in Quebec. Police soon recovered the arms, but not the money. A tip warned police of a bomb planted on a CN railway bridge, which they managed to detach and drop safely into the St. Lawrence.

Another half-dozen arrests shut down the ALQ, but it was quickly replaced by the ARQ (L'Armée révolutionnaire du Québec). In an attempted 1964 robbery of a Montreal gun shop by five of its members, one revolutionary shot the store manager dead. During an ensuing shoot-out with police, a second store employee was shot and killed. All told, police arrested 13 ARQ conspirators, and most went to jail. An FLQ publication later blamed the fatalities on the stupidity of the two dead anglophone store employees, and demanded the release of all the arrested murderers as "prisoners of war" under the Geneva Convention.

Though 1967 was fairly quiet in Québec, a small mob of youthful separatists attacked and damaged the Centennial Train in Montréal, knocking down a Mountie in the process.

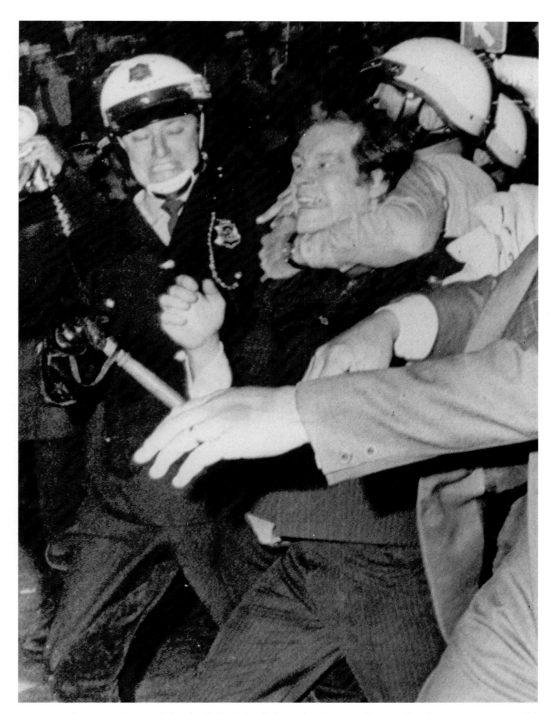

Pierre Bourgault, a leading light of the separatist party the RIN, was arrested in the same St.-Jean-Baptiste riots in 1968 in which Trudeau was attacked. The RIN disbanded that year, and most of its members joined the Parti Québécois.

Photos: Canadian Press Images

Late that year Queen Elizabeth II visited Canada, but any hopes that her presence would rally federalist sentiment in Quebec were soon dashed. British Navy frogmen had to guard the royal yacht *Britannia* moored at the docks in Quebec City, and there were (or seemed to be) more riot police than spectators sullenly lining the Queen's procession to the Quebec Legislature. As she passed, some of the sparse onlookers catcalled "Vive Elizabeth Taylor!"

This mocking cold shoulder infuriated British and anglo-Canadian opinion. While the Queen was being boycotted and insulted in Quebec, Pearson, to mollify Quebec, was forcing closure on the debate in Parliament to rid Canada of the Red Ensign, beneath which (it was inaccurately asserted) English-Canadian soldiers had fought and bled in two world wars (see page 70).

As a great many anglophones saw it, Pearson's Maple Leaf substitute flag symbolized no national achievement at all, just a vague hope that Quebec would someday get over its self-absorbed funk and join the modern world.

The Quebec Legislature had already passed a unanimous resolution demanding that the British Union Jack not appear in the new flag. A year earlier, the two main party leaders, Jean Lesage and Daniel Johnson, had agreed that as far as Quebec was concerned, Confederation had failed.

In 1965, the FLQ made an informal alliance with the Black Liberation Front in the U.S. There were more bombings and attempted bombings, and more arrests. After a brief lull, militancy resumed on a larger scale in 1966. In April, there were more robberies of money and arms, and in May the FLQ intervened in a Montreal strike by blowing up the employer's office, killing a secretary and injuring three others.

Another strike that month was bombed, without injury, as was a washroom at a provincial Liberal election rally in Montreal's Paul Sauvé arena. In June, separatists, for the first time, assailed the reviewing stand of the St.-Jean-Baptiste parade. In July, the FLQ suffered its own first fatality, when 16-year-old Jean Corbo accidentally blew himself up transporting a bomb to a textile plant.

Separatist agitators Pierre Valières (left) and Charles Gagnon confer with their lawyer, Michel Proulx, following extradition back to Canada in 1967. Already heroes of the international left, their incarceration on flimsy evidence became a *cause célèbre* in Quebec when chaos descended in 1970.

Five thousand protestors (above) occupied the campus of Montreal's McGill University in March of 1969 to demand that it become French-only, like other Quebec universities. Though the demand was refused, the university administration spent the rest of the century trying to satisfy demands for ever-increased bilingualism.

Photos: Canadian Press Images

Police knew who the real brains behind the FLQ were, and chose now to charge them, even though they had no evidence linking the two to any specific crime. One was a journalist, Pierre Vallières; the other was a sociology teacher, Charles Gagnon. Both came from working-class family backgrounds.

The pair fled to the U.S. where, instead of hiding, they upped the ante by staging a public hunger strike on the steps of the UN building in New York. By the time they were extradited back to Canada, they had become headline heroes of the left, both in Quebec and in leftist circles around the world. Stokely Carmichael, who had just launched the violent Black Power movement, sent a sympathy telegram (in English) to "our brothers in the FLQ," and two then-famous socialist filmmakers joined a petition drive in France to get them released.

Bringing Vallières and Gagnon home might have been a mistake. A cheering section at their trial required courtroom arrests; they launched – and eventually won – an appeal of their murder convictions; they wrote ceaselessly from prison, and served as iconic martyrs during the October Crisis of 1970. It was while in prison that Vallières wrote a best-selling book, *White Niggers of America*, about the alleged oppression of the French by the English.

Canada's centennial year, 1967, found the FLQ weakened by arrests and the Quebec public in a better mood, but the respite was brief. By 1968, bombs were exploding again.

During the St.-Jean-Baptiste parade – the same one in which protestors threw rocks at Trudeau (see page 126) – radicals elsewhere were overturning and burning cars, and throwing rocks, bottles and acid at police. Mounted city police rode into the crowd wielding nightsticks, while demonstrators fought back with steel bars.

In March 1968, the separatist RIN party broke up. Most of its members joined René Lévesque's new and growing Parti Québécois, but a more radical splinter group set up as the FLP (Le Front de libération populaire). Its activities were more tactical than the FLQ's – disrupting federalist events, staging counter-events, and defacing and destroying federalist symbols.

By the fall, a recession was setting in, unemployment was rising and radical new student groups were popping up on Quebec's expanding campuses. Two other state-funded sources of separatist agitation and subversion were Lester Pearson's new Company of Young Canadians and the CBC French broadcasting service.

September brought a rash of student strikes and sit-ins, shutting down campuses. Police cleared out the sit-ins, the main effect of which was to create a new underground student network, the MSP (Mouvement syndical-politique). Aggressive campaigns commenced to make McGill University French-speaking, and to suppress English in schools in immigrant areas. These and similar moves led to increasingly rowdy demonstrations.

Then the first taxi strike broke out, shutting down access to Montreal's airport. Striking drivers overturned and burned limousines, and firebombed buses. The FLQ resumed its own regular blasting program, starting with strike-bound liquor stores. Dozens more bombs – some found and defused in time, others not – were planted at the Liberal Reform Club, three different industrial company headquarters, and in Eaton's department store in Montreal.

In December, the home of the Murray Hill taxi company president in Westmount was blown up, three more bombs were removed from a trucking company, a bomb exploded harmlessly outside Montreal's city hall, one was dismantled in the National Revenue office, and a mailbox exploded outside the Ottawa office of Secretary of State Gérard Pelletier.

Trudeau commented that year that he was more apprehensive about the danger of domestic insurrection than of what might happen on the other side of the Berlin Wall.

Worse lay in store in 1969. Sabotage became more frequent, and strikes more violent. On February 13, a bomb exploded on the trading floor of the Montreal Stock Exchange. When 300 people recovered their senses amid a rubble of shattered glass and scattered paper,

The bombed trading pit of the Montreal Stock Exchange, February 1969. Though the charge damaged mainly a back wall and the ceiling, and was less deadly than many other blasts elsewhere, it injured 27. Bombings and hoax warnings had become so common in Montreal that a previous notification by telephone was ignored.

Photo: Canadian Press Images

A soldier armed with an automatic rifle stands guard on Parliament Hill, October 13th, 1970. Trudeau summoned troops to Ottawa three days before they moved into Montreal. When asked how far he would go to combat separatist violence, Trudeau famously retorted, "Just watch me."

Photo: Canadian Press Images

no one was dead, but 27 were injured. The FLQ had called in an advance warning, but warnings had become so frequent in Quebec, and were so often false, that business had proceeded as usual.

In May, as a new bomb went off every seven to 10 days, the FLQ dynamited the office of the St.-Jean-Baptiste Society in the town of Sherbrooke, causing security officials to forbid a scheduled visit there the following week by Trudeau. The prime minister reluctantly submitted, but declared, "If the Quebec population – if the leaders – give in constantly to

The same night in 1968 that Trudeau faced rock-throwers, rioters burned vehicles and fought back with steel bars against mounted city police.

Photo: Canadian Press Images

this kind of blackmail, decisions will always be subject to veto by a few guys who want to throw bombs. And if that is allowed to happen, it's the end of freedom in this country."

More street-level rioting and turmoil surrounded the Union Nationale leadership contest between moderate federalist Jean-Jacques Bertrand and his hard-line nationalist rival Jean-Guy Cardinal. In June, separatists pulled down and decapitated the statue of St. John the Baptist as it was carried in the parade procession.

On September 28, the FLQ blew up the home of Montreal Mayor Jean Drapeau, completely demolishing it. The mayor was not at home, and his wife and son escaped injury.

The worst came on the night of October 7, when the Montreal police themselves went on strike, accompanied by the city's firemen. Mobs of separatists and communists attacked (yet again) the Murray Hill taxi yard, where buses were rammed into the building and cars were burned, and gunfire erupted, killing a plainclothes Quebec provincial policeman. Rioters then headed downtown, yelling, smashing and looting without resistance from anyone. Five banks were robbed.

The Canadian Army had been called out to guard city hall and other key sites, but was otherwise under orders not to intervene. Police returned to work the next day to arrest the lawbreakers.

And so it went from 1969 into 1970, each short lull followed by renewed violence, readings of the Riot Act, armed robberies, clashes with police, waves of arrests, and communiqués and explosions from the FLQ.

Amid this rising turmoil, two events set the stage for the dramatic climax of the October Crisis of 1970. One was the election by a large majority on April 29 of a federalist Liberal government under a new premier, Robert Bourassa. The second was the police discovery, in February and June, of separate plots to kidnap the Israeli and U.S. consuls in Montreal.

When the crisis came and Trudeau invoked the War Measures Act (see page 160), he did it with the solid support of English Canadians.

By now, they were growing sick of Quebec. If this was Premier Jean-Jacques Bertrand's idea of Quebec's right to "work in French" and "organize its community life," Canadians elsewhere were ready for martial law.

■ ■ ■ ■

The October Crisis

Trudeau invokes the war measures act

Quebec's political violence climaxed in 1970 with the sixty-day ordeal known as the October Crisis. It began in Montreal on a pleasant autumn morning.

Monday, October 5: the Cross kidnapping

At 8:15 a.m. a gardener was raking autumn leaves across the street from 1279 Redpath Crescent, an impressive stone house on Mount Royal with a view of the Expo 67 site. It was the home of James Cross, 49, the British trade commissioner.

The gardener paid little heed to the driver waiting in a black LaSalle taxicab. Three young men, two carrying bundles, had left the cab and rung the bell. Cross, still in his bathrobe, was upstairs with his wife Barbara dressing for work. When their Portuguese maid opened the door, the three men directed her back into the house at gunpoint, announcing, "This is the FLQ!"

While one man with an automatic rifle guarded her, the other two went to find Cross. They ordered him down on his bedroom floor, dressed him, and hurried him out under a raincoat to the cab, pushing him to the floor of the back seat, and blinding him with a blacked-over military gas mask. The taxi pulled a fast U-turn and vanished down Redpath Crescent. Still unaware anything was amiss, the gardener then saw a woman burst from the house and stand sobbing on the front steps. He wondered at first if her husband had beaten her. Police took 20 minutes to arrive, having been given the wrong address.

Although the abduction marked a new and long-expected escalation in Quebec political violence, the initial reaction in both Ottawa and Quebec City was subdued – far calmer than it would have been in, say, the United States. Police immediately set up checkpoints at bridges and borders, without success. Premier Robert Bourassa went ahead with a scheduled trip to New York, and Parliament took notice of the event but expressed no alarm.

A ransom note sent to Montreal radio station CKAC later that day said that Cross would die unless seven demands were met. Four of these were later abandoned. The three demands that stuck were: media publication of an FLQ manifesto; release of 23 FLQ "political prisoners" in jail for robbery, arson, manslaughter and conspiracy; and safe passage of the kidnappers to Cuba or Algeria.

An FLQ photo of hostage British trade attaché James Cross halfway through his 60-day captivity. Though his kidnappers were not needlessly harsh, he regularly overheard them discussing whether they should kill him, and he lived in dread of a police raid.

Trudeau announced on Tuesday that the federal and Quebec governments would work together to resolve the matter, and Quebec Justice Minister Jérôme Choquette said that the governments would work for a peaceful conclusion.

Ignoring conflicting pressures from Ottawa and local police, CKAC broadcast the manifesto that same day. Although it was read without expression, it was a 15-minute tirade against English capitalist oppression, calling Jean Drapeau a dog, Robert Bourassa a flunky, and Trudeau a faggot ("tapette").

Although police had an impressive track record of convicting FLQ terrorists, and soon were pretty sure who they were after now, they had no idea where to look. Early Wednesday they rounded up 30 suspects, but discovered nothing and had to release them. By week's end they had conducted 1,001 raids under judicial warrant, and had detained and released 44 men and women.

A Wednesday noon FLQ deadline passed and was extended. On Thursday Trudeau told Parliament he would not surrender the government of the country to terrorists, Quebec's doctors started an unrelated province-wide strike, and Premier Bourassa went to New York to promote business investment.

In a series of communiqués, the kidnappers identified themselves as the FLQ's "Libération cell." It was later determined to consist of six or seven members – one of them a McGill University engineering professor from Britain, Nigel Hamer. The four abductors were Jacques Lanctôt, Jacques Cossette-Trudel, Pierre Séguin and cab driver Marc Carbonneau. Other cell members were Yves Langlois and Cossette-Trudel's wife, Louise Lanctôt.

Jacques Lanctôt's brother, François, had been in jail since June awaiting trial for conspiracy to kidnap the U.S. consul. Jacques had been implicated in the earlier conspiracy too and was free on bail. In their excitement, the kidnappers had forgotten to don their masks, and on Wednesday Barbara Cross identified Jacques Lanctôt's police photograph. By the end of the week police were also broadcasting the face of Marc Carbonneau.

In fact he and the gang were hiding in the rented first-floor apartment of 10945 Avenue des Récollets, a house in north Montreal, and keeping Cross in a small bedroom. They were treating him well enough, but he could hear them in the next room listening to newscasts and deciding whether to kill him. He sensed they really did want to negotiate passage out of the country, for themselves and their imprisoned comrades, rather than die gloriously in a shoot-out.

Meanwhile, far to the south, an aging yellow Valiant sedan was speeding homeward from Texas containing three more FLQ members and the mother of two of them. Rosa Rose was neither involved in nor supportive of political terror, but her sons Paul and Jacques were. With them on their holiday was another "Felquiste," Francis Simard.

They had heard a radio news report in Texas about the Cross kidnapping. They judged that the Canadian government

Laporte kidnapper Paul Rose leaving prison in 1982, and (inset) police mug shot of Jacques Rose. Lévesque called them "sewer rats," and by the time they were dug out of their underground rural hideaway they looked like it.

Photos: Canadian Press Images

would not give anything for the return of a minor British bureaucrat, and resolved to raise the stakes. Driving day and night, they were back in Montreal by Thursday. By Saturday they had selected their victim.

Saturday, October 10: the abduction of Laporte

Pierre Laporte, age 49, was Quebec's transport minister and deputy premier. He lived in St. Lambert on the south shore, across from Montreal. With Bourassa now back from New York, Laporte had been summoned that afternoon to a Cabinet meeting in Montreal to decide what to do about Cross.

Pierre and Françoise Laporte earlier in 1970. The Rose brothers decided the FLQ needed to capture someone who mattered more than a minor foreign functionary like Cross. As deputy premier, Laporte was the second-from-the-top in Quebec's political hierarchy.

Photos: Canadian Press Images

At 6:15 p.m. Laporte was in his front yard passing a football with some kids and waiting for his wife, Françoise, to finish dressing for supper. He had just listened to the media statement of his colleague, Justice Minister Jérôme Choquette, saying that the only concession the kidnappers would get was safe passage in exchange for James Cross; there would be no release of criminals.

Just then four disguised men drove up in a green Chevrolet, and two leaped out with automatic rifles. In seconds they forced Laporte into the car and drove off. His 18-year-old nephew, Claude, managed to get the plate number, which a shocked and terrified Françoise telephoned to police along with a description of the car.

Within minutes, bridges and major intersections all through the greater Montreal area were closed off. However, hours passed and neither the car nor Laporte was found.

In fact the four men – the Rose brothers, Simard and another accomplice, Bernard Lortie – had fled only 10 minutes east to nearby St. Hubert, not into Montreal. There they holed up in a rented house on Armstrong Street, and kept their prisoner handcuffed, blindfolded and unfed. Dubbing themselves the "Chénier cell," after a martyred hero of the 1837

Patriote uprising, they dropped off their first communiqué while their prisoner and was still in the back, gagged, bound, blindfolded and covered in coats.

The Chénier gang had indeed upped the ante. Laporte was a Quebecker, a leading light of the Quiet Revolution, and the second-highest political figure in the province. For the next six days near-panic prevailed.

Sunday, October 11: Laporte pleads for his life

Three successive Chénier communiqués, all delivered to CKAC, warned that unless their demands were met by 10 p.m. that night, Laporte would be killed. One contained a handwritten note from Laporte to the Premier, "Mon cher Robert," pleading for an end to police searches and release of the prisoners, to save his life. "We are in the presence of a well organized escalation...After me it will be a third, a fourth, a fifth...It would be as well to act now, to avoid a bloodbath..."

This FLQ combination of sweet reason and naked intimidation successfully divided and nearly paralyzed the Bourassa Cabinet.

Police knew that the FLQ was tiny, underfinanced, disorganized and inept, and that half its accomplices were already in jail. They also knew, however, that it had the open and growing sympathy of leading leftist figures in unions, campuses, revolutionary organizations, the Parti Québécois, culture and media all through the province. At any moment the situation might gravitate from selected acts of terrorism by a few, to a general uprising. Across the western world it was the age of "radical chic," of Black Power, Che Guevara and Ho Chi Minh, and Quebec society was riddled with it.

Parti Québécois leader René Lévesque had called the kidnappers "sewer rats," but said in the next breath that alleged manipulation in the recent provincial election had caused an exodus of his younger members to the FLQ. Bourassa was saying privately that these were just "kids from our own neck of the woods," and surely they would not kill; yet he knew as well as anyone that in seven years they had planted 200 bombs, injured dozens, and killed seven people, some of them deliberately. And everyone could see that this new Chénier cell holding their friend and colleague Pierre Laporte, whoever they were, were a nastier bunch than the Libération cell holding Cross.

Five minutes before that evening's 10 p.m. FLQ deadline, Bourassa came on the radio to say that negotiations would need more time, and that if the demand to release those he now consented to call the "political prisoners" was to be met, mechanisms must be put in place to do it.

That same holiday weekend, federal ministers in Ottawa were considering the pros and cons of invoking the War Measures Act to speed up police investigations and dampen revolutionary enthusiasm in Quebec.

The rented house in St. Hubert where Laporte was held and murdered. It was only a ten-minute drive from where he was taken, and outside all the city roadblocks.

Thanksgiving Monday, October 12: "Just watch me"

Now a third – fictitious – "Nelson cell" near Quebec City started issuing kidnapping threats. Meanwhile, negotiations began with the FLQ, between a Quebec government lawyer and Robert Lemieux, a radical lawyer who was already in jail on charges of obstructing police.

That evening, 500 Canadian Forces troops, armed with machine guns and in battle dress, landed by helicopter in Ottawa from Petawawa to guard senior political figures, diplomats and federal institutions. The deployment was within the ordinary civil-law power of the federal government.

When challenged by CBC reporter Tim Ralphe why there were armed soldiers in Parliament, Trudeau uttered a famous televised response: "Well, there are a lot of bleeding hearts around who just don't like to see people with helmets and guns. All I can say is, go on and bleed, but it is more important to keep law and order in the society than to be worried about weak-kneed people." How far would he go to stop the FLQ? Answered Trudeau, "Just watch me."[1]

There were news reports that evening, denied by the government, that Canadian Forces troops were converging on Montreal. The rumours were true. Lévesque says in his memoirs that the operation began in Valcartier at the same time as the Ottawa deployment, and that Trudeau was just waiting for Bourassa to invite the soldiers into Montreal.

Tuesday, October 13: civic election debates cancelled

Of 121 candidates for Montreal's city council and others, 31 were affiliated with FRAP (Front pour l'Action Politique), which had officially endorsed the FLQ manifesto broadcast on Tuesday. Montreal Mayor Jean Drapeau now cancelled civic election appearances.

Wednesday, October 14: prominent Quebeckers urge compromise

A new communiqué materialized claiming to have the joint approval of both FLQ cells. It refined the list of demands, and endorsed Lemieux (who was now out of jail) as the negotiator. This was the first indication the two cells were in contact with each other. It was about now that Cross overheard his captors remark about their Chénier comrades, "Laporte's dead."

Later that day, a "common front" of provincial political and labour leaders endorsed exchanging "political prisoners" for the two kidnapped men.

---

1. His wife Margaret recounts in her book *Beyond Reason* that Trudeau had earlier told her chillingly that if she and their children were ever held for political ransom, he would make no deals. This made no sense to her. "You'd let them kill me rather than come to terms?" she asked, incredulous. "Yes," said Trudeau. "Yes, I would."

When Trudeau declared a state bordering on martial law in Quebec, Liberal support in English Canada rose to an all-time high.

Photos: Canadian Press Images

Heading the list of signatories were Parti Québécois leader René Lévesque and Claude Ryan, prominent publisher of the newspaper *Le Devoir* and later provincial Liberal leader. They said "an atmosphere of almost military rigidity" in Ottawa was making a peaceful resolution impossible. Trudeau was furious, and never afterward forgave any of the signers. Premier Bourassa said the government had not yet decided what it would do.

In fact, it had.

Thursday, October 15: the army moves into Montreal

At 2 p.m. the Quebec government announced that it had asked Ottawa, under the "aid to civil powers" provision of the National Defence Act, to send in troops to assist the overwhelmed police, "to protect certain places and persons."

Immediately, one thousand "Vandoos" soldiers of Quebec's Royal 22nd Regiment, in battle dress and with small arms, rolled into Montreal and Quebec City to guard homes, offices and vehicles of senior political figures, and to establish a controlling presence at key public locations, especially major campuses. In successive days, the number of deployed troops, mainly in Ottawa and southern Quebec but as far afield as the University of Toronto, reached 10,000.

Parliament and the Quebec Legislature both went into emergency sessions.

That evening, a small public fundraising meeting of FRAP at a city arena suddenly swelled to a mass rally of 2,000 students and activists, who chanted FLQ slogans and were harangued by leading separatists and revolutionaries.

At 9 p.m. Bourassa left the Legislature to issue his government's final offer: they would allow six hours for the kidnappers to surrender the hostages in exchange for safe passage out of Canada, and they would recommend parole for five of the 23 FLQ criminals. Nothing more.

Three official letters were then signed by Quebec and Montreal government officials and couriered to Ottawa, citing a state of "apprehended insurrection" and asking the national government to invoke the War Measures Act suspending civil liberties in Quebec.

Friday, October 16: the War Measures Act

By 3 a.m. the FLQ had made no reply to Bourassa's ultimatum.

At 4 a.m. on October 16 the federal Cabinet formally activated the War Measures Act, announcing it publicly at 5:15 a.m. It would allow police in Quebec to search and arrest without warrant, and to hold suspects secretly without charge for 21 days, and without right of appearance ("habeas corpus") for 90 days. It made any association (past or present) with the FLQ, or equivalent groups, a criminal act – including belonging to them, financing them, transmitting their communications, espousing their aims and ideas, endorsing their actions, harbouring their members or in any way assisting their activities.

Police in Quebec were poised. Before the sun was up they had swept Montreal and Quebec City, questioning thousands and locking up 250 people. Over the next week the number would almost double.

In Parliament, still in emergency session, NDP and Conservative opposition members demanded to hear what justified such Draconian police powers. Regional Expansion Minister Jean Marchand replied that radical and violent groups had infiltrated key positions at all levels of government in Quebec, and that the FLQ had thousands of machine guns cached, and enough dynamite to blow up downtown Montreal. All of which was pure, paranoid fantasy, but the Opposition of course did not know that. Whether the Liberal cabinet knew it to be false is open to question. Except for Trudeau, the Quebec members were sounding almost hysterical.

Trudeau went on television later that day to warn the kidnappers that they would be "ceaselessly pursued" if they harmed either hostage.

Saturday, October 17: Laporte's murder

Both FLQ cells were lying low, having said nothing since Wednesday. On Friday, Laporte – manacled, starved and half-blinded – had flung himself through a window and was halfway out before they dragged him back.

On Saturday, one week to the hour after taking him, members of the Chénier cell strangled him to death with his gold crucifix chain, loaded his corpse into their green Chevrolet, and drove it to the nearby St. Hubert airfield. It took three calls to CKAC before anyone checked it out. Police arrived at 11:15 p.m., and an hour later a bomb technician opened the trunk.

It was Canada's second political assassination since Confederation in 1867. Trudeau told news cameras it was the "cowardly act of a band of murderers." Margaret Trudeau wrote in her memoirs that Trudeau then went home and wept, aging before her eyes.

There was a massive national outpouring of grief and anger the next day, vigils on Parliament Hill, and a viewing of Laporte's body on Sunday evening in Montreal. Thousands of people paid their respects.

A letter that day from Cross himself said that he was well, and that the only danger to his life would come if police tracked down where he was.

December: arrests

In the wee hours of Monday, October 18, police broke into the Chénier hideout at 5630 Armstrong. They had been asking the public for leads on the whereabouts of Paul Rose, and a St. Hubert neighbour recognized the photo on television. Inside the two-bedroom house they found all the proof they needed to convict, but the murderers had fled.

After Laporte's funeral on Tuesday, tensions slowly subsided and the pace of special WMA "detentions" slowed.

Warrants were issued for Paul Rose, Francis Simard and Bernard Lortie.

After killing Laporte the gang had relocated to the apartment of Paul Rose's girlfriend in the city, at 3720 Queen Mary Road. There they had contrived a small hiding place by building a false wall in a large clothes closet.

The four cell members remained here for almost three weeks while police systematically searched elsewhere. Finally, however, someone thought to check a telephone number that had been scribbled on a scrap of paper found at the St. Hubert murder site. It led on November 6 to a knock on the Queen Mary Road apartment door. The Rose brothers and Simard got into the closet in time, but Lortie was arrested. Undiscovered by police for two days, the trio emerged from their closet when the coast was clear and moved to an abandoned and out-of-the-way farmhouse at St. Luc, 20 miles southeast of Montreal. There, beneath the basement, they excavated a dank hideaway.

As more days dragged by, the only question was whether James Cross would survive the inevitable arrests. The RCMP closed in on the Libération cell on December 2, capturing Jacques Cosette-Trudel and his wife Louise that evening when they left the apartment. When they failed to return and the heat

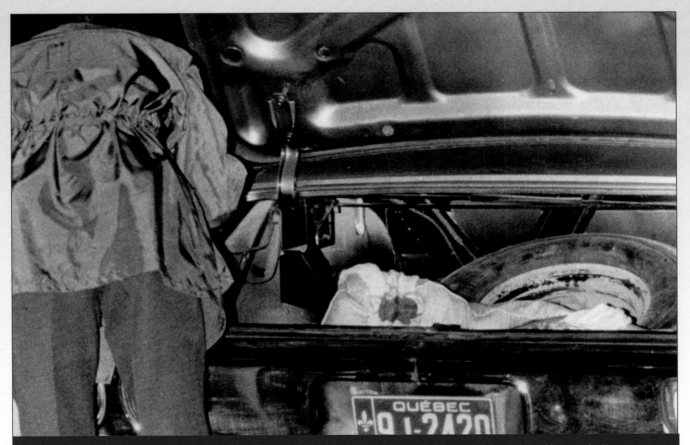

The trunk of the car where Laporte's body was found. Bourassa called them "just kids from our own neck of the woods" who surely would not murder. He was wrong.

in their house was turned off, the other cell members, knowing they'd been found, painted "FLQ" in the window and tossed out a pipe containing a note demanding safe passage. They handcuffed Cross to a doorknob, and waited.

At 11 a.m. on Thursday, a lawyer entered the apartment to confirm that Cross was alive. He was on his mattress, gaunt, 22 pounds lighter than on October 5th, but smiling. "Are you all right?" asked the lawyer. Cross replied, "Oh, I'm fine – considering the circumstances."

He remained with his captors while they drove, armed but under police escort, to the Expo island, where several weeks earlier an exchange facility had been set up with the Cuban government. There, after 60 days of captivity, Cross was released to the Canadians. His first call was to his wife in Switzerland. He then called his boss, the British high commissioner in Ottawa. All he said was, "Cross here, reporting for duty." Meanwhile, the Libération cell members – including the Cossette-Trudels and Jacques Lanctôt's wife and child – were boarding a Canadian military jet to Cuba.[2]

The Chénier cell was discovered on December 27. The three emerged from their underground tunnel cold and haggard. They surrendered their only remaining weapon – a rusty shotgun – and went off to jail.

Aftermath

The four Chénier men were all charged with kidnapping and murder, but because they refused to testify against each other, it was impossible to prove who did what. Jacques Rose was eventually convicted of lesser charges, sentenced to eight years, was paroled in 1978, and (to René Lévesque's lasting disgust) was given a standing ovation at a Parti Québécois convention in 1981. Paul Rose, Lortie and Simard were all sentenced to 20 years or life imprisonment. Paul Rose was paroled in 1982.

The ironic reality – much discussed ever since, especially in Quebec – was that in the end the kidnappers were apprehended by police doing the usual police things in the usual methodical way. It didn't require the War Measures Act.

Less than fifty of the almost 500 people detained under the Act were ever charged under its Draconian guilt-by-past-association provisions, and fewer than a dozen were convicted. Few of the detained had any business with the FLQ; most had none. They were kept for several weeks in detention, questioned aimlessly, released in due course, and later compensated by the Quebec government.

The real purpose of invoking the WMA in peacetime was political. This was admitted by some federal Liberals at the time and obvious enough. It was to end the sense of turmoil and violence-for-a-cause that pervaded Quebec.

Soldiers guarding the crowd at Laporte's funeral. The purpose of invoking the War Measures Act was entirely political, to suppress unrest. If anything, it diverted and distracted the police.

Photos: Canadian Press Images

Whether or not it cost one man his life (perhaps a softer response would have allowed Laporte to live, although this is far from certain), in this respect it succeeded.

Political terrorism ended abruptly in Quebec, while it continued for the next decade or longer in Europe, Latin America and the Middle East. According to Richard Gwyn (*The Northern Magus*), the reason heads of state admired Trudeau was not for his occasional flights of parlour Marxism and his anti-nuclear pronouncements. It was for his utterly inflexible line against domestic terrorism.

Quebec nationalists have said ever since 1970 that the Trudeau government's aim was to crush the democratic movement towards sovereignty. Trudeau always denied it, but they offer considerable evidence that he and the federal Liberals saw all separatism as insurrection. If that truly was the federal aim, it failed, and may even have backfired. In 1976 Lévesque became premier, and the sovereignty option continued to grow.

One thing is clear. Invoking the War Measures Act was the most popular thing Trudeau ever did. Gallup reported 85-percent public support for it. Political violence has never been an option Canadians tolerate, and if it took the War Measures Act to stop it, they considered it a price worth paying.

---

2. They found the workers' paradise little to their liking, and soon moved to France. Homesick, they eventually returned to Canada one-by-one to serve relatively brief prison sentences.

Pierre Trudeau and his new bride Margaret at a sugaring-off party west of Montreal in March 1971. Margaret is returning a peace sign given to her by some nearby children.

Photo: Canadian Press Images

By the end of 1970, Trudeau had lost his political shine.

Celebrity visitors John Lennon and Yoko Ono had come and gone, and so had the 1960s. The mood of the 1970s was colder and angrier. As Trudeau himself later put it, "the Love Generation of the '60s was moving towards the Me Generation of the '80s."

English support for the War Measures Act had been overwhelming – and along with it, Liberal support in the Gallup poll spiked from 42 percent to an all-time high of 57 percent in one month. But the increase did not necessarily come from people who would vote Liberal in an election. It came mainly from people who were fed up with Quebec. The War Measures Act tarnished Trudeau's credentials among centre-left academics, civil libertarians, union leaders and the like, who agreed with Tommy Douglas that invoking wartime powers was like "using a sledge hammer to crack a peanut."

In Quebec, though most people approved of Trudeau's hard line, it had strengthened the flow of disenchanted voters towards René Lévesque's nationalist Parti Québécois.

In 1971, as the Liberals slid steadily back down to 37 percent in the Gallup poll, it was becoming fairly clear that Trudeau had fallen short of all three of the Great Expectations he had set – peace with Quebec, power to the people, and prosperity for all. The honeymoon was almost over.

It was not quite over, however.

On March 15, 1971, the nation was astonished to hear that the previous evening the prime minister had secretly married in Vancouver. His bride was Margaret Sinclair, daughter of James Sinclair, an international cement company executive and former St. Laurent fisheries minister.

Nor was the marriage a Las Vegas whim. It had been in the planning for at least six months, but hardly anyone outside the immediate Sinclair family knew about it, and only 12 people attended.

Margaret Sinclair had been seen twice on the prime minister's arm in Ottawa. But he dated many young women, and though Margaret was strikingly beautiful, she was not in this regard exceptional. Nobody realized – even her parents, initially – that Trudeau was smitten with her, and the couple had kept both their liaison and their plans perfectly concealed.

Sinclair was a Simon Fraser University English Literature undergrad, a West Coast flower child who had studied poetry, toured what she called the "hippie trail" in Morocco, and sewn her own wedding dress. She said they wanted children together, adding that she was her own person and did not intend to become "just a rose in his lapel."

She was so attractive, and it was all so charmingly unexpected and intriguingly unconventional, that Canadians just chuckled and joined John Diefenbaker in wishing the couple well. To younger people, it promised in some vague way to preserve the innocent optimism of the 1960s amid the angry disappointments of the emerging decade.

Trudeau made no apology for the fact that, at 22, Margaret was less than half his age (51), though he had been torn by doubts about it for months. Neither did her mother Kathleen, who was herself two years younger than the groom; he was, she observed, "young at heart."

At first the marriage was a happy one, and it did Trudeau a lot of good – personally and politically. Not only did it humanize his public image, which needed it after the War Measures Act, but it also turned his empty government mansion on Sussex Drive into a real home. Sundered from his Quebec friends and family by his position and his workload, he was showing distinct signs of feeling trapped and lonely; and now that he was embarking on his second half-century of life, perhaps he was feeling his mortality as well.

The fact that his bride came from a very different generation and an entirely different cultural milieu should perhaps have dissuaded him. But it didn't, and the public, for the most part, found the match endearing and daring – typically Trudeauesque. It gave Canadians a little northern Camelot all their own. On Christmas Day of 1971, nine months and 10 days after the wedding, Margaret gave birth to Justin, the first of their three sons. It was all so perfect.

■ ■ ■ ■

Maggie T.

A marriage gone terribly wrong

Pierre Trudeau's flower-child bride, Margaret Sinclair, was widely and angrily denounced when the marriage ended and she took off to Toronto in 1977 to visit the Rolling Stones.

She was condemned as childish, spoiled, bad-tempered, drug-addicted, unhinged, superficial, ambitious, ungrateful and promiscuous. All of which she plainly was, and all of which now caused people to question why Trudeau had married her in the first place. Many shook their heads and said they had expected it all along.

According to Margaret in her 1979 memoir *Beyond Reason*, Trudeau himself had predicted it. While considering their engagement, he had been worried that her wild past might expose them to blackmail, and he demanded a detailed account of it. As she gave it, he remarked sadly more than once, "I know you'll leave me one day."

Trudeau refused to say anything about their marriage in his memoirs, but Margaret had plenty to say in hers.

She soon realized, she wrote, that Trudeau was no more a real playboy in his bachelor years than she was a real hippie. It was mostly for show. He was far too Catholic and guilt-driven to cut it as a playboy. He wouldn't even let her take birth control. She found it weird, but didn't mind.

When she first met Trudeau in Tahiti in 1968, she was 19, had already had a high-school abortion, and he was "too old and too square" to be of much interest – though there was something about her that clearly caught his attention. She was then in love with a French Adonis named Yves Lewis, a water-skiing instructor and the son of the man who founded Club Med.

But it was destined not to be. As she got more interested in making peace and making babies, Yves got more interested in collecting arms and making revolution. She left him, went on a six-month sex-and-drugs tour of Morocco, and then went home to Vancouver to mope.

And then, clear out of the blue in August 1969, a year after becoming prime minister and 18 months after he had chatted with her on the beach in Tahiti, Trudeau called her and took her on a restaurant date atop Grouse Mountain. She was now a little wiser and he was far more important, and things now looked different. She found him to be an intent and sympathetic listener. Despite having virtually nothing in common, to their mutual surprise they actually enjoyed each other's company.

Dropping her off at home, he suggested – as he usually did with beautiful young women – that she come by for supper if she was ever in Ottawa. Margaret says she silently resolved then and there that he would marry her. She promptly moved to Ottawa, got a starting-level sociology job with the Department of Manpower, and called him up.

They saw each other on weekends over most of the next year, usually in private. Margaret found their two public appearances together totally intimidating, and his private intellectual conversation with friends too far above her, conducted in a language she didn't speak.

"Don't worry about her," Trudeau once told some old friends as they discussed deep matters in French over supper, while Margaret smiled uncomprehendingly. "She wouldn't understand even if we were speaking English."

The worst barrier was not French, it was cultural. As she commented in her memoirs, "Culture to me was rock music."

That, and smoking pot – something Trudeau implored her to stop doing, but to which she returned whenever she was lonely, anxious or depressed. As she often was.

Margaret Trudeau in a brooding moment during her stellar performance in the 1974 campaign. Though she successfully portrayed herself as a lovestruck newlywed and proud young mother, in fact she was already being dragged down by manic depression.

Photo: National Archives of Canada

Margaret and Pierre in the fall of 1972. Though married only a year and still putting a brave and happy face on things, Margaret was already writing privately that she was terribly lonely.

Photo: National Archives of Canada

Before their marriage she would seethe out of sight as he publicly dated glamorous women, most notably actress Barbara Streisand. But she had the consolation that it was to her that he always returned, and by summertime 1970 they were in love, he for the first time. He was in some ways as emotionally immature as she was.

When Trudeau proposed in the late summer or fall of 1970, Margaret was still game, but both Trudeau and, later, her mother had severe misgivings. However, her mother had no real say in the matter, her father was not told until a little later, and Trudeau – busy with the October Crisis and its aftermath – let himself be talked into it.

Amazingly, the wedding remained absolutely secret from the fall of 1970 until March 4, 1971, when Trudeau flew west with a formal suit, ostensibly to go skiing. Even his executive assistant, Gordon Gibson of Vancouver, knew nothing.

Margaret insisted in her book that the marriage was initially a happy one, but that she soon felt trapped in his palatial prime ministerial "prison" on Sussex Drive. Like Trudeau, she had been sundered from old friends and was prevented by her exalted position from making new ones. How she got her copious supply of marijuana, surrounded as she was by plainclothes Mounties, she never said.

It would be easy to think she should have found something useful to do – but what? Trudeau wanted her out of public view and out of harm's way. He said she should write, but she had no gift for it. She liked being with people and doing things.

Except for fairly frequent stilted and uptight affairs of state, which terrified and repelled her, she had little to do except have

babies and raise them, and much of the second part was done for her. Trudeau was at home most evenings, but usually immersed in work he told her almost nothing about. Her days were filled with irritations caused by staff, most of whom she would have happily fired and not replaced, and police bodyguards, who exasperated her.

When packing her things to leave in 1977, she says in her book that she found a note dated November 1972 which read: "I am so lonely. I should be happy. I am married to a man who loves me, and I have a wonderful baby. But I am terribly unhappy." She had been married little more than a year.

Apart from her three children, the high point of Margaret's marriage was the election campaign of 1974, which she was invited to join. She did exceedingly well, not just accompanying her husband but often foraging off on her own assigned missions. Crowds loved her, and the fact that she loved Trudeau. Soon media pundits spoke of the "Margaret factor" in the Liberal recovery from their crippling "Land is Strong" fiasco of 1972.

Alas, her happiness was brief. As soon as the election was over she was back at Sussex Drive, to quarrel with servants and security staff, suffer the intimidations of protocol as gracefully as possible, and smoke pot in her upstairs hideaway. Two months after the election she had a fierce argument with Trudeau, ran screaming outside to kill herself with a carving knife, and was admitted to hospital in Montreal for stress.

Things went steadily downhill from there. She took more and more pot, and more "freedom trips" on her own, less now to see her mother than to try to track down Yves in France, and have an affair with Ted Kennedy. She and Trudeau now quarrelled

In January 1971 the Trudeaus had their first son, Justin, baptized at Notre-Dame Cathedral in Montreal. Soon after this Margaret began quietly falling apart, a victim of manic depression, but few were aware of it then.

Photo: Canadian Press Images

Margaret dancing up a storm at Studio 54, a New York disco, as Trudeau lost an election in Canada. Between her outrageous behaviour and tell-all interviews, she left Trudeau psychologically hamstrung.

Photo: Canadian Press Images

constantly, and when he came home in the evening he'd come upstairs not to kiss her, she wrote, but to sniff her, to see if she'd been using drugs.

By March 1977 they had concluded it was hopeless, and Margaret left on an unannounced three-month trial separation to work as a photographer. Her first professional venture was to attend a Rolling Stones concert in Toronto, and an after-hours party, which scandalized the country.

Worse was to follow, mostly in the form of risqué photos and tell-all interviews about her affairs, her teenage abortion, what made Trudeau tick, etc., leading up to the publication of *Beyond Reason* on the eve of the 1979 election. A famous news photo (see above) showed Margaret dancing merrily at New York's Studio 54 the same night her husband led his party to defeat.

She never made it as a photographer, nor as a TV host, nor as a movie actress – all of which she tried as she faded from public view. Her real skill was marrying, which she did again.

Their three sons usually stayed with Pierre, who by all accounts was a diligent and loving parent. Margaret came to stay regularly after the breakup, but caused such disruption that more distance was necessary.

They divorced in 1984 so she could marry Ottawa real estate developer Fried Kemper, with whom she had two more children. However, when the Trudeaus' youngest son Michel, was killed by an avalanche in B.C. in 1998 Margaret suffered a second breakdown, leading to a second divorce. She remained in contact with Trudeau, and was at his deathbed in 2000.

Margaret divulged in 2006 that she had bipolar disorder – something that many people had figured out for themselves years before. Her misbehaviour went beyond mere moral failure. Nothing could explain her erratic, up-and-down, self-destructive "flightiness" better than manic depression.

After Trudeau's death, she remained a valued advocate for the mentally disabled.

The "Just Society" Trudeau promised always had an economic context to it.

It is never wise to rely for economic insight on political news media and political leaders. Politicians deal in rhetoric and public perceptions, not facts, and reporters cover what the politicians, not the statisticians, have to say. Besides, journalists are notoriously poor at math, and statistics, coming months after the speeches, are of more use to historians.

Anyone reading Canadian contemporary news coverage of the Pearson-Trudeau era would conclude that they were times of constant government restraint and painful fiscal rectitude. That's how politicians talked, and it's what reporters wrote.

But the fiscal commentary of the time was quite disconnected from what was actually happening in the national accounts. Even after discounting monetary inflation and population growth, government spending was surging upwards throughout the period, as indeed it had been doing since the Second World War.

Finance minister Edgar Benson leaving the Commons after delivering his 1969 budget. The rhetoric was of austerity, while the reality was double-digit percentage increases in spending.

Photo: Canadian Press Images

Between 1947 and 1977, real (inflation-adjusted) spending per Canadian by all three levels of government more than quadrupled.

And never did it increase more at the federal level than when Pierre Trudeau was prime minister.

Between 1967 and 1977, the actual (inflation-adjusted) amount Ottawa spent per citizen doubled.

Thus, it is hard now to connect the constant cost-control, anti-inflation rhetoric of the politicians with what they were, in fact, doing.

The challenge facing Trudeau's government when it took office was an emerging phenomenon called "stagflation."

Neither the phrase nor the problem was unique to Canada. Stagflation was afflicting, in varying degrees, other modern economies because democratic governments had all been expanding their public spending faster than private investment could increase production of consumer goods. The result, after 30 years, was a combination of monetary inflation and stagnant employment.

The inflation happened because central banks were expanding currency and credit faster

Regional Economic Expansion Minister Jean Marchand. His "Marshall Plan for Atlantic Canada" terminated the region's steady recovery of economic independence.

Photo: National Archives of Canada

than the economy increased real goods and services. The stagnation resulted from governments raising taxes and making it increasingly easy for low-wage earners to quit working, or get paid for new public sector jobs of little real value.

It would take 30 more years for politicians and voters to grasp that, beyond a certain point, government spending reduces prosperity instead of increasing it, and that government cannot "create jobs" in any sustainable or useful sense.

Price inflation above 2 percent annually was (and is) assumed to be too high. In 1968, inflation hit 4 percent, and the following year it was 5 percent. At the same time, unemployment was rising again to Diefenbaker-era levels–above 5 percent. This frustrated earlier hopes during the Pearson years that unemployment would keep declining to its long post-war average of 2 percent.

According to standard post-war economic theory, if unemployment was rising, prices should be static, and vice versa. But the theory had ceased to fit reality, and people were unnerved by the new certainty that everything would cost noticeably more every month.

Trudeau's first government had to choose, therefore, whether to fight inflation by spending less, or fight unemployment by spending more.

In the end, it did both and neither. It opted to spend more while pretending to spend less.

In his 1968 and 1969 budgets, affable, pipe-smoking Finance Minister Edgar Benson claimed with a long face to be curbing inflation rather than easing unemployment, to the outrage of union bosses and the quiet satisfaction of bank presidents. He levied an anti-inflation surtax on incomes, a policy White Paper was ordered, and Trudeau talked about Ottawa setting a stern example of austerity.

There were some token program cutbacks – the cancelling of a planned winter works scheme, for example – but nothing significant. In reality, Canada's long government-spending surge continued. Federal spending (not counting transfers to provinces) rose a generous 9 percent in 1969, to 10 percent in 1970, and 10 percent again in 1971 – twice the rate of inflation.

The federal civil service increased during the three years by over 22,000 employees, or 9 percent – more than twice as fast as population growth.

Provincial governments, funded in large part by Ottawa doubling federal transfers for shared-cost social programs, increased their collective spending in the same three years by 13 percent, 8 percent and 20 percent, and their employee head count by over 34,000.

Yet the more the provinces received, the more they demanded. And the more the federal government claimed to be retrenching, the more it spent.

One thing that really was cut back – and perhaps the only thing – was further mention of the "Just Society." It drowned in a tide of rhetoric about inflation control. But while the phrase disappeared, an attitude and expectation of "equal prosperity for all" remained as robust as ever.

■ ■ ■ ■

owhere did the disconnection between politics and economics become more obvious and destructive than in Atlantic Canada.

One of the first moves of the first Trudeau government was the assignment of Jean Marchand to create what was described as a "Marshall Plan" for poor regions, especially Atlantic Canada.

Without generous federal help, the region could neither catch up nor keep up – or so it had long been assumed.

Atlantic Canada had an unfortunate history. At the time of Confederation in 1867, the Maritime provinces – Nova Scotia, in particular – were Canada's industrial heartland. (This was not true of poor Newfoundland, clinging to its cold granite rock; but it was not to be a part of Canada for another 82 years.)

As economist Fred McMahon would recount in his award-winning 2000 analysis of the region, *Retreat From Growth*, Nova Scotia came into Confederation with only one-sixth of Canada's population, but one-third to one-half of its steel, glass, cotton, sugar and banking enterprises.

Nova Scotia-built commercial sailing ships could be found in every port of the British Empire.

But all of this value-added enterprise and industrialism, McMahon explains, depended on the free international trade of the mid-19th century.

Above, the face of aboriginal poverty in Schefferville, northern Quebec, 1970. At right, cod fishing on the Grand Banks of Newfoundland was little changed from the first half of the century.

Photos: Canadian Press Images (above), National Archives of Canada (opposite)

As trade barriers rose around the world in the late 19th century, and continued to do so into the 20th, the Maritimes were cut off. Transport was expensive, and they were too far from the thriving towns of Ontario and the West to benefit from Canada's manufacturing tariffs. They were increasingly barred by tariffs from access to the huge consumer and industrial markets of the U.S. and Europe. And they had too little agricultural land to build a larger local market of their own.

So they stalled. Jobs withered, and people moved out. It became a deeply ingrained regional assumption, said McMahon, that a job, once lost, was gone forever. The normal expectation of progress – that new industries replace older ones – was not the Atlantic experience.

Clinging to what jobs they had left, Maritimers became economic reactionaries. In 1908, Nova Scotia passed a job-saving law banning mechanization of the fishery, and the new

Squid harvest in Holyrood, Newfoundland, 1964. The days of dories and hand-jigging should have been ending, but weren't. Federal subsidies were turning the region into a living museum.

Photo: National Archives of Canada

steam-powered trawlers dwindled from 10 to three. A large 1920s U.S. investment pitch to turn Nova Scotia into the "fish pier of America," using steam trawlers and new freezer technology, was killed by political resistance from inshore fishermen and fish processors.

By the post-war period, Maritimers had thoroughly succumbed to an attitude of dependency (in the later phrase of future prime minister Stephen Harper, a "culture of defeat"), and national politicians, riding a buoyant economy, were in an accommodating mood.

The first regional transfer programs began in the 1950s, aimed mainly at equalizing provincial spending on schools and hospitals.

Almost instantly, the regional economy perked up. Unemployment went down, from two percentage points higher than the national average to virtually the same level by the end of the 1960s, as job-creating private-business investment reached the national average. Average personal earnings, though still lower than elsewhere, began catching up too, growing noticeably faster than the national average. Education levels also began rising.

McMahon says that while the early assistance was helpful, mainly the region was experiencing the natural economic catch-up that comes with cheaper modern transportation and better finance. All around the world, it has been shown that poorer regions close the gap with

New technology, in the form of snow-mobiles and framed buildings, had done little to change the economic livelihood of this trapper and stone carver in remote Lake Harbour, Nunavut, in 1970.

Sealing remained a lucrative though dangerous seasonal business until the 1970s. Here in 1977 a sealer working the ice floes off Newfoundland prepares to load the whitecoat seal pup pelts he has just skinned. Urban animal-rights protests were already destroying the market.

Photos: Canadian Press Images

richer ones if they keep their taxes, wages and production costs lower than their high-cost competitors. Had the Trudeau government simply left things alone, all Canadians – especially Atlantic Canadians – would have been better off.

Instead, the Trudeau government inflicted a double blow – first in the form of massive federal industrial investment, and second in special regional entitlements to Unemployment Insurance (later renamed Employment Insurance, or EI). This was equivalent to stepping on the gas pedal and the brake at the same time – paying local governments and businesses to create jobs, and paying workers not to do them.

Over time, the combination proved ruinous to the work ethic and self-reliance of the whole region.

Where Maritimers had long ago concluded that every old job, no matter how outmoded, was worth preserving, under the new federal regime they concluded that any new job, no matter how useless, was worth creating. The lesson quickly sank in that security depends on how you vote, not on what you do.

Jean Marchand – much encouraged by Atlantic MPs and premiers – established a whole new federal department named DREE (the Department of Regional Economic Expansion). Although it operated in the more sluggish areas of all provinces, especially eastern Quebec, its influence was most pervasive and pernicious in Atlantic Canada.

By 1971, having absorbed a number of smaller federal programs and agencies into itself, DREE began pouring new money into the region for four contradictory purposes: (1) for major public infrastructure in urban centres, to enable a rural migration to jobs in larger towns and cities; (2) to finance rural projects that allowed whole small communities to qualify for EI and stay where they were; (3) to subsidize a few large, inefficient regional dinosaurs such as the Cape Breton coal mines; and (4) to start thousands of small private businesses that would compete for workers and customers with unsubsidized small private businesses.

DREE alone would have been bad enough, but at the same time Ottawa granted the region special concessions on Employment Insurance aimed at preserving seasonal farming, logging and fishing livelihoods in remote villages and outports.

This inaugurated what became notoriously known as "Lotto 10-42" – working for 10 weeks in a fish plant to "stamp up" for EI benefits, and taking the rest of the year off.

In 1969 Canadians were shaken by the voyage of the 1,000-foot oil tanker *Manhattan* from the eastern seaboard, through the Arctic Ocean and across to Prudhoe Bay on the northern coast of Alaska. Although accompanied by a Canadian Coast Guard vessel, the *Manhattan* did not have Canadian permission to enter what Canadians considered their own "internal waters" – a concept and a claim which Americans have never accepted. The Americans hoped that shipping the oil south would prove cheaper than building a pipeline across Alaska to Valdez, but it did not. The *Manhattan* loaded a symbolic barrel of oil and dead-headed home. The trip was never repeated, and the question of whether Canada may close the Northwest Passage to shipping remained unresolved into the 21st century.

Photo: Canadian Press Images

Not that Maritimers who did this were necessarily lazy. Many were tradesmen who were paid under the table for their services, creating a thriving underground local economy.

As more and more federally funded make-work jobs opened up and were shared within the community – painting the cemetery fence, directing traffic at the local garbage dump, producing tourist knick-knacks – even the hard traditional fish-plant jobs started to go begging. By the early 2000s, in regions with double-digit unemployment, Atlantic fish processors were flying in temporary workers from Eastern Europe.

Taken together, these measures produced the bizarre economic phenomenon of rising wage levels in an area of rising unemployment. By 1980, 80 percent of the Atlantic economy was government-generated – up from 40 percent in 1965. By the end of the century, it still hovered in the 70-percent range. By comparison, the government share of the overall Canadian economy (at all three levels) rose from 25 percent in 1965 to peak at 50 percent in 1993.

■ ■ ■ ■

As the first Trudeau government's mandate ran out, Canadians started taking stock, and most didn't like what they saw.

The government's few successes were of debatable merit. The only clear win was the forceful amalgamation of many dozens of feuding provincial agricultural marketing boards into a national system of fixed prices and production quotas.

Official Languages had increased Quebec's federal role without winning Quebec's federal loyalty. An unexpected 1971 constitutional deal with the provinces just as unexpectedly collapsed when Quebec Premier Robert Bourassa first agreed and later backed out.

Government, far from becoming more participatory, was said by many to have given way to rule by bureaucrats – by a "supergroup" of arrogant technocrats centred in the Prime Minister's Office and Privy Council Office.

The imposed 1971 conversion of the Canadian economy from English imperial to French metric units of measure, lauded by some, was derided by far more as a useless, expensive and confusing attack on traditional culture.

Inflation, though checked to 2 percent in 1971, returned to 5 percent in 1972.

NATO commitments had been chopped by half, and Canada's once-proud military was being decimated – yet government was getting bigger.

Social advocates were accusing Trudeau of having sold out the "Just Society" to business lobbies, while business accused him of being soft on unions, friendly with Communists and hostile to the U.S.

An ambitious tax reform attempted in 1969, aimed at eliminating investment tax breaks ("loopholes") and favouring low-income earners, had been demolished by an outcry from business. What little reform was left, when it was reintroduced in 1972, made the tax code so complicated that even tax experts said they weren't sure what they meant.

A brave 1969 proposal by Indian Affairs Minister Jean Chrétien to abolish his own department, and eventually Indian reserves and special Native status, had hit a brick wall of resistance. Instead, by 1972 support payments to treaty Indians had doubled, with a $3 million top-up to finance a plethora of Native lobby groups who were now fruitlessly and frequently conferencing at taxpayers' expense to think up new demands.

In the West, where, to quote historian Desmond Morton, "Trudeau had a gift for making enemies," and where, as Richard Gwyn puts it, even the rose in his lapel bugged people, the recurrent problem of unsold prairie wheat had returned. When Trudeau said candidly he wasn't sure there was much Ottawa could do about it, he provoked lasting hostility. The problem was now being solved by rising world markets, not by the Liberals.

The last provincial Liberal government in the West, and the second-last in Canada, was defeated in Saskatchewan in 1971. The West had now become a battleground for the Conservatives and the NDP. In four years, Trudeau had permanently redefined the Liberals as the party of eastern Canada, obsessed with Quebec and indifferent to the economic priorities of the West.

Unemployment was back up to 7 percent, and Trudeau was feuding publicly with Ontario Premier John Robarts over federal management of the economy.

With Canada in this fractured frame of mind, time ran out, and in September Trudeau visited the Governor General to seek an election writ.

■ ■ ■ ■

Quebec premier Robert Bourassa and Ontario premier John Robarts in 1971. A constitutional patriation deal that unexpectedly came together just as unexpectedly collapsed when Bourassa went home and backed out of it. Under the Victoria Formula, Ottawa, Ontario and Quebec would all have held unilateral vetoes over future amendments; smaller provinces would have had to combine.

Photo: Archives of Ontario

By Trudeau's own later admission, the ensuing campaign was inept.

Knowing that Trudeaumania had passed, and encouraged by his isolated, intellectual, personal court in the PMO, Trudeau imagined he would look his best holding a "conversation with Canadians" rather than fighting an election.

A Toronto ad agency dreamed up the surreal slogan, "The land is strong," which was untranslatable into French and sounded ridiculous in English. In reality, the land was angry, apprehensive, divided, frustrated and disappointed.

In his memoirs, Trudeau described his 1972 election approach as highly reasoned, in effect saying to voters, "Here's what we've accomplished in the past four years, and here are our plans for the next four. If you like them, then vote for us."

Trudeau never did understand, wrote Christina Mc-Call, one of his premier biographers, in her book *Grits* (1980), that what he considered the "politics of reason" was nothing more than his own unreasonable insistence on doing what interested him.

It no longer interested most voters. A majority opted either for Stanfield's Conservatives or the New Democrats under their feisty new leader David Lewis.

When ballots were counted on October 30, it looked at first as if the Conservatives had won 109 seats to the Liberals' 107. It took six days of recounts to reverse those numbers and give the victory to the Liberals.

Even so, it wasn't much of a win. The Liberals were a whopping 55 seats short of a majority. The NDP had jumped from 22 seats in 1968 to 31. Quebec's back-country Créditistes had held their ground with 15. The Liberals were down to seven seats in the West, and the Conservatives to two in Quebec.

Trudeau in adversity was always at his best.

Far from feeling chastened by his brush with political death, he was energized. He hated to lose anything, and vowed to win next time. Wearing a fringed Indian buckskin jacket, he went wheeling up to the front door of the Governor General's residence in his Mercedes convertible to accept the prime ministership.

Many people have said this near-loss sparked a change in Trudeau. From now on, he sounded less like a philosopher-king and more like a regular vote-hustling party politician. His bottom line was no longer "What is right?" but "What's popular?"

"Nine-tenths of politics appeals to emotions rather than reason," commented Trudeau somewhat petulantly. "I'm a bit sorry about that, but this is the world we're living in, and I've had to change."

The "Land is Strong" election of 1972 saw the NDP under David Lewis gain a solid hold over a Liberal minority government. Lewis derided "corporate welfare bums" who had received generous tax concessions and subsidies from the Liberal government. Trudeau always denied that the NDP exerted much influence, likening them to seagulls noisily accompanying a ship at sea, thinking they were steering it. All the same, Liberal policy turned sharply to the left, and never really shifted back.

One of the new hardball political advisers to gain Trudeau's ear was Jim Coutts, who originally served in Pearson's office in 1964. Newly installed PMO pragmatists such as Coutts had no real philosophy except to hang on to power, whatever that required.

Photos: National Archives of Canada

However, in another way he became much more genuine after 1972. He became openly socialist, which was an ideology he had believed in, in one way or another, his whole life.

In his first mandate, Trudeau had tried – perhaps unsuccessfully – to preserve a centrist Liberal balance between the competing interests of commerce and of wage earners.

Given his left-wing reputation and short tenure in the Liberal Party, he had initially felt he had to at least feign enthusiasm for capitalism, continentalism and free enterprise – things that the Liberal Party always believed in. But even though after 1972 ideological left-wingers such as Ivan Head were gone from the PMO, the political manipulators who replaced them were not traditional Liberals either.

Now, with the NDP's David Lewis holding the balance of power (assuming Quebec's aimless Créditistes could be kept on side, which usually wasn't hard), Trudeau could be as socialist as he liked, as long as he could convince Canadians it was what they wanted.

Over the ensuing months, Trudeau fired his cerebral senior PMO advisers, and brought back the hard-nosed Grit backroom boys he had driven out four years earlier. Lalonde was now a member of Parliament, so Trudeau asked an Albertan named Jim Coutts, a famous political operator with whom he had first worked in Pearson's office, to run the PMO. Together they shunted out intellectuals such as Ivan Head, and replaced them with party-savvy mechanics. Some of Pearson's more effective anglophone political heavyweights, most prominently Keith Davey (who had been appointed a senator), were restored to grace and favour.

Until now, Trudeau had respected the constitutional fact that social programs are provincial responsibilities. "No new medicares," he had often said, and "no more free stuff."

With President Richard Nixon, he had ratified what was a continental oil policy in all but name, and he had abandoned issues of Canadian economic nationalism to the NDP.

All this changed with the Liberals' minority predicament in 1972, and never changed back.

■ ■ ■ ■

Civil war on skates

The Eastern Hockey Establishment was never the same after
WHA founder "Wild Bill" Hunter was finished with them

by Eli Byfield

The 1970s would see an epic battle between professional hockey club owners, culminating in an old-fashioned, bench-clearing brawl. The new West took on the old "Original Six" eastern establishment. From among the many pugilists, two figures stood out. Although on opposing sides, both would go down as heavyweights of hockey history. And, when the fight was finally over, each would emerge bloodied but, in his own way, victorious.

William Dickenson Hunter was born into hockey in Saskatoon in 1920. His father, Jack, was the district director of the postal service for northern Saskatchewan and Manitoba, and very involved in sports. He was general manager of the Saskatoon Quakers hockey club, and had played pro in the old Winnipeg senior league.

Son Bill formed his first competitive sports team at age 17. He served as a fighter pilot in the Second World War. Upon returning home in 1944, he worked briefly in radio before opening Hunter's Sporting Goods store in North Battleford, Saskatchewan. Famous for his red hair, blue eyes and fiery locker-room pep talks, Hunter went on to own, coach and manage teams all over western Canada. A conflict with a referee earned him the moniker "Wild Bill," and it stuck.

In 1965, Hunter took over the major junior Edmonton Oil Kings – the Detroit farm club. Saying that he wanted to be his own man, the new general manager refused any payment, and Red Wings owner Bruce Norris didn't argue the point.

Under Hunter's management, the youthful junior team won the Alberta Senior Hockey League, beat the southern Alberta and British Columbia champs, and played a best-of-seven series against the Estevan Bruins for a shot at the Memorial Cup.

The semifinal matches were tightly contested. Game five saw the Oil Kings up three games to two. Hunter had no desire to play the last game in Estevan. Before game six, he told his boys he had absolute faith in them, and to prove his conviction he pulled out a fistful of airline tickets for the final in Toronto. They won the contest, playing, in Hunter's opinion, their best game of the year. The Oil Kings went on to beat the heavily favoured Oshawa Generals, a club led by a young defenceman named Bobby Orr. In 1966 – Hunter's first season as general manager – the underdog Edmonton franchise brought home the Memorial Cup.

The next season Hunter formed the Canadian Major Junior Hockey League, soon to become the Western Hockey League. Clubs such as the Regina Pats and Estevan Bruins came over from the Saskatchewan Junior Hockey League. A new team, the Calgary Buffaloes, likewise believed Hunter's promise that an amalgamated league could better compete with Ontario and Quebec than could four provincial ones.

The new league rocked a lot of boats. Many National Hockey League (NHL) owners opposed it, including Bruce Norris. Smaller farm teams were easier to manage and, as Hunter saw it, easier to shortchange. The Canadian Amateur Hockey Association, which Hunter despised, barred the "outlaw league" (an expression Hunter loved) from Memorial Cup contention in its first year. However, the WHL saw a steady influx of teams. The NHL accepted the inevitable, as more fans lined up behind the "Dub."

Although western teams continued to win nationals at about the usual pace, the WHL, as it came to be called, generated interest in new locales. Wild Bill was first and foremost a western man, bringing big-league hockey to towns such as Edmonton, Saskatoon and Medicine Hat. His quest incurred the wrath of eastern owners and the adoration of western fans.

By the mid-'60s, the NHL was a swamp of colluding interests. The American game was utterly dominated by the Norrises, known as "the family that owned the NHL." Ontario-born American entrepreneur James E. Norris, once the world's largest cash grain buyer, launched the Detroit Red Wings in 1933. Upon his death in 1952, he effectively bequeathed the league to his two sons: James, and Bruce, Bill Hunter's first NHL boss.

James D. Norris bought the Chicago Blackhawks with his father's help. James Jr. also inherited a significant stake in Madison Square Gardens, home of the New York Rangers. In 1949, he served as founding president of the International Boxing Club of New York. The Supreme Court objected to the club monopolizing title fights, and it was shut down after a ten-year run. Even worse for family prestige, however, were the two sons' admittedly close ties to a New York mobster, Frankie Carbo.

The second brother, Bruce, wrestled control of the Detroit Red Wings from his sister Marguerite in 1955. Not one to be

Tireless promoter Bill Hunter was told by the NHL that Edmonton could not possibly sustain a professional team.
So he created a new league, turned their comfortable world upside down, and proved them wrong.

Photo: Canadian Press Images

outshone by his older brother, he managed to accumulate convictions for fraud and tax evasion while plunging the then champion Red Wings into a 42-year Stanley Cup drought. Under Bruce, the Wings did at least manage to dominate the American farm team system. Other Norris-controlled teams did suspiciously little to close the gap.

Hockey players at that time were ridiculously underpaid, compared with other athletes. Hunter said they were treated like "serfs on skates." Labour unrest was frequently punished by exile to the minors. In 1957, Bruce Norris even traded Red Wings captain Ted Lindsay to perennial loser Chicago Blackhawks for the crime of organizing.

In 1967, the league took the first steps towards reform when the NHL Players' Association was born. The league added clubs in Philadelphia, Minnesota, St. Louis, Oakland, Los Angeles and Pittsburgh, despite the hard-liners' objections. In 1970, Vancouver and Buffalo enlisted too.

But to much of the NHL old guard, expansion remained at best a necessary evil, to be undertaken as slowly as possible. Hunter's proposal for a pro team in Edmonton was greeted with little enthusiasm by the league, even after he offered to buy and move the struggling Pittsburgh Penguins. League president Clarence Campbell, a westerner himself, told Hunter he must

have been "smoking something." Campbell declared: "It'll never happen."

Then, in the early '70s, Dennis Murphy and Gary Davidson – two Californians who had never watched a game before – started the World Hockey Association. These unlikely founders came to Hunter with an audacious notion: a rival league to compete with the NHL. Citing the NHL's intransigence regarding expansion, they argued the time was ripe. The WHA would embrace European players and pay far higher wages than the grasping NHL owners. Moreover, the new league would ignore the "reserve" clause, whereby players were forbidden to sign with different teams for one year after their contracts expired.

The Americans' business case actually made some sense. Their only problem was that they knew nothing about hockey. Hunter once met them at an LA Kings game, and he recalled that as the centremen bore down for the opening faceoff, Davidson leaned in and asked, "What are they doing?"

Ever the optimist, Hunter agreed to lend a hand, lining up franchises in Calgary, Saskatoon and Winnipeg. He decided to start one of his own in Edmonton. In November of 1971, 12 teams were formally announced, four of which had never skated. The NHL owners smirked. No one had seriously threatened NHL supremacy since the Western League of the mid-'20s,

Toronto Maple Leafs owner Harold Ballard was Hunter's arch-nemesis and went to his grave hating the WHA after its first act was to snatch four of his players.

and, as far as they were concerned, Bill Hunter and his friends were no threat now.

If Hunter represented a challenge to the eastern establishment, Edwin Harold Ballard embodied all the worst qualities of it. Born in Toronto in 1903, his father, Sidney, owned Ballard Machine Supplies Co., at one time a leading ice-skate manufacturer. Harold would spend five of the almost nine decades of his life with the most established team of all: the Toronto Maple Leafs.

Hunter actually liked Ballard, and regarded him a genius in business. But the westerner said there were two Harolds. One was a "tremendous philanthropist in private." The other pinched pennies, hated Europeans and had no desire to share the limelight with more Canadian teams. From its inaugural season, Ballard would be the most obstinate and vocal opponent of the WHA.

Unlike Hunter, Ballard always showed greater aptitude as a manager than he did as a coach. His first – and last – major coaching job was with the senior amateur Toronto National Sea Fleas. Although he managed them to the Canadian championship in 1932, he brought disaster the following year as coach. His decision to bench captain Bruce Paul aggravated several veterans, causing them to quit mid-season. Ballard shrewdly attempted to salvage the year by entering the World Championships in Prague. His ploy badly backfired, however,

when the Sea Fleas lost the final to an American team.

Ballard managed several Toronto-area teams during the Depression. During the Second World War, he won a long-desired place within the Maple Leafs organization as president of the farm team, the Toronto Marlboros.

In 1957, Conn Smythe, the founder of the Leafs, resigned as general manager, and Harold Ballard got a big break. He took a seat on the hockey operations committee chaired by an old friend, Conn's son Stafford Smythe. The "Silver Seven" committee helped shape the last powerhouse Maple Leafs team of the 20th century, which won four cups in the 1960s. In 1961, Ballard partnered with Stafford and *Toronto Telegraph* owner John Bassett to purchase the team. After considerable wrangling and double-crossing, Bassett was forced out in 1971. Six weeks after that, Stafford died, and Ballard then bought his friend's stake, making him majority owner.

The new owner quickly earned a reputation for outrageous conduct and miserly management. In 1972, he was convicted of fraud and grand theft on 47 counts: the charges included using corporate funds to renovate his cottage, and claiming his sons' motorcycles as hockey equipment. Ballard received a three-year sentence, and, while he was incarcerated, a Maple Leafs scout exploited his boss's absence to sign Börje Salming, a talented Swedish defenceman. Ballard later incinerated Foster Hewitt's

NHL star Bobby Hull put the WHA on the hockey map in 1972 when he signed with the upstart Winnipeg Jets for $1 million.

Photos: Canadian Press Images

legendary broadcast gondola to clear space for private boxes – something the Hockey Hall of Fame badly wanted to preserve.

Once on the radio program *As It Happens*, Ballard shocked CBC listeners by telling popular hostess Barbara Frum that "they shouldn't let females on the radio." "You know where they're good, don'tcha?" he went on to inquire. His response to the outrage of women's groups was not contrite.

Also, Ballard feared the league's decision to put names on jerseys would result in reduced program sales. He satisfied the edict by sewing white names on the white shirts, and blue names on the blue. He further outraged fans by selling all the Toronto Stanley Cup banners. Ballard was so despised that even his substantial charitable donations were suspect. Montreal Canadiens superstar Ken Dryden likened him to "a wrestling villain."

Ballard was as indifferent as the rest to the WHA in 1972, but not when the new league scooped four of his Leafs, including superstar goalie Bernie Parent. The following year, Paul Henderson and Mike Pelyk deserted too. Those who remained threatened to quit during negotiations. Rather than compete, Ballard vowed to destroy the new league.

It might have been easy had it not been for Bobby Hull. "The Golden Jet" was the star of the Chicago Blackhawks throughout the 1960s and into the early '70s, and was perhaps the greatest left-winger ever. When he jokingly told reporters

he'd join the WHA for $1 million, Winnipeg owner Ben Hatskin took him up on it. Hatskin and Hunter cleverly persuaded the other owners to contribute to a $1-million-dollar signing bonus. Hull's unprecedented five-year, $1.25-million-dollar deal brought some badly needed credibility to the WHA. Thus, "the Golden Jet" became a Winnipeg Jet. His departure from the NHL rocked the hockey world, and pulled other stars along, too. In 1973, even Gordie Howe came out of retirement to join his sons Mark and Marty on the Houston Aeros.

The WHA kicked off its season in 1972-73, and it differed noticeably from the older league. The calibre of play was significantly worse, as superstars were backed by mediocre teams. Second, clubs became increasingly reliant on European players to supplement a shallow talent pool. Unlike in the NHL, names such as Anders Hedberg and Ulf Nilsson were not uncommon. Third, exorbitant salaries stretched many teams to the breaking point. Teams were constantly going broke, getting sold and having to move, often in mid-season. The Los Angeles Sharks became the Michigan Stags and then the Baltimore Blades. A third move to Seattle was contemplated in 1975, but the team folded after less than four years in the league. This was typical.

Franchises that failed to implode through their own incompetence were often targeted by rival NHL teams. When it became clear that the new league would keep going, the NHL hastily added franchises in Atlanta and Long Island – the latter a proposed WHA location.

Harold Ballard got a chance to settle two scores when John F. Bassett, the son of Ballard's former partner, brought the Toros to town in 1973. They struck a deal to lease Maple Leaf Gardens at $15,000 per game. Ballard later demanded an additional $3,500 per night to use the television lights. He also forced them to build their own dressing room, at a cost of $55,000. The vengeful NHLer even famously removed the cushions from the home bench for the Toros' games, telling an arena staffer to "Let 'em buy their own cushions!" The younger Bassett finally had to move the club to the famous hockey town of Birmingham, Alabama, in 1976.

Clearly, the market could not sustain two professional leagues. Merger talks began as early as 1973, but the growing acrimony between the owners made negotiations less than cordial. The WHA crew resented the NHL establishment's bullying tactics, but beyond that there was a moral difference of attitude. The newcomers felt the old league's inflexibility had justified competition. The NHL crowd despised the interlopers and scavengers who had mushroomed salaries and picked apart their elite league. To the NHL, the WHA's problems were the inevitable result of misbegotten business plans that started teams in markets too small for pro clubs.

In 1976, after failing to buy out his partners, Hunter sold his Edmonton Oilers to B.C. investor Nelson Skalbania. Between the NHL, the other WHA clubs (particularly the American ones)

Wild Bill Hunter learned in 2000 he was good enough for the Order of Canada, but he never did make it into the NHL Hall of Fame.

Photo: Canadian Press Images

and feuding partners who were by this time suing one another, the old hockey man had had enough. He let the team go for what he felt was a terrible offer, and a promise to keep them in Edmonton.

The 1978-79 season found the WHA on thin ice. From its 14-team peak in 1974-76, membership had dwindled to six. In truth, only Edmonton, Winnipeg, Quebec and Hartford (Connecticut) were deemed viable.

John Ziegler, the new NHL president, managed to hammer out a deal very favourable to the old guard. NHL teams would be allowed to reclaim lost players. Each newcomer owed $6 million in franchise fees. The WHA won only two concessions before it capitulated. Each expansion club could protect two goalies and two skaters. And, most importantly, in addition to Hartford, all three Canadian franchises were to be included. (The NHL had hoped to exclude the Quebec Nordiques.)

Then on March 8, 1979, the NHL Board of Governors rejected the proposal. Although 12 of 17 NHL teams wished to accept, under the rules it needed the support of 14. All three Canadian NHL teams joined Boston and Los Angeles to prevent the merger. The main stumbling block, unsurprisingly, was Harold Ballard. As payback for the gutting of his roster seven years earlier, and to avoid having to split the *Hockey Night in Canada* revenue pot six ways, he led the faction demanding unconditional surrender.

There the deal might have died. The NHL would undoubtedly have crushed the WHA shortly, but the destiny of the sport was, in the end, determined by one of those rare but truly Canadian popular uprisings. A well-timed public boycott of Molson Canadian beer products in Edmonton, Winnipeg and Quebec forced the hard-liners to acquiesce. The *Hockey Night in Canada* sponsor brought Montreal and Vancouver in line. That was enough. The Board of Governors approved the merger on

March 22, despite Harold Ballard's reservations.

Ballard would go to his grave in 1990 still bitter at the WHA for blowing up players' wages and wrecking the league. By the turn of the century, even Hunter agreed the players had gone too far. Indeed, nothing could curb the inflation until 2005. The salary cap imposed that year came at the cost of a players' strike and the loss of the 2004-05 season.

The Leaf boss beat the WHA, but lost on all the issues. In addition to skyrocketing pay, the once-95-percent Canadian league grew steadily more European. Ballard's Leafs would go for more than 40 years without winning a Stanley Cup – the second-worst record of the original six. He never fielded a winning team as sole owner. Despite his induction into the Hockey Hall of Fame in 1977, he went down as one of the most infamous villains in the history of professional sports.

Bill Hunter should have been inducted into the Hall of Fame, but never was. He remained an object of loathing to the establishment. He had one more try. In 1982, he offered to buy the St. Louis Blues. Securing commitments for 18,000 season tickets and an 18,000-seat arena, Hunter proposed a move to his hometown, Saskatoon. The NHL board of governors refused, and they took over the club themselves.

Hunter's legacy would be preserved instead by his old team, the Edmonton Oilers. Under the ownership of Peter Pocklington, the Oilers won five Stanley Cups in seven years, and assembled one of the greatest teams in the history of the game. Likewise, although the other three WHA survivors ended up relocating in the mid-'90s, the Whalers and Nordiques would bring cups to North Carolina and Colorado respectively. From 1979 to 2008, former WHA clubs won more championships than had the original six.

Wild Bill left his mark on the sport. He helped assemble a league that changed the NHL forever, and introduced players such as Wayne Gretzky, Mark Messier, Mike Gartner and Ken Linseman. When he died in 2002, his business cards said, "Bill **Hunter, Sports Entrepreneur, Not Retired."**

Unlike Harold Ballard, Hunter was remembered fondly by thousands. As former Edmonton Oilers president Patrick LaForge once mused: "If there is a Mr. Hockey for the fans and the community of northern Alberta, northern Saskatchewan, maybe all of western Canada – I don't think anybody outranks Bill Hunter."

The people's admiration of him was demonstrated at the Oilers' first game as an NHL team on October 18, 1979. Among the NHL dignitaries assembled for the historic occasion were Bruce Norris and president John Ziegler. Edmonton Mayor Cec Purves and Premier Peter Lougheed spoke before the opening faceoff. Then a low rumble from the crowd grew steadily to a loud roar. There were tears in Hunter's eyes when he recognized the chant. "We want Bill! We want Bill! We want Bill!"

They didn't get Bill, but they knew he was watching. He probably still is.

Over the next two years, Trudeau's second government tilted heavily towards program spending and economic nationalism.

To placate economic nationalists – a rising political force in English Canada – the government activated a Foreign Investment Review Agency, which had been on the drawing board back in 1968. It screened foreign (mainly American) takeovers of large Canadian-owned companies to ensure they were in the national interest as Ottawa defined it.

The government further loosened social spending. Total federal disbursements rose 20 percent in 1972, 13 percent in 1973 and 29 percent in 1974.

Most notably, Ottawa intervened heavily when OPEC (the Organization of Petroleum Exporting Countries) choked back the global supply of crude oil and tripled the world price in the fall of 1973. In Canada's five easternmost provinces, which all relied on foreign sources, a barrel of offshore crude rose almost overnight, from $3 to $10.

Ottawa's solution to this crisis was to impose an export tax on oil and natural gas leaving the country from western Canada to the U.S., to subsidize consumption of foreign oil landed in the East.

This provoked anger in the West, especially in Alberta, where the new Progressive Conservative regime of Peter Lougheed had taken office in 1971, ending 36 straight years of Social Credit administration. One of the government's first acts was to double provincial oil and gas royalties. Trudeau's export tax – and a subsequent decision to make royalty payments non-deductible for federal income tax purposes – Albertans saw as a direct attack on their constitutional ownership of the resource.

Similar Alberta scorn and hostility greeted a new federal crown-owned oil company, Petro-Canada, created to give federal regulators practical insight into a complicated but essential industry dominated by multinationals.

A notorious bumper sticker now appeared in Calgary: "Let the eastern bastards freeze in the dark!"; this set off a furor of humourless East-versus-West media insults. The confrontation, and the federal attitude behind it, also inspired Calgary petroleum geologist John Rudolph to found the Independent Alberta Association, the first in a series of western separatist and quasi-separatist political groups.

Lougheed, though he was an ardent and unswerving federalist, soon became Trudeau's most effective and implacable opponent in the West.

Alberta had gone from four Liberal seats in 1968 to none, and Liberals had become rare throughout the West. To sweeten and soften western attitudes, Trudeau spent a great deal of public money and personal political capital on a much-touted 1972 Western Economic Opportunities Conference in Calgary with the four western premiers.

Peter Lougheed, shown here being sworn in, became premier of Alberta in 1971. Soon afterward the Organization of Petroleum Exporting Countries (OPEC) tripled the international price of oil, leading to major confrontations between Ottawa and the petroleum-producing provinces of the West, especially Alberta.

Photos: National Archives of Canada

Trudeau opened the conference by promising western industries federal subsidies, stabilizers and protectionist measures. To his surprise and chagrin, he was blindsided by Lougheed and the westerners, who argued forcefully for less federal money – and less federal interference. It marked perhaps the first time that the federal side was put off its game by superior strategy from the West. It would not be the last.

Despite these setbacks, the Liberal government survived for over a year. Between its cheap oil policy, and the salutary effect on employment of massive federal spending, by early 1974 the Liberals had rebounded to the mid-40-percent range in the polls.

Seeing their chance, they brought in a budget scandalously rich in spending, considering that inflation had just passed from single to double digits. The plan was inflationary enough to repel the Tories, and generous enough with upper-income tax breaks to offend the NDP. On May 8, 1974, the budget was defeated, and an election was called for July 8.

A 1973 bumper sticker perfectly expressed the rage of many Albertans when Trudeau's government froze the domestic price of oil and slapped a heavy export tax on crude being piped from the West to the U.S.

■ ■ ■ ■

Trudeau, Liberal minister from Winnipeg Jim Richardson, and Lougheed at the Western Economic Opportunities Conference in 1972. Never before had the western provinces so completely blindsided a federal government.

Photo: Glenbow Museum

Of the two perennial issues of federal politics – Quebec and economics – only the second loomed large in 1974.

Inflation was starting to cause panic.

Stanfield campaigned, stolidly and stubbornly, for a mandate to control wages and prices, even though economists had already concluded that where controls had been tried, they hadn't worked. But Stanfield wanted them anyway. Polls showed that most Canadians supported controls before the election campaign, after the election, and long after the subject had ceased to matter.

The sole time most Canadians did not support wage and price controls was on July 8, 1974, when they voted in a solid 141-seat Liberal majority.

Trudeau campaigned better in 1974 than in any of his five national elections. This was no serene "dialogue with Canadians" as in 1972; it was classic politicking. He sang with seniors, backslapped at union halls, ate hot dogs at ethnic fairs and whistle-stopped throughout the Atlantic. And his wife Margaret went with him, dressed femininely and casually,

Pierre and Margaret Trudeau with campaign organizers in 1974. The euphoria of a renewed majority did not last long, as one misadventure after another befell the new government.

Photos: National Archives of Canada

Maggie and Pierre hoedowning at a Liberal picnic on Centre Island in Toronto Harbour towards the end of the 1974 campaign. Both performed brilliantly throughout the campaign.

Photos: Canadian Press Images

looking on adoringly, discreetly nursing six-month-old Sacha to one side, or striking off on her own to spread the message.

Margaret's artless habit of saying whatever entered her pretty head terrified Trudeau's new political handlers, Keith Davey and Jim Coutts. For example, she famously provoked snickers from a large Vancouver crowd by saying about her husband, "He's a beautiful guy. He taught me a lot about loving."

The handlers need not have worried. Seeing this cloistered creature up close for the first time, Canadians fell for her the same way Trudeau had (except in Quebec, which did not see her because she could not speak much French). Prominent journalist June Callwood wrote dotingly in *Maclean's* about Margaret's "ethereal smile and rapt eyes full on her husband," saying

The Trudeaus take a whistle-stop tour of the Maritimes in 1974, harkening back to the Diefenbaker era. Inset, Margaret waves to an adoring home-province crowd in Penticton, British Columbia, after explaining that Pierre was not aloof and arrogant at all but was a "very warm, loving human being."

Photos: Canadian Press Images (inset), National Archives of Canada (below)

that her "truthfulness and trust are like the artistry of a high-wire act, all guts and beauty."

This was a mere six weeks before she headed off to the U.S. to an affair with Senator Ted Kennedy.

Trudeau, meanwhile, was ridiculing wage and price controls with the kind of vicious wit Stanfield could (or would) never master. Trudeau's most famous epigram this time was "Zap, you're frozen!" It was easy to control wages, argued Trudeau, but it was impossible to control prices. It would impoverish workers and enrich capitalists.

As ever, paradox piled upon contradiction. By supporting wage controls, Stanfield, a thoroughly "red" Tory, was arguing a case for a capitalist class he himself belonged to but didn't much like. Trudeau, a thoroughgoing intellectual socialist, was arguing a pragmatic libertarian case for laissez-faire he himself rejected. Canadians ended up voting against something most of them believed in. And the Liberals were about to implement something they had ridiculed and promised not to do.

The subsequent disillusionment of Canadians with national politics could perhaps be traced back to 1974.

The resurgent Liberals had hit a high point when Parliament resumed. With 141 seats out of 264, they no longer needed to fear the PCs (with 95) or the NDP (with 16).

The next five years, however, would prove the Liberals' worst under Trudeau, and perhaps their worst in the 20th century. Everything went wrong, both with unity and with the economy.

The first sign of trouble was with Margaret Trudeau, whose

behaviour after 1974 became increasingly bizarre. In Christina McCall's unsurpassable description, she resolved to wreak vengeance upon the man who had kept her "well-shod and pregnant in his prime ministerial fortress."

As the marriage disintegrated to nothing over the next five years, and Margaret's revenge grew ever more vicious and more public, Trudeau became almost paralyzed. His success as a leader had always depended upon his being mysterious, personally successful, and unpredictable. To preserve this, he had always scrupulously kept his private life private. By the time Margaret was finished demolishing his privacy, Trudeau was just another cuckold with a screwed-up marriage, of which the public knew many of the most intimate, lurid, petty and depressing details.

Added to this was the fact that Trudeau himself was now a different person, surrounded by different people than in 1968. He had become political and imperial. His costly new swimming pool at Sussex Drive, his new bulletproof silver Cadillac, his ostentatious world

A media double-standard: in the 1974 campaign, to show he could be athletic too, Conservative leader Robert Stanfield entertained news photographers with his football prowess. After throwing, catching and running impressively, the 60-year-old Stanfield fumbled the ball once, and the photograph was printed all over Canada. In sharp contrast, when 55-year-old Trudeau fumbled a flyball while playing outfield against the Ottawa press corps in 1975, the picture was hardly seen at all. The lesson? Avoid stunts during campaigns, especially if you're a Conservative.

Photos: Canadian Press Images

tours, his increasingly unilateral, sweeping and inconsistent decisions, and the angry exodus of old political friends and potential rivals from his Cabinet all bespoke a prime minister convinced of his own invincibility.

Most of this would take five long years to unfold.

■ ■ ■ ■

Homecoming queen Margaret Trudeau returning to the prime ministerial residence on Sussex Drive after a late-night Liberal whoop-up at the Chateau Laurier Hotel celebrating their 1974 majority victory.

Photo: Canadian Press Images

The CN Tower

For three decades Toronto's engineering marvel set a world record

by Joanne Byfield

It took three years to build, and when it opened in June 1976, the CN Tower, at 553.33 metres high, was the tallest freestanding structure in the world. The needle soaring above dozens of surrounding highrises has been the signature feature of Toronto's skyline ever since.

The structure was conceived as a communication tower in the late 1960s. The city's boom saw an explosion of highrise office towers which increasingly blocked radio and television signals. Canadian National Railway and its architectural and building partners decided to include a Sky Pod partway up, at 346 metres, to house a revolving restaurant, and an observation deck at 446 metres. They gambled correctly that the tower, in addition to improving communications, could become a

major tourist attraction. The CN tower is used by all the major television, radio, wireless, cellphone and paging companies in the Toronto area. In addition, over two million tourists ascend the tower each year.

Construction cost $63 million ($252 million in 2008 dollars). It employed over 1,500 workers, and required 40,524 cubic metres of concrete, 129 km of post-tensioned steel, 4,535 tonnes of reinforcing steel, and 544.2 tonnes of structural steel. The building is 29 mm, or one inch, off plumb.

To assemble the mast on top it took a Sikorsky helicopter, dubbed "Olga," to position the 44-piece, 102-metre antenna. The chopper first had to dismantle and take down the crane used to pour the pouring. Then thousands of people in

surrounding office towers and on the streets watched as Olga lowered pieces of the antenna into position, the heaviest weighing 7.2 tonnes.

The CN Tower attracts more than tourists. It is struck by lightning 40 to 50 times a year. Every surface that could be hit is attached to copper strips running down the tower and connected to 42 seven-metre buried grounding rods.

Between its base and its pinnacle, the temperature varies as much as 14 degrees Celsius. degrees. In 1995 the CN Tower was declared one of the Seven Wonders of the Modern World by the American Society of Civil Engineers.

In 1995 CN sold the tower to the Canada Lands Corporation, a federal crown corporation. In September 2007 it lost its status as highest structure in the world to the Burj Dubai, an office and residential tower in Dubai, United Arab Emirates. It was still under construction in 2008, and builders had not revealed what its final height would be.

Designed to send radio signals down into the surrounding concrete canyons, the CN Tower was declared one of the Seven Wonders of the Modern World by the American Society of Civil Engineers in 1995. Built around a hexagonal concrete core, poured continuously into a specially designed moving "slip form," three tapering buttresses – or "brackets" – were added for strength. A freezing rainstorm with high winds in March of 2007 required police to close the Gardiner Expressway and clear surrounding streets for fear of falling and blowing sheets of ice sliding off the Sky Pod 346 metres above. One chunk of ice smashed a taxi window on King Street, almost half a kilometre to the north.

Photos: Jupiter Images (opposite and above right), Canadian Press Images (above right)

Trudeau's personal problems aside, the first thing to go obviously wrong was the economy.

Inflation hit 10 percent in 1974 and 12 percent in 1975 – levels unseen since Canada's expansionary boom early in the century. But, unlike then, when a modern nation appeared out of a large, cold, empty wilderness, in the inflation of the 1970s new investment was sluggish and unemployment remained stubbornly high, rising from just under 5 percent in 1974 to almost 8 percent by 1979. Captains of business and industry did not trust any economy subject to the caprice of Pierre Trudeau, and it was easier than ever for the unemployed, rather than accept a job less satisfying than the one they had lost, to await better times on Ottawa's now-more-generous unemployment insurance.

As business lost confidence and workers slacked off, governments continued to increase their spending, and Ottawa set the pace. From 1973, federal spending (excluding transfers to provinces) went up by 29 percent in 1974, 22 percent in 1975, 9 percent in 1976 and 12 percent in 1977. The provinces, aided and abetted by Ottawa, were little better. The idea that government spending somehow creates prosperity was deeply entrenched.

This in turn opened a permanent annual revenue shortfall and a rising national debt. By 1977, the federal deficit (the annual shortfall) had reached $8 billion, and the accumulated federal debt had ballooned to $50 billion – a number that alarmed anyone who paid attention to such things. For instead of going into productive infrastructure, as it had in previous inflationary times, or even into making war material, most of it now was directed to making people more comfortable and less productive.

With inflation came labour strife. As Richard Gwyn recounted in *The Northern Magus*, the clear winners were public-sector unions – from the nation's posties to local school boards. Canada-wide, the average wage settlement in the first half of 1975 was 18 percent, when more time was lost to strikes than in the entire period of 1960 to 1965. One teachers' union in Ottawa managed to extract a one-year contract increase of 34 percent. In 1974 and 1975, Gwyn reported, Canada had the worst strike record in the developed world, except for Italy.

Inflationary uncertainty so unnerved people that they instinctively hankered for the good old wartime days of Mackenzie King, C.D. Howe and a managed economy. Even the normally free-market C. D. Howe Institute came out after the 1974 election urging federal controls. Though controls had already failed in both Britain and the U.S., the conclusion Canadians had reached by now was that it was better to do something – anything – than to do nothing.

One man who disagreed with "doing something – anything" was Finance Minister John Turner, a corporate lawyer. Having taken on the finance portfolio at the worst possible time, Turner was privately expressing dismay at the wasteful level of federal spending, and had concluded that just as Ottawa could no longer run its own operation with the efficiency it once did, neither could it run the Canadian economy. Solutions would have to be business-driven, or they would not be found. Trudeau, on the other hand, believed government could manage anything it had to. He believed in free-market capitalism only as long as it worked, and in 1975 it appeared not to be working at all.

There now emerged between the two men the first real rift since they had competed for the leadership seven years earlier. Two things were bothering Turner. He thought any system of controls would do more harm than good. He also had the feeling that Trudeau should bestow upon him a suitable Cabinet promotion (such as deputy prime minister) to

Conversion from Imperial units of measure to metric was phased in through the decade. It was probably one of the most unpopular and resented decisions of the Trudeau years. It began with weather reports in 1970, and ended with retail fuel sales in 1980. Efforts to make hard metric measurements mandatory were thwarted when the Mulroney Conservatives abolished the federal Metric Commission in 1985, and allowed goods to be sold in either metric or Imperial measure. Imperial remained in common use, especially in food products, cooking, agriculture and construction well into the next century.

Photo: National Archives of Canada

signal that he, Turner, was heir apparent. Otherwise, he had probably gone as high as he would ever go.

Trudeau knew better than anyone that Turner, with his movie-star looks, decisive speaking style and confident, competent air, was more popular than he in English Canada. He was even fairly popular in Quebec. Turner had assiduously maintained his own power base in the party, and his own perspective on events. He was as educated as Trudeau, as intelligent, as athletic and as competitive.

The one thing he lacked was Trudeau's moral certitude and resolve; he liked to be liked. Trudeau didn't care to be liked, as long as he won.

From July 1974, when Trudeau shared his election-victory stage with Margaret and

John Turner, until the summer of 1975, Turner felt increasingly trapped. Convinced that finance had become his political graveyard, he had asked for a new portfolio; Trudeau would bestow only lesser ones, amounting to demotions. So Turner fretted and fumed at his cottage on Ontario's Lake of the Woods all summer, and went in to Trudeau's office on September 10 and quit. Trudeau could have prevented it by offering Turner a better position, but he didn't. Six months later, Turner left Parliament altogether after 14 years, and joined the Toronto corporate law firm McMillan Binch.

In the meantime, Trudeau was in an economic crisis and was short one finance minister. He prevailed upon Energy Minister Donald Macdonald, a Toronto MP and one of his earliest caucus supporters, to forgo his plan to leave politics, and to take the reins Turner had dropped. Macdonald was no more a fan of wage and price controls than Turner had been, but he agreed to consider them. He soon realized, as did the whole Cabinet, that whether they worked or not, they had become a political imperative.

On Thanksgiving Day, October 13, 1975, Trudeau went on television to announce the government would do what he had said only a year before it would not do: control wages. For the next three years, an Anti-Inflation Board would restrict individual wage increases to $2,400 per year in companies with 500-plus employees, as well as in trade unions and professions.

Finance Minister John Turner, shown here packing up his office in 1975, quit the Cabinet in September and left Parliament in 1976. His departure did little to diminish the popular assumption that he was next in line for the leadership, and prompted a longing among growing numbers of Liberals for Trudeau to quit.

Photos: Canadian Press Images

In March 1976, thousands of union members picketed Parliament Hill over wage and price controls. Though they had campaigned against it in 1974, the Liberals later realized that in fact most Canadians wanted inflation to be curbed, and it proved to be one of their more popular measures.

The goal was to hold inflation to 8 percent in 1976, and then cut it to 6 percent, and then to 4 percent.

Despite such a blatant reversal, Canadians were not outraged – most, in fact, told pollsters they were relieved. Whether or not the program made much difference – and plenty of people said it made none – inflation sank to 8 percent in year one. Although it did not then go down as intended, it did hover below 10 percent until 1980. Then it shot up again into double digits.

■ ■ ■ ■

In 1976, another reversal occurred – one which shook the Canadian political system.

On November 15, René Lévesque's separatist Parti Québécois won a massive surprise victory in Quebec, rising from the meagre six seats it won in 1973 to 71. The Bourassa Liberals sank from 102 seats to a mere 26. The Union Nationale revived enough to capture 11 seats, but in many areas it served only to split the federalist vote and let the PQ win – what Lévesque in his 1986 memoirs referred to as the "dream scenario."

With perfect symbolism, Robert Bourassa was defeated in his Mercier riding by a separatist rookie, Gerald Godin – a poet he had needlessly locked up under the War Measures Act in 1970.

That night, above a hubbub of revolutionary glee, a slouched little chain-smoker took the microphone in the Paul Sauvé arena. "I have never been so proud to be Québécois!" declared Lévesque, a CBC broadcaster whose familiar throaty rasp many Quebeckers had come to trust over the past two decades. "We are not a little people; we are now closer to something like a great people!"

Lévesque could only guess why Bourassa, holding every seat except eight in the National Assembly, had gone to the polls a year early.

Bourassa's government had been plagued by corruption scandals as bad as those of the Maurice Duplessis regime in the 1950s. Bourassa's unwieldy 1973 majority, wrote Lévesque

Quebec premier Robert Bourassa hamming with young Liberals at Grand-Mère in 1973.

Photos: Canadian Press Images

in his memoirs, "encouraged appetites so numerous and so insatiable that the administration seemed little short of a free-for-all."

Bourassa knew – indeed, everyone did – that the Parti Québécois was now, suddenly, gaining ground. In its first two elections, in 1970 and 1973, it had been the party of left-wing, working-class, east-end Montreal. Now it was all through rural Quebec and the Gaspé, it was strong in Quebec City, and it had made key converts in the upper echelon of the provincial bureaucracy.

What Bourassa could not know – Quebec being Quebec – was how strong the shift would prove; he gambled that it was better for the Liberals to go sooner than later.

René Lévesque, flanked by party stalwart Lise Payette, led the Parti Québécois to its first provincial victory in 1976, eight years after founding it, and after two previous election defeats. The PQ's triumph prompted a large outflow of anglophone residents and Montreal corporations.

The Union Nationale, which had almost vanished in 1973, revived a little by claiming a significant share of anglophone voters: those who wanted to punish the Liberals for making Quebec officially unilingual-French in 1974. The Liberals were further weakened by a large swath of Liberal francophones voting PQ to punish English Canadians for making such a fuss in June about bilingualizing federal air traffic control.

Others, offended by Liberal graft, saw René Lévesque and his new party as honest. Neither was it necessarily even separatist. After a huge internal clash with its hard-line separatist faction in 1974, the party had resolved that, if elected to govern, it would hold a referendum before making any move towards sovereignty. At this time the sovereignty option was

René Lévesque— the great adversary

Quebec's provincial response to its federal champion Trudeau

The two figures who dominated Canadian politics in the 1970s, Quebec Premier René Lévesque and Prime Minister Pierre Trudeau, were more than once described as "two scorpions fighting in a bottle."

In politics and personality they were opposites. Trudeau was religiously puritanical, physically fit, seldom drank and never smoked. Lévesque was a lifelong gambler, chain-smoker, drinker, agnostic and womanizer. Trudeau presented himself as an intellectual, Lévesque as an anti-intellectual. Young Trudeau was anti-war essayist, young Lévesque a front-line war correspondent. Trudeau was respected, even revered in Quebec. Lévesque was loved.

Lévesque was born in Gaspé in 1922, three years after Trudeau, in direct line of descent from a Robert Lévesque who arrived in New France nine generations earlier. As a boy he was close to his father, a small-town lawyer who died (as Trudeau's did) when he was in early adolescence.

Lévesque decided at an early age he had no interest in religion, and then, despite his mother's insistence, that he had no interest in law. He joined the U.S. Army in 1944 as a war correspondent, served as a translator in France, and witnessed the liberation of the Nazi extermination camp at Dachau. He later joined the French division of CBC and reported on the Korean War.

Later in the 1950s he became Quebec's first serious television current affairs host, with a popular weekly program on world events called *Point de mire* (On Target). He slid into politics when Jean Lesage recruited him to run as a Liberal against the decrepit Union Nationale in 1958. He won easily in Montreal-Laurier and immediately became Minister of Hydroelectric Resources and Public Works.

As with Trudeau, fate seems to have lured him willingly along. He thought Quebec's privately owned electric utilities held the key to its economic future, and against serious Cabinet opposition he successfully provincialized the ownership of them. He cleaned the corruption out of the Quebec's notoriously corrupt public works system. When Lesage, fearing Lévesque's personal popularity, made him welfare minister, Lévesque used it to take social responsibility away from the Catholic Church for which he had no respect, and handle it with a new secular government bureaucracy as it was everywhere else.

Lévesque as a young war correspondent in Korea, wading a stream en route to the front in 1951.

Photos: Canadian Press Images

Although he never had any interest in constitutional matters, Lévesque concluded that Canada was of no political use to Quebec, and vice versa. He saw Canada not as 10 politically united provinces but as two natural trading partners. He wrote this in the nationalist *Le Devoir* newspaper in 1967, and it finished him in the Liberal Party. Not that he was surprised; he was moving in a very different direction, towards a new partnership with Canada, which he called "sovereignty association."

Quebec's two extant separatist parties had no more liking for something as soft and fuzzy as "sovereignty association" than the Liberals did. In October the Liberals drove him from the party, and not many members left with him. In 1968 he and

One of the most bitter disappointments in Lévesque's career was the 1973 Quebec election, which saw his upstart party boxed in with only seven seats, the same number it had won in 1970.

several hundred separatists and quasi-separatists formed a Movement for Sovereignty Association, which the following year became the Parti Québécois, though Lévesque found the name too presumptuous to like.

Until 1970, Lévesque remained a member of the Quebec National Assembly (MNA) for Montreal-Laurier, and was the natural leader of the new party. With the 1970 election his situation changed, however, when seven PQ MNAs were elected, but not Lévesque. It became even more disheartening in 1973, when PQ seats were reduced to six and Lévesque himself lost again.

In his 1986 *Memoirs* Lévesque referred to this period as the "long march." He was living in Montreal, struggling to keep the party going, and to keep in touch with his distant Quebec City caucus, and to contain the PQ's ever-turbulent separatist faction, and to make a living. To the federalist Liberals he was a separatist, and to the separatists he was a cop-out. After the 1970 War Measures Act, about three-quarters of PQ members abandoned the party, at least for a while.

Then came the great turnaround in 1976 (see page 200). By then Lévesque knew the party would move ahead. How far they would get would depend on some fairly intricate vote-splitting between the PQ, Liberals, Créditistes and Union Nationale. From Lévesque's perspective it went perfectly, and he was swept into government with 71 of 110 seats and 41 percent of the vote.

The Parti Québécois governed as the Liberals had done since the Quiet Revolution – from the left and on French-nationalist principles. Only, they were only more extreme. They were generally more honest than the Liberals, but their nationalism often carried an ideological charge that offended

Lévesque, as when passing Bill 101 in 1977, the Charter of the French Language. Lévesque often said, and seemed to honestly mean, that the point was not revenge on the English. His sole intent was the maintenance of a French Quebec through majority rule at home and a new federal relationship with Canada.

From the outset he served as the moderator between the separatists and others who could be called "associationists" – that is, between those who wanted complete independence and those who wanted a new arrangement. He found the original separatists who had come into the party with Pierre Bourgault a serious challenge. By 1976 the hard-liners had moderated, and were now led by a Péquiste, Jacques Parizeau. Parizeau accepted, however begrudgingly, that the gradualist approach of the larger, softer faction led by Claude Morin was the only way forward. Lévesque always positioned himself between them. Both with sovereignty and with social democracy, he was never harsh or ideological, though he often had to be firm.

When the PQ lost the 1980 sovereignty referendum, René Lévesque lost his spirit. He became impatient, fretful and discontented, and his second election victory in 1981 didn't really change that. The crushing personal loss he suffered from Trudeau in the constitutional struggle later that year finished him.

He lingered as premier until his party began falling apart around him. After his defeat by Robert Bourassa's Liberals in 1985 he quit as leader and returned to journalism. He died in 1987, and will be long -and well-remembered in Quebec.

favoured by less than one-quarter of Quebec voters. Trudeau himself had conceded that a vote for the PQ was not in itself a vote for separation.

Thus, the PQ vote rose from 30 percent of the popular vote in 1973 to 41 percent in 1976, the Liberals plunged from 55 percent to 34 percent, and the Union Nationale rose from 5 percent to 18 percent – just enough, in just the right places, to defeat the Liberals.

This development occasioned at least moderate alarm in English Canada. Bilingualism had been simmering across Canada as a source of resentment, flaring now and then into open hostility.

English Canada reacted angrily in 1974 when Bourassa's government had severely curtailed anglophone rights in Quebec with Bill 22, and when Ottawa did nothing to stop it. It meant that while the rest of the country must now officially accommodate French, Quebec would no longer officially accommodate English.

In June 1976, a federal proposal to allow both languages in air traffic control at major airports across the country, instead of just English, led to a nine-day strike by traffic controllers that was backed by airline pilots. Air travel abruptly stopped, and anglophone grassroots opinion hit the media like a firestorm. Ottawa was forced to reconsider, and

Trudeau and Cuban dictator-for-life Fidel Castro singing a duet during Trudeau's visit to the island in 1976. Photos such as this convinced conservative Canadians that Trudeau was a Communist fellow traveller.

Photos: National Archives of Canada

When Liberal popularity rebounded briefly after the Parti Québécois victory, Trudeau's political advisers, Keith Davey (above) and Jim Coutts (inset), argued strongly but in vain for Trudeau to call an early election.

Photos: Canadian Press Images (top), *Saturday Night* Magazine (bottom)

Jean Marchand quit the federal Cabinet in disgust. An expert inquiry concluded years later that bilingual control posed no safety risk; but from the perspective of English-speaking Canada, neither did it serve any practical good.

After the PQ won, Trudeau downplayed the significance.

He appeared on television to congratulate the new premier on his solid electoral win, and said that Canada could not and should not be held together by force. He promised practical co-operation and constitutional reform, and ended with what is probably the most compelling case for national unity.

"There is a deeper bond than that of blood," he said. "If the Canadian nation is to survive, it will only survive in mutual respect and in love for one another."

Lévesque said he would see if these promising words had any substance, and proceeded with Bill 1 – the Charter of the French Language (later renumbered Bill 101). This was Bill 22 times three, and it swelled an exodus of anglophone companies and families from Quebec that Bill 22 had started.

According to the polls, English Canada did not react much to Lévesque until he went to speak to the Economic Club in New York in late January of 1977, where he compared Quebec's imminent departure from Canada to the secession of the 13 American colonies from Britain two centuries earlier. The Canadian dollar, which had been weakening anyway, suddenly sagged further, and by October it would reach its lowest exchange level since 1932.

English Canadians, especially in Ontario, suddenly felt that the nation really was in danger, and started re-embracing bilingualism and Trudeau Liberalism.

In July 1976, after the air traffic strike, the Liberals had hit their lowest response on the Gallup poll since 1968, registering 29 percent. In 1977, they began to rise again, and by summer were back above 50 percent.[5]

Jim Coutts in the PMO and party strategist Senator Keith Davey urged Trudeau to head now for an election. Yes, it was a year early, they admitted, but conditions would never be better.

---

5. The Liberals' highest Gallup poll result was 59 percent in 1970, after imposing the War Measures Act.

Canadian unity was in peril, and Canadians saw Trudeau as the sole saviour. Strike now, they urged, while the unity iron is hot; for when the public focus returns to the economy, as it inevitably will, the Liberals will lose.

Any other leader in the history of the Canadian Liberal Party would have followed their advice; but not Trudeau. It wasn't so much that he disagreed (though he did protest that it would look opportunistic – as if that ever mattered), but that he was paralyzed. His marriage had blown up, his wife was insane, and his three young children lived in dread of abandonment, as children in such a plight always do. He simply couldn't take two months away to lead an election. Coutts, Davey, the Liberal Party and Canada would have to wait.

In his disastrous campaign of 1979, Trudeau took a moment in Calgary to try lassoing one his aides. His marriage and his government both having failed, he was in a mean and hostile mood.

One of the factors blackening Trudeau's mood was the plight of his three motherless sons (from the front, Michel, Alexandre [Sacha] and Justin) waiting back in Ottawa while their father campaigned.

Photos: Canadian Press Images

While everyone waited for Trudeau to feel more engaged, Canada (once again) did not collapse, the economy continued to languish, month-by-month the government looked more erratic and inept, and the Liberals' golden moment turned to lead.

It now came out that the RCMP had significantly broken the law at least four times to infiltrate and demoralize the Quebec nationalists.

A report from the Commissioner of Official Languages said that federal bilingualism was not working.

A federal task force on national unity concluded that federal policies were too centralist and intrusive, and that a more flexible approach was needed. Trudeau's response was to threaten to patriate the Constitution from Britain unilaterally, without provincial consent.

By the summer of 1978, Trudeau was showing signs of megalomania, compiling Nixonesque "enemies" lists of media and politicians, ordering a presidential-style, bulletproof

silver limousine, and holding Cabinet meetings dressed like Lawrence of Arabia. This private indulgence was followed by public clothing choices – berets, corduroy suits – almost as outré as those which had caught the public fancy a decade earlier; but Trudeaumania was long over, and now they merely looked out of place.

The leader's protracted waiting forced him to call 15 by-elections in October of 1978. Despite running numerous star candidates, the Liberals lost every one except the two in Quebec. By now, they were back down to a 35-percent rating in the Gallup poll, and they held a bare majority (133 seats of 265). So they hung on into their fifth year, grimly hoping.

They did recover somewhat, but not nearly enough. On March 26, Trudeau asked the Governor General to dissolve Parliament, and the campaign began.

To the Liberals' horror, Trudeau performed even worse than in 1972. He yelled at unemployed protestors: "Why don't you get off your ass and get a job?" He snarled at the media, insulted his audiences and called questioners "stupid." Everywhere he went, he affected a lone, "gunslinger" pose, and substituted a massive backdrop Canadian flag for the engaging persona that he had lost.

Photos: Canadian Press Images (top), National Archives of Canada (bottom)

CANADA   MARCH 1, 1976

TIME

Tory Leader
Joe Clark

THE
WINNER

75 CENTS

■ ■ ■ ■

Yet even then, the Conservatives only half-won the election.

Three years earlier, Stanfield had stepped down, having lost three consecutive elections, and the Conservatives had chosen a somewhat nervous, somewhat pompous, generally decent leader named Joe Clark, who was from Alberta.

Despite his youth, he had mounted a skilful leadership campaign. In a crowded field of 11 candidates, he had positioned himself as the best compromise between two stronger front-runners from Quebec: Brian Mulroney and Claude Wagner.

Though a better-than-average parliamentarian, in person and on television Clark was woefully lacking in confidence and appeal. Perhaps he was just too young – at 36, he was the youngest man ever to lead a major national party.

His first great challenge as leader was to win six by-elections in May of 1977, just as the Liberals were rising in the wake of the PQ victory. The PCs lost not only the five seats open in Quebec, but also a Prince Edward Island riding they had held since Diefenbaker's era. It was an inauspicious beginning.

But since then, Trudeau had managed to do everything wrong, and in 1978 he had lost more by-elections than had Clark.

Still, despite that, in the May 1979 election, Clark's PCs came in six seats short of a majority.

They rose from 98 seats to 136, while the Liberals shrank from 133 to 114.

Clark needed Quebec's six Social Credit MPs, led by Fabien Roy, if they were to master the 282-seat House. With the Créditistes on side, he had a majority of one seat; but then he annoyed them by not allowing them formal party status in the House (the conventional minimum was 12 seats), making them unreliable allies.

As so often, the Tories' disadvantages were more obvious to voters than to themselves. They had a bad habit of believing their own press releases. They had been 16 years out of

Try as he might, John Diefenbaker never could take Joe Clark seriously.

Photo: Canadian Press Images

With Governor General Edward Schreyer looking on, Privy Council Clerk Michael Pitfield accepts the oath of office from Clark. One of the first things Clark did was fire Pitfield.

Photo: Canadian Press Images

office, they were divided internally and they were down to a mere two seats from Quebec.

However, their biggest liability by far was their leader. Personally, Clark was so unimpressive that he invited derision. Trudeau was physically small, but on television he looked big. Clark was the opposite. As Dalton Camp gently observed, "He is a hard man to find in a crowd."

John Diefenbaker, who had tried to take Clark seriously and had given up, was less kind.

When the 1979 election was over, the Chief remarked acidly, "Canada celebrated the [International] Year of the Child by electing Joe Clark as Prime Minister."

■ ■ ■ ■

PART THREE

1979-1982

Terry Fox near the end of his run in northern Ontario.

In an eight-year struggle for control of the country, Pierre Trudeau thoroughly defeated Joe Clark. Despite his parliamentary skill, Clark suffered two fatal weaknesses: lacking support in Quebec, he needed to reconcile the competing interests of Ontario and Alberta, and

"Welcome to the 1980s"

Trudeau returns in triumph to finish his life's work

Joe Clark's brief term of government is usually referred to as an "interlude." Officially, it lasted nine months – from June 1979 to March 1980. In practical fact, it lasted six.

Clark's government provides a cautionary lesson to any opposition party that wins an election with 36 percent of the vote. Having first overpromised, as opposition parties usually do, it had to repudiate its commitments, and then had to worry about appearing incompetent or insincere.

From the outset, there was a fatal delusion among the Tories, emanating in large part from their leader, that they had defeated the Liberals. The truth – obvious to everyone else – was that the Liberals had defeated themselves. Canadian voters, as is so frequently their wont, had not elected a new government; they had punished an old one. As Jeffrey Simpson recounted in his book *Discipline of Power*, written immediately after the Clark government fell, this faulty assumption produced a chain of mistakes.

By the time the shortest Parliament in Canadian history had assembled in October, Clark – wrongly imagining himself to be poised on an electoral landslide like Diefenbaker in 1957 – had decided to govern as though he had a majority. As a result, his record was one of compounding errors unrelieved by notable successes.

The Clark government is perhaps the only one that has sunk in popularity almost from the day it took power.

Its first mistake was that it stopped polling (a miscalculation the Liberals have never made). It assumed it was secure because it assumed the Liberals understood that Canadians had rejected them, and had especially rejected Trudeau. In fact, the Liberals had finished the May election 4 percent ahead of the Conservatives. (The Liberals lost anyway; their surplus of popular support in Quebec could not add to their seats.)

Bereft of internal polling intelligence, the Conservatives did not see public opinion turning strongly against them over the fall. When the November Gallup poll plotted the Liberals

19 points ahead of the Conservatives, the Tories dismissed it as impossible.

Any twinges of fear they might have felt about their tenuous position vanished when Trudeau announced tearfully to caucus on November 21 that he would quit as leader in the spring. From that point on, the Conservatives assumed they were bulletproof – at least for a year while the Liberals regrouped.

The second Tory mistake concerned an embassy. In a blatant election pitch for Jewish votes in Toronto, Clark had promised that, if elected, he would move the Canadian embassy in Israel from Tel Aviv to Jerusalem. Though it would badly upset Arabs, and served of zero advantage to Canada, he moved quickly to deliver on this promise in July, provoking a threatened Arab oil embargo and boycott of Canadian exports. Then, instead of backing down, Clark sent Bob Stanfield on a fact-finding mission to the Middle East. There were no new facts to find, however, and the delay served only to keep the fiasco in the news.

Clark's next miscalculation was to pursue his firm resolve to privatize the Liberals' new crown corporation Petro-Canada. Most Canadians and half his own Cabinet thought this foolish. While Tory ministers and deputies argued among themselves over whether and how to do it, the Iranian Revolution sent the price of oil soaring from US$14 a barrel to US$40, and evening newscasts showed Americans lined up for blocks to buy gasoline. Canada's supplies were only marginally more secure.

Rightly or wrongly, most consumers saw government-owned Petro-Can as a hedge against global uncertainty and a useful check on the hated multinationals which dominated the Canadian industry. Clark and his government were scorned in the media and in Parliament as they shifted from one position on Petro-Can to another. Only after the government had been defeated did Clark settle on a final position – miles removed from his first – and by now he was fighting an election.

Clark was briefed by Trudeau in June 1979 on an upcoming prime-ministerial trip to Japan. Trudeau then took the summer off while Clark's government plunged in popular support. Trudeau later recalled in his *Memoirs* that Clark was in fact "a far stronger opponent" than his successor, Brian Mulroney.

Photo - Canadian Press Images

Misfortune number four – probably unavoidable – was to get caught between the colliding demands about oil pricing from the provincial Conservative governments of Ontario and Alberta. Alberta was demanding 85 percent of an escalating world price for its oil, and Ontario wanted petroleum resources nationalized under Ottawa's constitutional power to appropriate strategic assets in the national interest. Politically, Clark needed support in both provinces, but he could please neither; and the time it took to contrive a shaky agreement with Alberta hobbled his government.

Fifth was an internal clash between ministers who wanted to slash spending and taxes, as Republican candidate Ronald Reagan was promising to do in the United States, and Finance Minister John Crosbie, who wanted to raise taxes.

Crosbie was a Newfoundlander of strong views, and one of only two ministers in Clark's government who had previous (provincial) Cabinet experience. He believed that federal spending could not be cut very much because over half of any federal budget consists of statutory expenditures: transfers to provinces, Employment Insurance, Old Age Security, etc. Reducing these would require difficult legislative amendments. And without spending cuts, tax cuts would simply fuel inflation, drive up interest rates and widen the deficit.

The annual federal deficit now ran to $12 billion, and inflation in 1979 was at almost 10 percent. To dampen this, the Bank of Canada lending rate hit 14 percent in October, which for most mortgage-and small-business borrowers meant 18 percent.

Joe Clark and Maureen McTeer, with their three-year-old daughter Catherine, enjoying their short sojourn in the prime-ministerial residence on Sussex Drive in 1979.

Photo - National Archives of Canada

■ ■ ■ ■

Rescuing Americans from Iran

Canada's Ambassador daringly saves six U.S. embassy personnel from Muslim militants

by Joanne Byfield

Prime Minister Joe Clark's tenure as prime minister was brief, but he presided over a remarkable, movie-quality Canadian foreign-affairs coup. In 1979 Canadian diplomats saved six American embassy personnel from the Muslim student revolutionaries who seized the U.S. embassy in Tehran, Iran.

On November 4, an armed mob of some 400 students, stirred by the "Great Satan" anti-West rantings of Muslim cleric Ayatollah Khomeini, stormed over the walls of the U.S. embassy and captured most of its 65 staffers. Amid the chaos, a handful of consular officers and assistants, including consular chief Bob Anders, walked out of the compound, and five of them hid in Anders' apartment. Anders himself hid elsewhere at first, and joined them later.

Anders knew they needed a safer place, and by all standards of international law they should have been able to claim the protection of the Iranian government. It was obvious, however, that the Iranian government supported the students and was not afraid of retaliation by U.S. President Jimmy Carter.

The escapees (four men and two women) spent a couple of days moving between a safe house owned by the British embassy and the home of a fellow American being held hostage. However, the Iranian staff in that house were suspicious of the guests, so they couldn't stay there.

Anders phoned John Sheardown, chief immigration officer at the Canadian embassy, and explained their plight. Sheardown, astonished that Anders was free, contacted his boss Ken Taylor, the Canadian ambassador. Taylor had been in Iran for two years and with the diplomatic service for 20, but he was not a typical civil servant. His expertise was in business, and he was flamboyant, outgoing and energetic. He had impressed his superiors earlier that year by arranging the safe exit of over 800 Canadians working in Iran as its secular-liberal government fell apart.

Taylor instantly agreed with Sheardown that they would hide the escapees. The question was...where?

The Canadian embassy was not a safe location. With the students now acting as a law unto themselves, the only safety lay in not attracting attention. The best bet was to split up the six, having two of them stay at Taylor's residence and the others at Sheardown's. The plan was to pass them off as Canadian tourists visiting for a few days. Taylor sent a top-secret cable to Ottawa explaining the situation and asking for approval.

It was risky. Sheardown's wife Zena was Guyanese and was not protected by diplomatic immunity – for what little such "immunity" might now be worth in Iran. Most of the diplomatic community had been intimidated, and refused to condemn the shocking complicity of the Iranian government with the students.

Canadian External Affairs Minister Flora MacDonald and Prime Minister Clark agreed that Canada would help the Americans. Everyone still assumed the hostage drama would last only a few days.

They were wrong. Over the ensuing weeks, the "house guests," as they were referred to in cable exchanges with Ottawa, rarely ventured outside the homes. They celebrated American Thanksgiving in hiding, wondering what the Carter administration was doing to get them and their compatriots released.

By early December it was obvious no negotiated release was imminent, and Taylor was getting nervous about what would happen to his house guests if the Americans staged a rescue of the embassy hostages. The Americans were not telling Canada their plans, but their focus was on the hostages inside their embassy compound. They considered the six with the Canadians to be safe. How, Taylor wondered, would they get both groups out at once?

The situation got more worrisome on December 7, when a Canadian reporter for Montreal's *La Presse* contacted the Canadian embassy in Washington to say he knew about the house guests. Jean Pelletier, who later co-authored the book *The Canadian Caper* with Claude Adams, was the first reporter to stumble onto the story. Pelletier agreed to sit on it, but it shocked Flora MacDonald that he knew about it at all, and it frightened Ken Taylor. For how long could the reporter be trusted? Who else knew, or would find out? They desperately needed to get their house guests home.

Taylor knew if word got out, his offices and home would be searched. He enlisted a friend, the New Zealand ambassador, to pose as a businessman and rent a suitably secluded villa. Though embassy staff would not normally do such things, there was no longer any diplomatic law in Iran, so others felt at liberty to break the rules. With that done, Taylor asked his staff, without telling them why, to stock the villa with furniture and food. If the situation arose, he could quickly send the Americans there. On December 12, Minister MacDonald was in Paris for a NATO meeting, but her real task was to meet with her U.S. counterpart,

Canadian diplomat and hero Ken Taylor, back on safe ground in France, after saving and evacuating six Americans from the Ayatollah's Iran. Even a Canadian newspaper reporter kept the secret.

Photo - Canadian Press Images

Cyrus Vance, to press him for help in getting the house guests out. Minutes before that meeting, she received an urgent message from Prime Minister Clark telling her that she must return to Canada that night for a House of Commons vote on the budget the next day, which the Conservatives might lose. She was unable to get a flight back to Ottawa, and it wouldn't have changed anything if she had. The Clark government was defeated anyway. (see page 220-222.)

Vance agreed with a Canadian plan to fly the Americans out of Iran disguised as Canadian business people, and the two governments arranged for false passports and travel documents. In early January 1980, Taylor booked 18 flights, just to be safe – six each on three different airlines. The "exfiltration" scheme (as it was dubbed) also called for the gradual return home of all Canadian embassy staff over a three-week period to get them out of danger of Iranian retaliation.

On January 27, the six "house guests" boarded a Swissair plane to West Germany, and thus to safety. Two days later, Jean Pelletier's story appeared in *La Presse*, and the story flashed around the world. Ken Taylor became an instant international hero.

Americans, who were stung by the lacklustre performance of the Carter government in freeing their hostages, were thrilled that some had been daringly rescued by Canadians. As Pelletier wrote in his book, "The outpouring of gratitude was so extravagant that Canadians were almost embarrassed."

By subsequent Middle East norms – in which torture and beheading of hostages became commonplace – the American hostages were not too badly treated by the Iranians. They were pushed around, assaulted, threatened and publicly humiliated. Thirteen women and blacks were released for political reasons two weeks after their capture, while 52 others were kept.

In April, the Carter administration tried to rescue the captives by military helicopter, but the mission failed. No helicopters ever reached Tehran, and one crashed, killing eight men. The hostages waited 444 days in captivity, and were freed on January 20, 1981, six minutes after Ronald Reagan was sworn in as U.S. President.

So when budget time came in early December, with Clark's support Crosbie did not deliver a much-promised $2-billion "stimulative tax cut." Nor was there a new Conservative allowance for homeowners to deduct mortgage payments from their taxable income, as in the U.S. This would have to come later, and in the end never did. Instead, Crosbie delivered an unpromised tax increase: an excise tax of 18 cents per gallon (4 cents per litre) on gasoline and diesel to reduce the gaping federal deficit by $2.5 billion. Crosbie described it as "a budget that faces facts," and "short-term pain for long-term gain."

Though Trudeau had decided in November to quit as leader, he told a few intimates that he would wait until January to announce it. Why he advanced his announcement to late November is not clear. Maybe, said chronicler Richard Gwyn, it was because he had a severe toothache and was depressed.

Not so, Trudeau told Christina McCall in 1985 (*Trudeau and Our Times*). To her, he broadly hinted that he was still hoping in 1979 to reconcile with Margaret by leaving politics, and he sensed that his leadership role was over. But then, he said to McCall, Crosbie brought down his budget, and "it had become obvious that Clark couldn't hold his party or the government together until the Liberals could be ready under a new leader to fight an election."

The best reconstruction of the sudden, spectacular destruction of the Clark government is Richard Gwyn's, in his book *The Northern Magus*. Amid the usual Ottawa swirl of conspiracy, posturing and fluke luck, it fell out like this:

Finance Minister John Crosbie, sporting Newfoundland sealskin mukluks, heads into the House of Commons to propose an additional four-cent tax on a litre of gasoline, causing the government's defeat by a united Opposition.

Photo - Canadian Press Images

November 22: The print media said two things about Trudeau's departure that mattered – that his legacy was on balance disappointing (which goaded Trudeau), and that the Tories were now secure until the Liberals chose a new leader (which reassured Clark).

December 3: The Gallup poll reported the Liberals at 47 percent of popular support in November, while the Conservatives were at 28 percent.

December 4: Liberal pollster Martin Goldfarb confirmed to *de facto* interim Liberal leader Allan MacEachen that the poll was reliable, and that the Liberals could now easily win an election; frantic internal follow-up polling ensued.

December 7: MacEachen, a grand master of the parliamentary chess game, told the party whip to ensure that every last Liberal MP was in the House for the upcoming budget vote –

even two who were in hospital.

December 11: Crosbie put his budget before Parliament. Trudeau told the media the Liberals would vote against it. The media shrugged this off, in Gwyn's picturesque phrase, as "ritualistic Opposition chest-thumping." The almost universal assumption, even among Liberals, was that enough Opposition MPs would miss the vote to let the government survive.

December 12: MacEachen stirred up the Liberal caucus to defeat the government, and "damn the torpedoes." All Trudeau added was that the budget was regressive and should be defeated, and that he would not lead them in the ensuing election "unless the sovereign asks me on bended knee three times." It was an allusion to a Chinese folk tale, and nobody in caucus had any idea what he meant. Most were already lining up behind new leadership candidates.

December 12: The Créditistes told the media they would abstain from the budget vote because they didn't like the 18-cent tax on gasoline. The media now began to suspect the Liberals really were going to defeat the budget and trigger an election.

December 12: In the Commons question period, MacEachen said quietly to Trudeau: "I believe the government will be defeated tomorrow. You'd better figure out what you're going to do." Smiling an inscrutable smile, Trudeau replied: "What does one do? One does one's duty, of course." This convinced MacEachen that Trudeau would stay on as leader, if necessary.

The *de facto* leader of the Liberals after Trudeau announced in November he was quitting the leadership was Cape Breton MP Allan MacEachen. Though he had harboured leadership aspirations of his own, he persuaded the caucus to stick with Trudeau and defeat the Conservatives.

December 13 (morning): Clark's steering team of ministers and staff spent an hour discussing routine matters as though nothing were amiss. Clark's agitated legislative assistant, Nancy Jamieson, blurted out: "I think we'll be defeated [tonight]. We don't have the numbers." She reminded them that only with all Tory and Social Credit MPs in the House could they beat a united NDP/Liberal opposition. Yet the Social Credit were not in support, and three (some accounts say six) Tory MPs were absent. Most problematic was the absence of External Affairs Minister Flora MacDonald, who was in Paris.

Jamieson's concern was dismissed by chief of staff Bill Neville, based on the Clark government's settled assumption that the Liberals would not dare trigger an election they were bound to lose.

December 13 (afternoon): Liberal MPs were indeed suffering doubts, as the recklessness of their previous day's resolve sank in. Six months after a defeat, with a discredited leader

intent on leaving, and with the divisive leadership selection process now well begun, they were going to bring down an elected government.

Front-running Liberal leadership candidate Donald Macdonald, no longer in Parliament and fearing the party was about to commit mass suicide, was pleading with the caucus, one-on-one over the telephone from Toronto, to leave Clark in power. Other MPs were desperately trying to re-engage John Turner, who had already said he wouldn't run.

Still sensing no change in their situation, the Conservatives decided not to delay the budget vote.

December 13 (evening): The Conservatives put their budget to Parliament, and were defeated 139 votes to 133.

December 14: Bright and early Clark went to the Governor General, and an election was called for February 18.

"The miscalculation was not so much one of arrogance as of innocence," wrote Dalton Camp in the preface to a book on the Clark interlude, *200 Days: Joe Clark in Power*, by Warner Troyer. "[The government] failed to comprehend the swiftness with which cynicism, opportunism, and an abiding lust for power could combine to revive a defeated Liberal party."

Clark chief of staff Bill Neville (left) in 1979. Assuming that Trudeau was gone and that the government was still popular, the party had stopped polling and proved wrong on both counts. Neville remained a senior Conservative operative under Brian Mulroney, and later became a lobbyist. Right, a bearded Trudeau returns from a summer canoeing in the Northwest Territories and touring Tibet to lead the Opposition. His political aide Jim Coutts told him bluntly to shave it off if he wanted to remain as leader. He soon did.

■ ■ ■ ■

Trudeau now told the Liberal caucus that he would resume his leadership only if they asked him with an overwhelming vote, and he reminded them of all the reasons they might not want him.

After he left them to discuss it, MacEachen immediately asked why, having caused an election, they would not want to fight it under the present, proven leader. That clinched it. Why would they not?

Though support was probably less than "overwhelming," and no vote was taken, the majority of caucus clearly agreed, as in turn did a very alarmed and distraught Liberal Party executive. The only part that may have surprised Trudeau was the skepticism expressed privately over the next two days by so many individuals he respected, including staunch allies and close friends from Quebec such as Marc Lalonde and Jean Marchand.

For four days he remained perfectly torn, veering back and forth, until, after an intense morning with Jim Coutts, he walked into a news conference on December 18 to announce that he would stay on and lead the party in one last election.

The factor that most drove him forward was Quebec's approaching referendum on

Clark campaigning in Niagara Falls, Ontario, in February 1980. He knew by the earliest opinion polls that he would lose the election.

sovereignty, and it was this that most alarmed his friends. They feared that he would lose the election and doom the federalist cause in Quebec.

René Lévesque's first four-year mandate was reaching an end, and he had committed to holding the sovereignty vote before it was over. On December 19, one day after Trudeau's decision to stay on, the Parti Québécois decided the wording of the question, and confirmed that the referendum would proceed after the federal election.

Lévesque said in his memoirs that he was not surprised that Trudeau "seized this un-hoped-for chance to be born again from his still hot cinders." Far from being discouraged, Lévesque claimed that he'd sooner face Trudeau than Clark in a referendum, because Trudeau was stiff and polarizing, whereas Joe was just a "nice, basically broad-minded guy."

How broad-minded and flexible Clark really was is open to question. He was still insisting on privatizing Petro-Can and declaring that the budget was right for Canada, even though it had just been defeated in the Commons, and even though Crosbie himself now suggested they propose a phasing-in of the excise tax, in three six-cent increments.

Close observers had noticed by now in Joe Clark an abiding fear of appearing weak. This made him even more rigid than Trudeau, but with less success. Positions he presented as principled appeared to many people just stubbornly wrong-headed.

The opening Tory pitch in the election was that the Liberals should have given the Conservatives a reasonable chance to govern, and that Trudeau should not be re-elected as prime minister.

Internal Conservative polling by Allan Gregg during the campaign's initial week – the first since August – revealed to the Tories something the Liberals had known for a month: the Conservatives were in deep trouble everywhere except Alberta.

According to Gregg, they began the campaign 21 percent behind in the polls. Their brief performance in government was rejected two-to-one across the country, and – even worse – Trudeau personally was now outpolling Clark three-to-one. These gaps were far too wide to close in a campaign. The Tory team put the best face on it they could, but to their great chagrin they knew they had been outflanked by an enemy they had wrongly assumed to be down for the count.

Liberal strategists Coutts and Davey knew that victory was theirs. They had only to wait for it, and not make mistakes. Just as the Liberals had defeated themselves the year before by having governed badly, now the Tories had done the same.

It left both parties with little to do except tear each other down. Trudeau kept a low profile, ducking a debate with Clark, minimizing media contact and appearing on stages crowded with other Liberal luminaries, where he promised this would be his last round as prime minister. He delivered speeches flatly and slowly – almost mechanically.

Clark summed up Trudeau's election pitch as, "Elect me and I'll quit." In reply, the Liberals fixed Clark with the moniker "the wimp."

There was nonetheless a consistent Liberal policy message, which strengthened as the campaign progressed. It was simply, "Make Alberta pay."

Trudeau began, pleasantly enough, in Winnipeg, promising to take western alienation as seriously as Quebec separatism.

However, in the crucial battleground of Ontario, the Grits became much more pointed and divisive. Trudeau would say that Clark, coming as he did from Alberta, wasn't as sensitive to Ontario's needs as the Liberals were. He cited criticisms of Ontario Conservative Premier Bill Davis and provincial Treasurer Frank Miller of the Conservatives' energy policy and gasoline tax, and implied that Clark and Alberta Premier Peter Lougheed were in

league, though he knew very well they had been bitterly at odds.

"We have to use energy as a tool of our industrial strategy," Trudeau told a typical election rally in Peterborough, "not as a bludgeon to destroy the competitiveness of [Ontario]. By driving Canada's energy prices up to 85 percent of world prices, that's what the Tories are doing to this province. And whether the Joe Clark Conservatives are doing it through ignorance, or policy, or weakness to some other part of Canada, I can't say."

As the Tory campaign foundered, the Liberal campaign strengthened. Trudeau, by the end, was back in top form, speaking without notes, and his handlers were thrilled to let him do it. It felt like 1974 all over again.

Towards the end, in a speech to the Halifax Board of Trade, Trudeau began hinting about new federal intervention in the oil business on a massive scale. The media didn't report it, but it did not escape the vigilance of Lougheed. "I read that Halifax speech," he recalled in a 2001 interview, "and I said, 'Wow, we're in for it.' I never foresaw anything as bad as the National Energy Program, but I sure expected a real attack."

Legend has it that Senator Keith Davey summarized the 1980 Liberal strategy as "Screw the West – we'll take the rest."

Whether he really said it, it hardly matters. It's what happened on February 18, 1980.

■ ■ ■ ■

"Well, welcome to the 1980s!" was Pierre Trudeau's hearty greeting to a joyful crowd in Ottawa's Château Laurier Hotel on election night.

The Liberals had captured 60 percent of the seats in the Atlantic provinces, 99 percent of Quebec's seats and 55 percent of Ontario's. The western returns had not yet been tallied due to time-zone differences, but they made no difference. The Liberals had already taken over half the seats in the House of Commons. The two western seats they picked up in Winnipeg were padding.

By stark contrast, the mood that greeted Clark and his wife, Maureen McTeer, in an arena that evening in Spruce Grove, Alberta, was heartbroken and grim. Little could be said

Trudeau at the Château Laurier Hotel in Ottawa utters his triumphant election-night greeting, "Welcome to the 1980s." The party took only two seats west of Ontario, but had all the strength it needed to do with oil and gas whatever it wanted.

Photo - Canadian Press Images

beyond "the people of Canada have spoken," and little was. Clark took it stoically, but Maureen was in tears. Her husband had reached power and had lost it. His career had peaked at age 40.

The lopsidedness of the result was stunning. The Liberal share of the popular vote was 23 percent in the West, compared to 42 percent in Ontario, 68 percent in Quebec and about 45 percent across the Atlantic. The Conservatives, by contrast, had pulled 35 percent to 40 percent across all major regions, except Quebec, where they got only 12 percent.

The situation was not new – just worse. As long ago as the Flag Debate of 1964, Quebec Tory MP Heward Graffety had said to the Liberal bench: "Let us recognise the fact that neither of the two traditional parties can truly call themselves national parties any more. I recognize that with our [small] 'corporal's guard' from Quebec, we [Conservatives] are no longer a national party in the great sense of the word. But with your corporals' guard from west of the Lakehead, neither are you."

In spirit, Canada had gone from the "two solitudes" – British and French – described by Canadian novelist Hugh MacLennan half a century before, to four solitudes: the Atlantic provinces, Quebec, Ontario and the West.

In the vacuum left by the departed British identity, Canadians naturally looked inward, and they found that the histories, economies and hopes of their four major regions were actually quite different and, in many key respects, in collision.

Westerners rejected the Liberals because westerners had never really accepted the original French-British theory of Canada. To them, Canada was an English-speaking, multi-ethnic country with one French province, far away and shrinking in importance. For a century, they had gambled that Canada's economic future lay in the West, and with the surge in resource values in the 1970s they knew now that it did. They were tired of being told by a French prime minister that the national interest was, by definition, contrary to their own.

Trudeau was rejected in western Canada because he refused to acknowledge any of this, and after 1980 he was loathed as no other national leader before or since; and it galled westerners that his popularity, amounting at times to adulation, was as strong as ever in central and eastern Canada.

■ ■ ■ ■ ■

On taking power, Trudeau's first challenge was to win Quebec's May 20, 1980, referendum on sovereignty.

To help win it, the new Liberal approach of "make Alberta pay" was brought into plain daylight.

Both sides had been preparing since December, before the referendum date was set.

Knowing that most Quebeckers – even most francophone Quebeckers – did not want to separate completely from Canada, Lévesque's "Péquistes" (PQ partisans) had never proposed "independence." They had advocated "sovereignty association," a more ambiguous and plastic concept. And because even this prescription was too strong for most voters to swallow, they now spoke of gaining "equality as a people."

Being certain that Quebec's diminishing anglophone minority would vote solidly "No," the Péquistes knew that to reach the required 50 percent, they had to persuade 62 percent of francophones to vote "Yes."

The Quebec government had phrased the referendum question to ask for a mandate to "negotiate a new agreement with the rest of Canada, based on the equality of nations." If the majority answer was "Yes," negotiations for a new arrangement with Canada would

Quebec separatist supporters throng a "Yes" meeting in Montreal during the 1980 sovereignty referendum. Outgunned by Liberal Ottawa, by the end they were lashing out wildly.

Photos - Canadian Press Images

proceed, and a second referendum would follow.

Anyone who actually read the referendum question (no more than 116 words in French) could understand that the government wanted legislative sovereignty within a continuing Canadian economic union. The question was straightforward enough, considering that this had been Quebec's main political interest for 20 years.

The new provincial Liberal leader, Claude Ryan, had organized the "No" campaign well, but he lacked the immense money and manpower of the federal Liberals. With the election won, the feds took charge of the referendum campaign. Jean Chrétien, now justice minister,

Trudeau addresses a "No" rally at Montreal's Paul Sauvé Arena. His arguments went from appeals to Quebeckers' self-interest to scathing sarcasm. Old people would starve and freeze, and Alberta would sell oil at OPEC prices.

"No" voters celebrate the federalist victory. The price was a Trudeau promise to deliver undefined constitutional guarantees that would satisfy French demands.

Photos - Canadian Press Images

ran it, while Trudeau stormed the province with an energy and passion unseen since 1968.

The federalists – Trudeau in particular – demolished the sovereigntist case at every level.

Lévesque could not deliver economic "association" with Canada, argued Trudeau, because all the other nine premiers had said they were not economically beholden to a sovereign Quebec. Nor could Lévesque promise "sovereignty," said Trudeau, because Quebec had just filled 74 of its 75 federal seats with a party solidly committed to preventing it. So neither sovereignty nor association could happen. A "Yes" vote, Trudeau concluded, would simply produce a stalemate that would be bad for Canada – especially Quebec.

That was the intellectual case, and it registered. Most Quebeckers had never thought of it from the perspective of English Canada. Having been spurned, why would they make any special concessions to Quebec? He followed it by pouring scorn on sovereigntist terminology. The original separatists of the 1950s and 1960s, said Trudeau, at least were honest enough to say what they wanted – outright independence – rather than hide behind weasel words that cloaked the same intent.

Then came over-the-top sarcasm. "Suppose," said Trudeau, "that Cuba or Haiti came proposing to 'associate' with us, because down there they like Canadian prosperity, or the Canadian countryside, or Canadian women...So they vote on it, and they agree, massively, 'Yes, we want association with Canada.' Would we, in the name of democracy, be obliged to accept them? Would our only choice be to consent – 'Well, yes, they voted for it, so we don't have anything to say in the matter'?" This was so preposterous, it always amused federalist audiences.

Next came an appeal to fear, heavily subsidized by federal advertising and street-level

Lévesque, flanked by his wife Corinne and with minister Lise Payette looking on, admits defeat on sovereignty, but assures his supporters it will one day succeed.

rumour-spreading. Quebeckers, especially the poor and elderly, would perish without federal transfers. This talk was everywhere, and it was all untrue. That Quebec has received more from Ottawa since the 1960s than it contributed is a well-established fact; but that it has reaped any real benefit by being subsidized is highly questionable.

Last came inducement – some would say bribery. Chrétien and Lalonde hammered away at the idea that if Quebeckers voted "No" to sovereignty, Ottawa would deliver Alberta oil at bargain rates. An independent Quebec, warned Lalonde, "would immediately, and I insist immediately, have to pay $3.8 billion a year more for its oil." Chrétien got Lougheed to publicly confirm that an independent Quebec would have to bid for oil like any other foreign country.

It worked, and, by the end, knowing they'd lost, the Péquistes began lashing out wildly and foolishly. Lévesque accused Trudeau of being English because his middle name was Elliott, and one of his ministers, a hard-line feminist named Lise Payette, accused no-voting women of being male-dominated.

Even so, the pro-sovereignty "Yes" vote was 40 percent on May 20. The francophone vote had split right down the middle, and the anglophone vote had clinched it for the "No" side. The Péquistes had lost – at least for now, conceded Lévesque. "The day will come," he told 5,000 crestfallen supporters in Montreal's Paul Sauvé arena, "and we will be here to greet it. À la prochaine!" (Until next time!)

It would come sooner than many probably expected.

T rudeau did not rest on his laurels. He plunged immediately into two other large projects he already had in preparation: patriating the Canadian Constitution from Britain, and wresting a federal share – in effect, a federal royalty – from provincial oil and gas production in the West.

There were, and always have been, two widely shared sentiments among Canadians about oil and gas. One is that they should be cheap; the other that they should be federal. Most Canadians in 1980 either didn't know or didn't care that under the Constitution oil and gas belong, as do all natural resources, to the Crown in right of each province.

In other words, they belong collectively to the residents of each province through their provincial government. This is a sensitive point in Alberta and Saskatchewan, because they had to struggle for 25 years (from 1905 to 1930) to win from Ottawa the same right of resource ownership that other provinces had enjoyed since Confederation.

Because Ottawa had no right to petroleum royalties, yet had undertaken to subsidize oil consumption under the Petroleum Administration Act of 1974, either the federal deficit or federal taxes would have to rise – or Ottawa would have to somehow arbitrarily impose a direct wellhead claim on western production. Trudeau knew it. Peter Lougheed and Bill Davis knew it. The whole country knew it.

Federal subsidization of Canadian consumption throughout the 1970s had had the double effect of increasing per-capita consumption (unlike in the U.S., where it had fallen) and swelling the federal deficit.

Trudeau, having watched Clark come to grief now that the price of oil was rising once again, had decided to take a hard line with Alberta. He had hinted in the election that in the

Trudeau had decided on a head-on confrontation with Alberta. Lalonde delivered one far more severe than anything the province had expected, imposing what was in all but name a royalty at the wellhead.

Photo - Canadian Press Images

Though shocked at the provisions of the National Energy Program, Peter Lougheed's Alberta government was prepared to respond, and did.

Photo - Canadian Press Images

next round of energy negotiations, the federal gloves would come off. Clark had been unable to bring forward a timely and acceptable federal budget because it took months to reach a national pricing scheme acceptable to both Alberta (the largest producer) and Ontario (the biggest consumer). Clark needed seats in both provinces.

Trudeau didn't. One-third of his majority caucus came from Ontario, and none of it from Alberta. He knew who and where his friends were.

Trudeau assigned to this daunting struggle his two toughest ministers, Marc Lalonde in Energy and Allan MacEachen in Finance. By the fall, they were ready with the National Energy Program (NEP).

It was announced with the federal budget by MacEachen on October 28, 1980. It included a wellhead tax on oil and gas production (in effect, an ownership royalty) and a continued and expanded tax on exports, and it held the price of oil at $17 a barrel – less than half the then world price of $40. It also offered major incentives to shift petroleum investment onto federal lands in the North from the provincially owned fields of Alberta, Saskatchewan and British Columbia.

Except for one brief, unsuccessful meeting that summer at Harrington Lake between Trudeau and Lougheed, there had been no consultation. Ottawa simply declared how it had decided the matter.

Lougheed was briefly stunned at the blatant constitutional illegality of it, but he and his government had been anticipating events as best they could. Two days later, the Alberta premier replied to Ottawa on province-wide television. Much of it went live across Canada, and Trudeau and his ministers watched it from his office.

Lougheed, his brow like a thundercloud, came as close to a declaration of war as any premier could. He said that "The Ottawa government has, without negotiation, without agreement, simply walked into our home and occupied the living room." The NEP was, he said, "an outright attempt to take over the resources of this province, owned by each of you as Albertans. We're facing a situation where more and more decision-making, more and more control, will be in the hands of the decision-makers in Ottawa, and your provincial government will become less and less able to influence your future and to provide for job security and opportunity."

Therefore, said Lougheed, starting in March of 1981, Alberta would reduce its oil output by 15 percent – or 180,000 barrels a day – in three phased cutbacks of 60,000 barrels over six months. This was to minimize as much as possible the loss to Albertans of Ottawa's forcible underpricing of their resource. Second, two oilsands and heavy oil projects worth $16 billion in new investment would have to be reviewed and perhaps suspended. Third, Alberta would challenge a new federal gas export tax in court.

"We are going to have a storm in this province," warned Lougheed. "But I think we've got enough strength and resolve to weather that storm."

Alberta was treading a fine line. If its cutbacks created genuine hardship – if it "let the eastern bastards freeze in the dark," to quote the now-notorious 1973 bumper sticker – it would give Ottawa the political and legal grounds to federalize the resource. If it cut back too little, Ottawa would ignore it.

It was later disclosed that, for this very reason, the team of Ottawa ministers and

The NEP caused such a heavy exodus of drilling equipment to the United States it actually showed up as a statistical spike in the province's export of manufactured goods. Within two months, 60 full-sized drilling rigs had gone south. Here, a smaller service rig crosses the border at Coutts, Alberta.

Photo - Glenbow Museum

By March of 1982, business bankruptcies had become common, oilpatch equipment was being dumped at auctions, and Albertans were seething. Here, Trudeau is hung in effigy at a machinery sale in Nisku, south of Edmonton.

Photo - *Edmonton Sun*

technocrats who designed the NEP expected, or at least hoped, Alberta's cutback would be more severe, or even total.

As it was, Energy Minister Lalonde dismissed the cutback as a "tantrum." The tantrum's cost to Canadian consumers, when the cutback came, would be $3.6 million a day, or 14 cents a day per person (the added cost of replacing 180,000 barrels of $17 Alberta oil with $40 foreign oil).

What surprised the Trudeau Cabinet as the fight dragged out, growing nastier by the month, was that the industry turned mainly against Ottawa, not Alberta. Despite the NEP's fairly rich drilling incentives, resource companies would not invest in a country so blindly determined to freeze the price of their commodity at such a low level. As for shifting more exploration northward onto "Canada lands," the NEP gave Petro-Can an automatic 25-percent "back-in" share of anything the private companies found.

Within weeks of the NEP announcement, drilling and service rigs were leaving Canada for the U.S., each taking with it 25 to 30 jobs and $1 million a year in local spinoff benefits. The industry guessed that at least 200 would leave that winter, and drilling was forecast to drop by 40 percent. As it turned out, they were not far off in their estimate.

Earl Joudrie, president of the Independent Petroleum Association of Canada, commented that even after some February 1981 adjustments favourable to the industry, "the basic stupidity hasn't changed." What Ottawa didn't get, said Joudrie, was that by restricting the new incentives to Canadian-owned companies, Ottawa was cutting off the industry from its traditional source of risk capital in the U.S. Eastern Canadians didn't invest in petroleum – Americans did.

In March 1981, as the first 60,000-barrel cutback took effect, Alberta won round one of its court case. An Alberta Court of Queen's Bench ruled that Ottawa had no right to tax

Peter Lougheed never accepted Ottawa's National Energy Program, but regardless, there had to be a pricing agreement on Canadian oil and natural gas. The schedule, worked out and sealed with a champagne toast in September 1981, would soon prove hopelessly optimistic. Meanwhile, Albertans resented their premier having made peace; Lougheed later privately described this famous photo as the most damaging of his political career.

Photo - Canadian Press Images

Between October 1980, when the NEP was announced, and Alberta's provincial election two years later, a wave of separatist sympathy washed through the province. It began with an address by Western Canada Concept (WCC) founder Doug Christie urging the western provinces to unite into a single new nation.

exports from three gas wells that had been specially drilled by the provincial government. It would take two more years, but eventually Alberta would win in the Supreme Court.

By now, Lalonde was starting to soften, and negotiations began, five months after the war had erupted. There was progress, but not enough to prevent the June cutback from kicking in. Lalonde imposed a two-cents-a-litre "Lougheed levy" on gasoline to pay for more imports.

By now, between marginally increasing the price of crude oil and increasing the gasoline tax, Ottawa had hiked the consumer price as much as Crosbie intended to. However, in the interval, pumps and prices had been converted from imperial gallons to litres (one gallon consisting of 4.55 litres), and consumers hardly noticed it.

When pricing negotiations began, Lougheed said there were 151 outstanding points of disagreement. By August, with the third incremental cutback looming on September 1, negotiations in Montreal between Lalonde and his Alberta counterpart, Merv Leitch, were reaching a conclusion. When reporters saw Lougheed arrive unexpectedly on September 1, they knew the war was over.

In the end, Alberta got most of the price it wanted at the outset. The price for "old oil" (already discovered) was to rise from $19 a barrel to $57. All "new oil" discoveries would start at $46 and go to $77 by 1986. The price of natural gas would be allowed to rise by similar percentages as well.

There was one large "but," however. Alberta and the industry would have to allow the federal-revenue share to increase, to approximately 25 percent, where before it had been negligible.

Lougheed and the Albertans were doubtful that prices would rise so high, but whether they did or not, at least there was a deal. To his lasting political regret, Lougheed was then photographed drinking a champagne toast with Trudeau, and everyone went home – if not happy, at least satisfied.

The industry, however, was decidedly unhappy. Having been excluded from negotiations, it found itself with only 44 percent of the revenue. (Alberta got 30 percent.) Neither the Canadian juniors nor the multinational majors thought there was enough left to justify exploration after two levels of government drew off 55 percent. Lougheed had to travel to New York to assure investors that there were still profits to be had in Alberta.

In fact, the international price of oil had already peaked and was on its way back to a 1982 close of US$30 a barrel, while the price of borrowing money reached 20 percent. Immediately, both governments had to start feeding some of their new gains back into the industry, as investment sagged and the Alberta economy entered a tailspin.

Years later, Lalonde was quoted by Alberta MP David Kilgour in his 1988 book *Uneasy Patriots* as saying that the NEP was not ultimately about oil at all. It was to stop Alberta from getting more powerful.

"The major factor behind the NEP," Lalonde explained, "wasn't Canadianization or getting more from the industry or even self-sufficiency. The determinant factor was the fiscal imbalance between the provinces and the federal government. Our proposal was to increase Ottawa's share appreciably, so that the share of the producing provinces would decline significantly, and the industry's share would decline somewhat."

The cost to Alberta was steep indeed. By 1983, the province was in a severe recession. Unemployment rose from 3.3 percent in October 1980 to 10 percent by December 1982 – this despite the fact that Canada's regulated oil price was going up constantly,

Warning Albertans not to vote "protest" in a general election, and opening up the provincial treasury, Lougheed crushed Kesler and his party in a November 1982 general election. Here, Kesler is crashing a Conservative campaign event in High River because Lougheed refused to debate him.

Photo - National Archives of Canada

even as the international price was coming down.

Also unforeseen was a significant surge in western separatism. Victoria lawyer Doug Christie organized the Western Canada Concept (WCC) and harangued large, angry public meetings in Edmonton and Calgary in November of 1980.

Christie envisioned a sovereign western Canada with no provinces, but his Alberta wing disagreed and soon broke away to form a provincial party. The Alberta WCC mushroomed to 12,000 members over the following year, and in a February 1982 by-election a 36-year-old WCC candidate, Gordon Kesler, a rodeo rider and oilpatch scout, was elected to the Alberta Legislature. After the NEP, polls showed popular support for outright separation had risen in Alberta from its usual low level of about 5 percent, to 23 percent.

However, Kesler did not remain long as MLA for Olds-Didsbury. The WCC did recruit a few credible academics and businessmen, but parties fuelled by rage seldom prosper, and many WCC candidates sounded unhinged. Within two years, the party suffered the same fate as the early independence parties of Quebec: it split between reformers and separatists. Many members wanted mainly "good government," meaning right-wing government; others wanted mainly to get out of Canada.

Kesler emerged the winner from a raucous August 1982 leadership convention, but whether he was really the leader was open to serious doubt. By now, he had said he was no longer a separatist unless all more moderate reforms failed; but there were still plenty of avowed sovereigntists all through his party.

Premier Lougheed initially expressed cautious sympathy with the separatists' frustrations, but not with their aims. However, once he had struck an oil-pricing deal with Trudeau, and after Kesler had won his by-election, Lougheed took a harder line, warning Albertans not to vote "protest" in the general election he called for November of 1982 because they might end up with a government they would regret.

As the Alberta economy deteriorated, Lougheed hiked provincial spending and received an overwhelming mandate – 75 of 79 seats, with 62 percent of the popular vote. The WCC took only 12 percent of the vote and no seats, and after struggling for a few more years receded into history. However, they did much better than Alberta's provincial Liberals, who took a mere 1.8 percent.

■ ■ ■ ■

The sinking
of the *Ocean Ranger*

A super-modern drilling platform sinks in the North atlantic, killing all its crew

by Joanne Byfield

By the 1970s, Newfoundlanders had been making a perilous living from the shallow waters of the Grand Banks continental shelf for four centuries. But for decades the fisheries had been in decline, and in the 1970s a new hope arose that oil might replace cod as the province's economic base. Particularly promising was the Hibernia formation, 300 kilometres east of St. John's. To probe it, Mobil Canada had brought over from Japan the deep-sea drilling rig *Ocean Ranger*.

The *Ocean Ranger* was the largest self-propelled semi-submersible drilling rig in the world when it was designed in 1976 by ODECO Engineers Incorporated. It had already drilled off Alaska, New Jersey and Ireland, and by 1981 was on contract to Mobil Oil Canada and ODECO Drilling of Canada for the Hibernia job. By February of 1982 it was working on its third Hibernia hole. Mobil had two other rigs in the Grand Banks – the *SEDCO 706*, 21 km northeast of the *Ocean Ranger*, and the *Zapata Ugland*, 48 km north.

Although seabed oil drilling was almost as old as drilling on land, and was reckoned to be no more dangerous, the Hibernia field would soon experience tragedy of a kind with which Newfoundlanders were all too familiar.

Early in the morning of February 15, with almost no warning, the *Ocean Ranger* capsized during a vicious winter storm off the Grand Banks of Newfoundland. Despite heroic efforts to save the crew, all 84 men (56 of them from Newfoundland) drowned in the icy, turbulent Atlantic Ocean.

It was the worst Canadian maritime disaster since the Second World War.

The Royal Commission on the Ocean Ranger Marine Disaster, jointly appointed by the federal and Newfoundland governments and headed by Newfoundland Supreme Court Chief Justice T. Alexander Hickman, interviewed 102 witnesses and recorded 14,281 pages of transcript to find out what happened. Their report, including phone and radio transmissions from the rig, gave a detailed description of its last hours.

In the dry, bloodless tone of all public inquiries, the report told a horrific tale.

The Grand Banks seas, being only 100 metres deep and home to conflicting currents, are notoriously dangerous. Early on Saturday, February 13, Mobil's private weather forecasts began warning of an approaching storm, with winds up to 70 knots (126 kilometres per hour), building to "gale- to storm-force west to northwest winds, heavy seas, flurries and freezing spray by Sunday night."

By Sunday morning, a revised forecast was predicting winds at 90 knots (162 km/h) and sea heights of 11 metres by 2:30 p.m. that afternoon. The message was sent to Mobil's shore base, where it was telexed to each rig. The *Ocean Ranger* received it at 8 a.m. on Sunday morning.

Such wild weather was not supposed to be of great concern to the drilling platform. That fateful Sunday, ODECO's shore-based drilling superintendent Jim Counts reviewed the day's operations with the *Ocean Ranger*'s toolpush (or crew chief), Kent Thompson, first at 7 a.m. and again at 11. Thompson told him that drilling operations were proceeding as usual, and the weather did not seem to be an issue. Counts went home shortly after 11 a.m. because the weather was deteriorating.

At 1:30 p.m., the forecast worsened, calling for poor visibility and even rougher seas throughout the night, culminating in sea heights of 14 metres by 8:30 a.m. on Monday. Despite the forecast, *Ocean Ranger* senior drilling foreman Jack Jacobsen phoned Merv Graham, Mobil's area drilling superintendent in St. John's, at 2 p.m. to report that the rig was drilling at 18 feet per hour.

Drilling continued as usual until 4:30, when onshore drilling foreman Peter Kapral advised the rig personnel to "hang-off" – meaning the process of suspending drilling without having to remove the entire drill string from the well.

At 6:47, Jacobsen phoned Graham at home to tell him the job of hanging-off had been completed. By now, the rig was heaving six metres, and the sea was spraying the drill floor. Also, due to the fierce winds and waves, the *Ocean Ranger*'s standby ship, the *Seaforth Highlander*, was almost 10 km away instead of the recommended 1.5 km to 3 km.

Just before 7 p.m., toolpush Thompson phoned Counts and told him that the winds were raging at 104 km/h, and the

Crewmen from the rescue ship *Hudson* unload one of the *Ocean Ranger's* dead in St. John's Harbour.

Photo - Canadian Press Images

heaves were up to almost seven metres.

Sometime between 7 p.m. and 8 p.m., the heavy waves broke a lower-level glassed porthole. Personnel on *SEDCO 706* overheard radio conversations between people on the *Ocean Ranger* about broken glass, water in the ballast-control room, a short circuit in the panel, indicator lights flickering off and on, and valves opening and closing on their own.

At 9 p.m., the *Ocean Ranger* called the *Seaforth Highlander*, now 11 km away, to see how it was faring, but did not request it to move closer. Jack Jacobsen mentioned the broken portlight to Mobil's Graham, and to personnel on the other two rigs, but said all had been cleaned up, and there were no other problems.

At 1 a.m. on Monday, February 15, Jacobsen phoned Graham at home and asked him to notify the Coast Guard that the *Ocean Ranger* was listing forward, and that the crew "were at-tempting to isolate the problem." Graham also called rescue helicopters.

Five minutes later, the *Ocean Ranger* contacted the *Seaforth Highlander*, now 13 km away, and asked it to come to "close standby." At 1:06, Graham, onshore, advised the Search and Rescue Emergency Centre about the *Ocean Ranger*. At 1:09, a MARISAT (a satellite communication system) operator in Connecticut picked up a distress telex from the *Ocean Ranger* which said they were experiencing a "severe list of 12 to 15 degrees to the port side" and in winds of 75 knots (135 km/h).

At 1:10, the rig's radio operator contacted Mobil's onshore radio operator and asked him to transmit a mayday. One minute later, Jacobsen called the *SEDCO 706* and said that the *Ocean Ranger* "was not coming back for us," and that they would need helicopters and supply boats for evacuation.

The two standby vessels for the other rigs, along with the *Seaforth Highlander*, all proceeded to the *Ocean Ranger*. At 1:30 a.m., the *Ocean Ranger*'s medic/radio operator, Ken Blackmore, in the last communication received from the rig, called Mobil's shore base and reported that the crew were going to lifeboat stations. He also asked for another mayday to be sent.

As the standby boats headed to help, the Rescue Coordination Centre (RCC) in Halifax contacted a rescue unit in Gander and asked them to send a helicopter crew to the rig. However, with icing blades in the forecast, the choppers could not fly. At 1:36, the RCC contacted SAREC (Search and Rescue Emergency Centres) in St. John's to issue an All Ships Broadcast to assist the *Ocean Ranger*. That broadcast was not issued for another half-hour.

The *Seaforth Highlander* was the first to reach the *Ocean Ranger*. At 2:11, the rescue ship saw the listing *Ocean Ranger*, flashing lights in the water, and smoke flares off the port beam. The flashing lights were attached to empty life jackets, floating in the water. At 2:14, they saw a distress flare off the starboard quarter.

The *Seaforth Highlander* spotted a lifeboat and approached, radioing back to Mobil. Graham later recalled sending instructions not to attach lines to the lifeboat to avoid capsizing it, but the crew never received the message. As the ship manoeuvred into position for rescue, four seamen went onto the afterdeck, and they could see the lifeboat was "holed on both sides of the stern from the waterline to the gunwale." Men were bailing water. The water was very rough, with swells over 18 metres and four-metre waves. The spray over the decks froze instantly, hampering the mens' visibility and movements, so they untied their own lifelines.

At 2:32, the *Seaforth Highlander* came alongside the lifeboat. In the storm and wind, they could not communicate but could see men moving on the lifeboat. After several failed attempts, they managed to throw two lines to the lifeboat, and each was fastened to both vessels. Seven or eight men from the lifeboat came out on the port gunwale. They were wearing hard hats, and some were warmly dressed, but others lightly, and some wore only pyjamas.

Almost immediately, according to the report, "the lifeboat began to roll slowly to port, away from the Seaforth Highlander, and within seconds capsized throwing the men who had been standing on the port gunwale into the sea and snapping the lines which had been attached to the *Seaforth Highlander*." It was 2:38 a.m. The lifeboat was spotted hours later with 20 bodies strapped inside, and despite valiant attempts to recover it, the boat sank.

The men on the rescue ship launched a life raft, but the men in the sea were now too cold to grab the lines or the side of the raft. Two were still holding on to the capsized lifeboat, drifting perilously close to the ship's propeller, so the captain shut it off. That caused the ship to be blown further away from the lifeboat and raft.

At 2:45, a second standby vessel, the *Boltentor*, saw the *Ocean Ranger* and approached with a searchlight. They saw no signs of the crew or lifeboats on the rig or in the water. The rig, according to several seamen, had a severe list, and the helicopter deck was almost in the water.

A third ship, the *Nordertor*, was still about 16 km from the site, but had the *Ocean Ranger* on its radar until 3 a.m., when it disappeared from the screen and was presumed sunk. The crews of the *Seaforth Highlander* and the *Boltentor* continued to try to rescue the men in the sea, hoping some might still be alive. They could see bodies in the water, but high winds of 60 to 70 knots (108 to 126 km/h) and 18-metre seas made them impossible to reach.

At 3:38, the *Nordertor* reported to the *SEDCO 706* that the *Ocean Ranger* had disappeared from radar, and the information was immediately sent to Mobil's shore base. Search efforts continued throughout the morning, and for five more days. Only 22 bodies were recovered. The official cause of the deaths was "drowning while in a hypothermic condition."

What caused the disaster? The commission determined that the broken portlight set off a chain of events that no one on the ship seemed to understand, and therefore did not take seriously. Certain design flaws in the rig meant that the broken light (which itself did not meet required standards) allowed water into the ballast-control room, causing short circuits in the indicator panel, which was not waterproof. That led to water coursing into the ballast, causing the list and eventually sinking the rig.

In addition, crews were poorly trained in management systems and emergency procedures, and there were no manuals or training programs to explain the technical systems on the rig. The rig crews were industrial workers, not mariners. For example, when the first severe weather warnings came in, the crew could have closed the deadlights over the port lights, which would have protected them from the waves which broke the light. When they thought they were emptying seawater from the ballast tanks to correct the list on the rig, they were actually letting more in. Once they decided to go to the lifeboats (an exercise they had not practised), the heavy seas and high winds made it almost impossible to launch the boats without damaging them. The commission assumed that the holes visible in the lifeboat seen by the *Seaforth Highlander* occurred during launch. There were not enough survival suits for the entire crew, which would have "appreciably lengthened the time of survival" according to the commission, and, if each man had had one, "there is a real probability that some of them would have survived."

The disaster, as ever, led to after-the-fact safety regulations that should have been in place to begin with.

W hile the energy war was being fought, Trudeau opened a second front – one much dearer to his heart. In fact, it was the same imperative that had propelled him into politics 16 years earlier: Quebec and the Constitution.

But constitutional reform now went far beyond Quebec. By 1980, energy and the Constitution were two fronts in the same war of Ottawa versus the provinces. As Lougheed put it in his broadcast address to Albertans following the NEP, Trudeau's emerging constitutional assault "could complete the [federal] takeover of our resources, which is [already] being engineered on a pricing and taxation basis."

Likewise, NDP Premier Allan Blakeney, though more centralist in his views than Lougheed, agreed that as long as Ottawa claimed the right to set oil and gas prices, Saskatchewan's resource guarantees were pure fiction. On this point, he disagreed with not only Trudeau but also his own national party. The West was the only place where the NDP could elect governments. That fact made the western provincial NDP leaders far less centralist than the national party.

Though Trudeau had scarcely mentioned reforming the Constitution in the 1980 election campaign, he ended the referendum campaign in Quebec with a bold promise, delivered on four occasions, to forge a new constitutional deal. He didn't say – and couldn't know – what the new deal would be. But he knew what he wanted, and he was resolved to get it.

Back in 1971, after Bourassa torpedoed his Victoria pact with the premiers, Trudeau had washed his hands of constitutional reform and vowed never to revisit it. He did not – indeed, could not – keep that promise. The country's worsening economic and political tensions required that some fundamental decisions be made.

At a deep level, the psychology of the country had changed in ways that Trudeau and his biculturally focused government chose not to acknowledge. Albertans John Barr and Owen Anderson described it thus in their 1971 book *The Unfinished Revolt: Some Views on Western Independence.*

"Now that we know there are not two solitudes in Canada, but many," they wrote, "we can all stop pretending that this is a united nation, or indeed a nation at all, in the modern, tight-knit nation-state sense of the word. It is really a collection of fairly parochial regions held together by a tenuous sense of a shared consciousness and a fear of American or other outside domination – but each area pursuing its own identity and its own sense of destiny."

The extent of this centrifugal tendency had grown compellingly clear by 1980.

To counter the devolutionist drift Trudeau had returned to the Constitution, even before the November 1976 election of a separatist government in Quebec. He began with a letter to all the premiers in April of 1975.

Quiet, low-profile conferencing over the next several years produced a lengthy list of disagreements and unknowns:

1. The rules for "patriation." Canada's Constitution was the British North America (BNA) Act – an 1867 statute of the British Parliament. Could Ottawa unilaterally assume legislative control of it, or was provincial consent required? If so, how many provinces, representing how many people? This dispute, and others, had undone all nine previous attempts to Canadianize the Constitution since Britain had washed its hands of the matter half a century earlier.

2. On the heels of the first point came another: how to amend a patriated Constitution? In the past, all amendments had been legislated by the British Parliament upon request by Ottawa, and – especially since 1931 – with varying but substantial degrees of provincial support. Quebec and Ontario assumed they each should hold a unilateral veto over changes. Ottawa agreed. But should all other provinces hold a veto? If so, the Constitution would be unamendable. So how many other provinces should it take to approve or block a proposed change?

3. Should the Charter of Rights and the French-language rights that Trudeau had insisted on since 1968 be added to the BNA?

4. Would it be right to clarify the vague assurances in the BNA Act of provincial resource ownership, provincial responsibility for social programs and civil rights, and modernize the outdated division of tax fields?

5. Should new responsibilities that had accrued by constitutional default to Ottawa since 1867 be shared with or reassigned to the provinces, such as broadcasting and culture, environment and family law?

6. Should provinces be granted a greater role in federal institutions, especially in the choosing of senators for Parliament and judges for the Supreme Court of Canada.

7. Should certain federal powers be restricted, two in particular: the right Ottawa assumes to spend federal money in areas constitutionally reserved to the provinces; and Ottawa's constitutional right to federalize anything it deems necessary "for the general advantage of Canada," from grain elevators to oil reserves.

Quebec premier René Lévesque hated constitutional abstractions as much as Trudeau enjoyed them. Here, they are going into a federal-provincial conference in 1979.

Photo - Canadian Press Images

Headway soon seemed impossible. Ontario wanted less decentralization, Quebec wanted more. Western provinces wanted much more meaningful guarantees of resource ownership and control than Ottawa was willing to give. The Atlantic provinces wanted ownership and control of offshore mineral resources and of the fishery, neither of which Trudeau's government would consider granting. They also wanted a permanent guarantee of Equalization.

■ ■ ■ ■

Many of these constitutional demands were new. But newest, and most problematic of all, was a constitutional-amending formula proposed by Alberta and backed by British Columbia.

The amending formula assumed and accepted until 1980 was the one unanimously agreed to in Victoria in 1971. It was simple enough: general amendments would require the support of Parliament and the legislatures of Ontario, Quebec, any two Atlantic provinces representing half the regional population, and the same in the West.

The now-premiers of Alberta and B.C., Peter Lougheed and Bill Bennett, had taken no part in the Victoria consensus, and both strongly objected to Quebec and Ontario gaining a constitutional status superior to that of the other eight provinces. As they saw it, all provinces, from smallest to largest, were constitutional equals with Ottawa, with equal but distinct legislative responsibilities. "Our country," said Bennett, "is above all a bargain – between people, between the regions and between the provinces." Said Lougheed, "Canada cannot be governed under a unitary system where all the basic questions are left to a central government to be resolved."

In February of 1979, they suggested a compromise based on the principle that all provinces are constitutional equals, and that therefore the general amending formula should require support from Parliament and any seven provincial legislatures representing at least half the population of Canada.[1]

By 1980, there was a strong desire for greater provincial rights among all the premiers elected since the Victoria conference. They were (standing, l to r) Peter Lougheed, Alberta; Angus MacLean, P.E.I.; Sterling Lyon, Manitoba; Allan Blakeney, Saskatchewan; Brian Peckford, Newfoundland; (seated, l to r) John Buchanan, N.S.; William Davis, Ontario; Trudeau; Governor General Ed Schreyer; René Lévesque, Quebec; Richard Hatfield, N.B.; Bill Bennett, B.C. The only ones who sided reliably with Trudeau were Davis and Hatfield.

Photo - Courtesy of Peter Lougheed

Federal constitution minister Jean Chrétien at the opening meeting, July 1980. While Chrétien was sweetness and light, Pitfield was in the background ensuring failure.

Photo - Canadian Press Images

The advantage of this was that it was simple, clean and less blatantly discriminatory. It more-or-less protected both outer regions from a constitutional gang-up by the rest of the federation. It restored, in part, the theory of "compact federalism" (the idea that Confederation was fundamentally a pact among provinces) without relying on the historical distortions that theory demanded.

But it had one overriding disadvantage: it denied Quebec the constitutional veto it had always claimed to possess to protect its internal language and culture. Mathematically, Lougheed's "7/50 formula" (as it came to be called) required that any constitutional amendment would need support from the Legislature of either Ontario or Quebec (to reach 50 percent of the population), whereas the Victoria formula required approval from both.

By 1980, Trudeau had been at the constitutional game long enough to realize that if he didn't somehow get the Constitution home from Britain, the paralysis would continue, and he would never get his Charter of Rights. Patriation was the key to all the rest.

---

1. The "7/50 formula" was an Alberta idea which, to make it more politically palatable in eastern Canada, was dubbed the "Vancouver formula." Alberta was seen by now as a polarizing force in national discussions.

The provincial premiers understood just as clearly that if Ottawa forced patriation without an amending formula and an updated division of powers, the provinces would soon become little more than glorified municipalities subject to federal dictate and depredation.

This was the set-up for the 1980-81 final play.

In July of 1980, with the Quebec referendum over, the provinces heard from federal Justice minister Jean Chrétien that patriation would proceed "as soon as possible." Unofficially, Chrétien warned that Ottawa would proceed unilaterally if necessary.

Given Ottawa's aggressive, inflexible mood, provincial governments consulted with each other over the summer, and met with the federal government in September. By now, it was obvious that (a) the provinces could not agree on what they wanted, and (b) Trudeau, expecting such a stalemate, would use it as an argument to convince Britain and the Canadian public to let Ottawa patriate unilaterally.

Any doubts about Trudeau's strategy were erased by a leaked memo in August from Privy Council Clerk Michael Pitfield advising the prime minister to proceed unilaterally as

The four-day, televised September 1980 conference failed as well, as Trudeau prepared for unilateral action. Quebec was drawing closer to the opposing provinces of the West.

Photo - Canadian Press Images

Lévesque, seen here in December 1980 denouncing Trudeau's constitutional plan in a speech to 14,000 Quebeckers, was not nearly as subtle and patient as his adversary.

Photo - Canadian Press Images

soon as the September meeting ended in an impasse. Though few premiers were surprised, most were angry, and they accused Trudeau of bad faith. The whole September conference had been simply for show.

This was followed in September by a second leaked federal paper, this one by then senior bureaucrat (later senator) Michael Kirby, which was even more explicit than Pitfield's on how to manipulate public opinion to move unilaterally.

The federal government offered a few last-minute concessions, but the two memos – combined with Trudeau's hard and hurried attitude – convinced the premiers that the concessions were insincere and cosmetic. The four-day televised meeting had been a waste of time.

On October 2, 1980, Trudeau put a resolution before the Canadian Parliament asking the British Parliament to approve patriation of the British North America Act to Canada, along with an added Charter of Rights, French-language guarantees, a commitment to Equalization, and the Victoria amending formula.

Among the provinces, he had only the governments of Ontario and New Brunswick in support. The six governments of Quebec, Alberta, British Columbia, Manitoba, Newfoundland and Prince Edward Island declared themselves opposed, while those of Saskatchewan and Nova Scotia, still hopeful of a negotiated agreement, remained neutral for the time being.

The only new and unexpected aspect of the federal resolution was a proposed referendum mechanism as an alternative, at federal discretion, to the Victoria amendment formula. For an amendment to succeed in this way, it would have to get referendum majorities in the same number of provinces called for by the Victoria formula. The difference would be that only Ottawa could trigger the process and set the question, and thereby circumvent the legislatures. Most provincial governments were more appalled than ever.

Trudeau was convinced that Canadians in all regions would normally prefer a stronger Ottawa to stronger provinces. He and his party had come, by now, to detest provincialism, and he assumed citizens did too. Whether he was right or not is impossible to prove. Subsequent experience – especially in Newfoundland, Quebec and the four western provinces – would suggest he was, in large part, wrong.

■ ■ ■ ■

A long, lonely road to hope

The lasting legacy of Terry Fox

by Joanne Byfield

Heroism, often enough, comes in unlikely forms. Surely one of the unlikeliest was Terry Fox, hobbling along the lonely, endless Trans-Canada Highway. He had set himself two seemingly impossible goals. One was to run across Canada on one good leg. The other was to raise $1 million for cancer research.

Even though cancer cut short his 1980 Marathon of Hope, he actually exceeded his financial target. By the time he died, he had raised almost 25 times more than his initial goal. By 2008, the annual run he inaugurated had raised over $400 million.

Terrance Stanley Fox was born in 1958 in Winnipeg, and grew up in Port Coquitlam, near Vancouver. He loved sports, and played with an almost obsessive intensity. In March 1977, at age 18, after ignoring a sore knee for several months, Terry was diagnosed with bone cancer. His right leg was amputated six inches above the knee, and he spent the next 14 months in chemotherapy. During his frequent visits to the hospital, he was touched by how many people – young and old – suffered from cancer, and how many died.

Then he read a story about an above-the-knee amputee who ran the New York Marathon. Terry could do better. That's when he set his goal, and over the next two years he ran over 5,000 kilometres to prepare.

On April 12, 1980, Terry dipped one foot into the Atlantic Ocean in St. John's, Newfoundland, and set off across Canada. On his first day, he ran 20 km through cold and snow. This was not good enough. To cover the 8,529 km to Vancouver in six months,

he would have to average 42 km a day. Which he soon did.

With little advance publicity, there was scant public interest when he came hopping into those first Atlantic communities. This frustrated him, and he would phone ahead to news media and city officials to set up meetings, but it often didn't generate much reaction. Still, in a few places – especially in Newfoundland in small communities such as Port aux Basques – he got a good reception and impressive donations.

Those who did see him were enthusiastic – even awed. A donor in Newfoundland spoke for many when he handed $50 to Terry's friend and support van driver, Doug Alward, and said, "I don't care if he makes it. He's really making a lot of people feel good."

His fame grew as he worked his way steadily westward through New Brunswick and Quebec. The sight of the grinning, grimacing, curly-haired, unstoppable, one-legged runner and his odd hop-skip method of running became a common sight on TV news and in daily newspapers. He had to take two steps on his good left leg for every step with the prosthesis on his right. The artificial limb caused blisters and cysts on his stump, making it bleed.

The Canadian Cancer Society, which he had persuaded to endorse the run, had insisted he first get medical approval from a heart specialist. According to Leslie Scrivener, author of the 1981 book *Terry Fox: His Story*, Dr. Akbar Lalani warned Terry that while his enlarged heart had withstood the stress of training, "you might die tomorrow because of it." He reluctantly gave his approval, but warned Terry that if he felt dizzy or short of breath, he should stop.

By the time Terry reached Toronto he was a national celebrity. On July 11 he spoke to a huge crowd in Nathan Philips Square, wearing a Leafs jersey given to him by Darryl Sittler.

Photos - Canadian Press Images

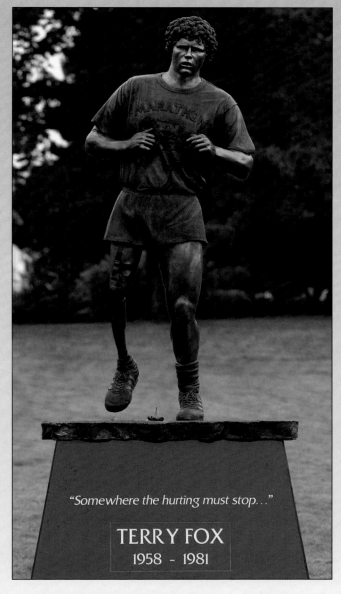
"Somewhere the hurting must stop..."

TERRY FOX
1958 - 1981

Terry Fox statue in Beacon Hill Park in Victoria. He never finished the run, but wildly exceeded expectations.

Terry, said Scrivener, had already experienced those symptoms during training, and mentioned them in his daily journal during the Marathon. He just didn't mention them to the doctors whom the Cancer Society had arranged for him to see along his route. In fact, he skipped the appointments. He was determined to complete the run and raise money. Now, he was hoping for $1 per Canadian – $24 million. He refused to be distracted by anything else.

Terry was so intensely focused that he often lashed out at Doug Alward and at his own younger brother, Darrell, who joined the trip when school ended in June. The two would en-

sure his favourite foods were ready, and they stopped every mile to give him ice water. Terry would erupt angrily at proposed schedule changes, or when he felt underappreciated or exploited by organizations or politicians. He was disappointed with the efforts of the Cancer Society representatives, especially in the Maritimes and Quebec, when he felt he didn't get enough exposure. Neither Terry nor his crew spoke French, and Quebeckers gave him short shrift.

But when the Marathon reached Ontario, interest exploded. Terry crossed the border between Quebec and Ontario to a cheering crowd, and was feted everywhere he went. Hundreds turned out to see and hear him in many communities, and money began pouring in.

In Nathan Phillips Square in downtown Toronto, an estimated 10,000 people celebrated his arrival. The Cancer Society estimated that $100,000 was raised that day – over half of it from pledges phoned in to radio station CKFM.

Still, Terry kept up his punishing routine, getting up at 4 a.m. or 5 a.m., running 10 or 12 miles, stopping for breakfast, speaking to groups, resting, running another 10 or 15 miles, and then often speaking at an evening event and doing media interviews.

Finally, on September 1, after 143 days and 5,373 km, Terry was forced to stop outside Thunder Bay, Ontario. On this last day, he ran with constant pain in his chest, and wondered if he was having a heart attack. He climbed into the van, and told Doug to take him to emergency. Tests showed that the cancer had returned in his lungs. Terry flew back to British Columbia and began treatment.

Money continued to roll in. Isadore Sharp, founder and president of the Four Seasons Hotels, whose son had died of cancer, told Terry that he would institute an annual event, the Terry Fox Run, to continue the Marathon of Hope. By February 1, 1981, the Marathon of Hope had raised $24.17 million (almost exactly $1 per Canadian). Terry was made a Companion of the Order of Canada – the youngest person ever inducted. He received many awards, and buildings, streets, parks and schools – and even a B.C. mountain – were named after him.

Terry contracted pneumonia in early June, and he died on June 28, 1981, at age 22.

The following September, the first Terry Fox Run saw over 300,000 participants raise $3.5 million, and annual runs held in over 50 countries since have raised more than $400 million. In 2005, the Terry Fox Foundation started the Terry Fox National School Run Day, which was one of the largest events in Canadian history with 9,000 schools and over three million students participating.

Isadore Sharp probably summed up Terry Fox's legacy best. "Terry did not lose his fight," he said. "Perhaps he finished all he had to do. Terry is like a meteor passing in the sky, one whose light travels beyond our view, yet still shines in the darkest night."

Trudeau's October 1980 resolution immediately hit roadblocks. Clark's Conservatives, ignoring pressure from their Ontario caucus, stalled it in every way they could, with enough success to force the resolution to go before a joint Commons-Senate committee for study and adjustment.

At the same time, provinces referred the federal resolution to appeal courts in Newfoundland, Quebec and Manitoba. Was it legal? They also had their agents general in London start lobbying British MPs to vote against it if and when it reached Westminster.

All of these efforts soon bore fruit. In London, Quebec's agent general caught the sympathetic attention of the Commons Foreign Affairs Committee, chaired by long-time Tory MP Sir Anthony Kershaw. It agreed, on November 5, to receive submissions from interested parties. This was a breakthrough because, instead of meddling in the politics of the United Kingdom, provinces opposing the resolution were now answering a Parliamentary request for information. Five provinces made submissions. Ottawa did not.

Roy Romanow, co-author of the 1984 book *Canada...Notwithstanding* and the Saskatchewan minister who took part in constitutional negotiations, recalled that the question in England was fairly simple. Did Britain still have a "guardianship role" with respect to the Canadian Constitution? The dissenting provinces said "yes," but Ottawa said "no."

Ontario premier William Davis, who was dismissed by other premiers as Trudeau's flunky, played a pivotal arbitration role at the end.

Photo - National Archives of Canada

The Kershaw committee, aided by an expert in Commonwealth law from Oxford University, held 10 meetings to consider the matter, and concluded in January of 1981 that the British Parliament was not obliged to approve a Canadian government resolution if, by doing so, Britain would significantly change the federal character of Canada, especially in the absence of any opinion from Canada's Supreme Court.

The "substantial objection" it had heard from half the Canadian provinces caused the Kershaw committee to think that the Canadian balance was indeed being altered. "We think that it would not be inappropriate," concluded the committee, "for the U.K. Parliament to expect that the request for patriation...be conveyed to it with at least that level of Provincial concurrence which would be required for a post-patriation amendment..." (This would mean endorsement from the legislatures of at least five more provinces than it already had, which it would never get.)

The Kershaw report raised little interest in England, but set off a political furor in Canada.

As a single parent, Trudeau sometimes took his children travelling. In June 1980 his eldest, Justin, met Pope John Paul II at the Vatican. How Trudeau squared his legalization of abortion and homosexuality with his Catholic beliefs remained unclear to many Canadians.

Trudeau met Margaret Thatcher in 1980 and assured her the patriation of Canada's Constitution would be a simple matter, and she was displeased when it disrupted her Parliament. They are pictured here chatting in 1982 at a conference in Versailles, France.

With the introduction of a "Charter of Rights", constitutional concerns suddenly moved beyond the small circle of Canada's first ministers to engage — and alarm — many social subgroups. Pictured here demanding inclusion in the Charter is Yvonne Peters of Saskatchewan, demonstrating on Parliament Hill in November of 1980 with the Coalition of Provincial Organizations of the Handicapped.

Photo - Canadian Press Images

The Trudeau government, unwisely, tried to use it to stir up patriotic resentment against the meddling British. Most Canadian commentary, however, said it was a reasonable and responsible conclusion.

By now, it was estimated that the provinces had recruited about one-third of British MPs from both main parties to vote against the federal resolution. The Cabinet of Margaret Thatcher was expressing polite but growing concern to Ottawa about a controversy it didn't need tying up Parliament. Trudeau had assured Thatcher the previous summer it would be a quick and simple matter.

In March of 1981, the Trudeau government — which had declined to appear before the British committee — wrote scathingly that the committee had been factually misinformed. This only made relations between the two governments worse.

Meanwhile, the Commons-Senate committee in Ottawa had been busy, holding 267

hours of hearings over 56 days. Liberal-dominated, most of its inquiry centred on the proposed Charter of Rights, and most of its witnesses were lobbyists for various special interests: feminists, aboriginals and civil libertarians. They convinced the joint committee to expand the Charter significantly.

The committee chose to deny homosexual lobbyists admission to the Charter, but Justice Minister Jean Chrétien assured them (correctly, as it turned out) that in due course they could be included by the judiciary. Pro-lifers failed to get the fetus protected, and later found the judiciary to be no help at all. The Conservatives tried to get property rights protected, but the committee's Liberal and NDP majority overruled them. The federal NDP had said it would vote against the Charter if property rights were Charter-guaranteed. When the joint

A breakfast meeting of the notorious "Gang of Eight" premiers opposing Trudeau. Though their position was outwardly strong, they had been weakened by internal division and distrust. They are, clockwise from left, Brian Peckford, Newfoundland; Allan Blakeney, Saskatchewan; Angus MacLean, P.E.I.; John Buchanan, N.S.; René Lévesque, Quebec; Peter Lougheed, Alberta; Bill Bennett, B.C.; (back to camera) Sterling Lyon, Manitoba.

Photo - Canadian Press Images

committee was done, the Trudeau government submitted an amended resolution to Parliament in February of 1981.

In April of 1981, the Parti Québécois was elected – again to general astonishment – with an even larger majority than before, further hampering the federal cause. Not only did it confirm that Ontario and Quebec (Canada's two original and largest provinces) held diametrically opposite views on the future of federalism, but it also weakened the Trudeau government's claim that, since the PQ lost the sovereignty referendum, the province's MPs were the constitutional wardens of Quebec. It also guaranteed that future conferences would be burdened by the unfortunate personal animus that had always existed between René Lévesque and Trudeau.

During the winter, Saskatchewan and Nova Scotia joined the six opposing provinces, creating what was dubbed the "Gang of Eight."

Between January and April of 1981, the three provincial appeal courts that had been consulted by the provinces in September of 1980 rendered their opinions. In split decisions, Manitoba (3-2) and Quebec (4-1) held in favour of Ottawa. Against this, the three justices of the Newfoundland court held in favour of the provinces. After this, Trudeau announced

that he would seek the opinion of the Supreme Court of Canada.

In April of 1981, the Gang of Eight produced a counter-proposal they entitled the Provincial Patriation Plan. It proposed simply that (1) the BNA Act be patriated with (2) Lougheed's 7/50 amending formula and (3) the right of any province to opt out of any federal program with full federal compensation. The Charter and the rest could be settled later.

Trudeau dismissed it, and Chrétien tagged the opt-out provision (insisted upon by Quebec) "sovereignty association by installment." Still, the provinces' minimalist approach was, in one way, astonishing: Lévesque had accepted it. It was the only time that any Quebec premier has ever been willing to relinquish the provincial claim on a unilateral constitutional veto. He was pilloried in Quebec for doing so, but he stuck to it. He still hoped the whole constitutional project would fail, that Ottawa would withdraw its resolution, and it wouldn't matter.

Spring gave way to a 1981 summer ceasefire, but hostilities resumed with renewed fury in the fall.

■ ■ ■ ■

The Parti Québécois had been weakened by its referendum loss in 1980, but was bolstered by an unexpected, larger-than-ever majority mandate in an April 1981 general election. It seriously weakened Trudeau's constitutional claim that his federal Liberal caucus represented Quebec's views. Pictured here are Lévesque and his wife Corinne Côté-Lévesque on election night.

Photo - Canadian Press Images

The climax of the drama was set for a final, last-ditch, four-day first ministers' meeting in Ottawa in early November.

Though the momentum had shifted noticeably to the Gang of Eight, their alliance was flimsy, and everyone knew it. They were united solely by what they didn't want – by what Romanow and his co-authors have called "the federal government's denial of their differences" – and not by any positive common aim. Some premiers actually liked Trudeau's Charter (or parts thereof), others hated it, and still others were focused mainly on resources – and Lévesque just wanted out of Canada. Nor was it only the premiers themselves whose views mattered. Within each delegation of ministers and expert officials there was a range of opinion.

The Gang's odds were bolstered considerably by the Supreme Court of Canada (SCC) on September 28. Its opinion on the Resolution to Amend the Constitution was really a statement of the obvious. No written law, said the nation's highest court, prevented Trudeau from doing what he planned, but it was contrary to convention. It clearly would affect provincial rights, and provinces traditionally had a say. The SCC refused to stipulate how many provinces were needed to satisfy convention, only that convention demanded a "substantial degree" of provincial endorsement.

Trudeau promptly declared his resolution vindicated: the court had supported his legal right to proceed. But in reality, the SCC had dealt the federal side a serious blow. In Britain, the whole Constitution rests on unwritten conventions, so to ask the Mother of Parliaments

The Supreme Court of Canada, in its first-ever televised session, ruled that Ottawa could legally patriate the Constitution unilaterally, but that custom required "substantial" consent from provincial governments – something that Trudeau clearly did not have.

Photo - Canadian Press Images

to approve a law that needlessly violated conventions was, in effect, to ask it to behave unlawfully. Under a conventional system, only dire need justifies ignoring or changing the normal practice; and what urgent need of state could the Canadian government point to?

Meanwhile, B.C. Premier Bill Bennett, as chairman of that year's premiers' conference, had met with Trudeau and was meeting with other Gang of Eight premiers to suggest that Ottawa was open to negotiation.

However, the few specifics he was able to offer from Trudeau convinced the more hard-line premiers that Trudeau was just trying to divide them and derail the Provincial Patriation Plan (PPP).

By November, though the Gang of Eight still existed, there were really three groups among the provinces. Ontario and New Brunswick were still pro-resolution, though they were losing faith in Trudeau's odds of success. There were three hard-line PPP provinces: Quebec, Alberta and Manitoba. The remaining five provinces, though still officially behind the PPP, were openly looking for compromise. Saskatchewan Minister Romanow and Ontario Attorney General Roy McMurtry were exploring alternatives with Chrétien. However, by late October, all compromise initiatives had failed, the battle-lines remained drawn, and the likelihood of a November impasse loomed large.

The meeting opened in a tense and suspicious mood in Ottawa's massive Government Conference Centre – a refurbished CN train station – on Monday, November 2, 1981. By now, nobody trusted anybody. None of Trudeau's offers had amounted to anything, and half of the Gang of Eight no longer really wanted to gamble everything on the PPP.

Trudeau, conferring here with finance minister Allan MacEachen at the final conference in November 1981, knew he had to draw Lévesque out of the Gang of Eight so the coalition would collapse. He succeeded.

Photo - Canadian Press Images

Trudeau started by saying he would not insist on the Victoria amending formula, but he refused to budge on the Charter or anything else. Ontario's Bill Davis said that he too would be willing to relinquish the Victoria formula, and with it Ontario's veto, if the other premiers would give ground on the Charter. New Brunswick's Richard Hatfield suggested a phasing-in of Charter sections, entrenching the most fundamental rights immediately and allowing further negotiation of the rest.

While the middle-ground provinces stayed at least nominally attached to the PPP, they proposed numerous possible alternatives, or expressed pious hopes that some other solution might be found. Even Quebec said it was open to a scaled-down Charter of Rights. It was left to Alberta's Lougheed to make the case for the Provincial Patriation Plan without compromise or addition.

Alternating between open and closed sessions, the conference continued through Tuesday and into Wednesday, with everyone seemingly disagreeing on a bewildering array of major but difficult points, while the whole country tried to make sense of it on television.

Into such complex but important political negotiations there usually creeps a subtle but powerful determination among the participants to come out with a successful result; and the more intractable the disagreements, the stronger the desire very often becomes. It's the secret ingredient of democratic self-government, and why such a chaotic system typically produces better results than any other. This mood of determination now took hold. Among the 11 governments involved, the only one immune to it was Quebec's.

By Wednesday morning the Gang of Eight had fallen apart, federal spirits had lifted, and Trudeau sprang his trap – an offer to Quebec to put the federal resolution to a national referendum. Lévesque, confident it would fail in Quebec, immediately agreed. The other premiers, certain it would pass in their provinces, were dismayed.

Photo - Canadian Press Images

By the end of Tuesday, the Gang of Eight had fallen apart, but this didn't mean that Ottawa had made any converts. Everything had become, in the B.C. phrase, "fluid." Minds had been forced open, lines were shifting and anything might happen.

What finally shattered the Gang of Eight was Trudeau's challenge to Lévesque on Wednesday morning to put the federal resolution to a national referendum. On pure impulse and with no warning, Lévesque accepted it. His seven provincial allies were astonished and dismayed: everyone knew that the language and process of a referendum would be federally controlled. When the morning session dispersed for lunch, Trudeau trumpeted to the waiting media that there was now a "new Quebec-Canada alliance," and he added with a mischievous gleam, "The cat is among the pigeons."

By the time Lévesque figured out that afternoon that he had given the game to Trudeau, the other provinces had been furiously repositioning without him, and continued to do so through the evening.

But for some time, Lévesque had already been feeling abandoned by his fellow premiers – "a bunch of Kiwanis presidents," in the description of one of his advisers. Lougheed was "the only one with real guts," in Lévesque's view. But Lougheed, like the rest, was a Canadian, and Lévesque sensed that the alliance-of-differences was shutting him out as the Gang began considering new options.

Lévesque bitterly told Stephen Clarkson and Christina McCall in 1986 (in *Trudeau and Our Times*, volume 1): "None of them [the other premiers] had a vision that couldn't be turned by a couple of cocktails. In the end, they patched [a deal] together. And Quebec was once again left in the corner."

Lévesque suffered two handicaps. First, by his own admission, he hated constitutional politics. Second, it was he – not Trudeau and the other premiers – who insisted that Quebec remain apart. It was how his mind worked, and the whole point of his political career.

Things now moved rapidly to a deal. The Gang met all through the evening in Saskatchewan's hotel suite, and produced the "Kitchen Accord," handwritten on a notepad. The Quebeckers were not invited, but all the other dissident provinces were, with communication to those on the other side and to the feds.

The deal was: if Ottawa would accept the 7/50 amendment formula, the Gang (excluding Quebec) would accept Trudeau's Charter – as long as governments could opt out of any adverse court rulings based on its individual-rights sections.[2]

When Trudeau, surrounded by his federal constitutional ministers and political chieftains,

"Now the cat is among the pigeons," Trudeau playfully told reporters. There was a "new Quebec-Canada alliance."

saw the "Kitchen Accord" on Wednesday evening, he at first rejected it, saying the country should instead go to a referendum on the original federal resolution. But among all his Cabinet allies – even Lalonde – he was alone in thinking so.

Then Richard Hatfield phoned, and, lastly at 10 p.m., Bill Davis. Both said they would no longer support him if he turned this deal down. That clinched it. Trudeau knew that even if his resolution passed a national referendum, it would fail in Britain if not one premier supported it. After quickly wresting three fairly minor concessions from the Gang, Trudeau gave in.

Lévesque was livid when he joined the Gang for breakfast on Thursday morning, and saw the proposal. They worried the Quebec delegation might boycott the conclusion of the conference. But it didn't. Lévesque showed up, and excoriated the lot of them.

A remarkable tableau on television greeted Canadians on the final morning of that historic event – Thursday, November 5, 1981. Against all hope, a deal had been struck. After nine failed attempts over half a century, Canadians would now have their own Constitution.

Yet, as this was announced, there was no celebration. Every face wore a frown.

■ ■ ■ ■

The final compromise pleased none of the central Canadian players – (from left) Ontario's Davis, Chrétien, Trudeau and MacEachen, and Quebec's Lévesque. All felt they had lost more than they gained.

Photo - Canadian Press Images

2. This "opting-out" right became Charter Section 33, the "Notwithstanding Clause." It applies only to Charter Sections 2 and 7 to 15.

Why "patriate" anything?

For a complex federal nation, Canadians are remarkably uninterested in their constitution

by Link Byfield

Most Canadians assume that government is something done for them rather than by them. As a result, we have a poor sense of how our system of self-government works.

Few Canadians in the 1960s and 1970s knew what a constitution is, why ours was somehow "in Britain," and why "patriating" it was necessary. It's unlikely that many citizens understand this today.

A constitution is the foundation of a nation's lawful authority, and the instrument by which citizens control governments (meaning Cabinets). Just as ordinary laws (such as the Criminal Code and the Highway Traffic Act) seek to restrain the behaviour of individual citizens, constitutions are supposed to guide and restrain the behaviour of governments.

Constitutions may be written or unwritten. Canada, being a hybrid parliamentary federation of provinces, has both written and unwritten (or "conventional") elements.

Until 1982, the written aspect of the Canadian Constitution consisted mainly of the British North America Act (still in force as the Constitution Act, 1867).

The BNA Act was an ordinary statute passed by the British Parliament in 1867. It established a federal union of four provinces (Ontario, Quebec, New Brunswick and Nova Scotia), and made specific allowances for an American-style division of legislative sovereignty between national and provincial governments.

Federalism was a concept foreign to the British parliamentary system, but the framers would not accept a system in which Ottawa decided civil rights and local matters. They had tried it in Ontario and Quebec as the united Province of Canada, and they felt it had failed.

Likewise, none of the Maritime colonies had any interest in being taken over by Quebec and Ontario. For Confederation to proceed, the division of powers and public revenues had to be negotiated and written down.

Because the BNA Act was a British statute upon which all Canadian governments relied for legitimacy, the only legal way Canadians could take control of it in 1982 was by an Act of the British Parliament transferring responsibility for the BNA Act to Canada.

The BNA Act had been amended numerous times over the previous century, but always by Britain, and always – where relevant – with the consent of most or all of the affected provinces. As firm believers in freedom and fair play, the British had always been very considerate of provincial and minority rights – far more so than Ottawa.

Over a century, the convention had developed that Ottawa alone could ask Britain for BNA Act amendments, and that Britain would show due regard for provincial rights and responsibilities.

The strange paradox of Trudeau's constitutional approach was that he expected Britain to observe the first convention (responding to requests for amendment from Ottawa), while ignoring the second (respect for provincial rights).

The gall of what he was asking for is, in hindsight, breathtaking. He expected the Mother of Parliaments to send him, without delay, a heavily amended Constitution which eight of 10 provincial governments opposed, and contrary to the advice of the Supreme Court of Canada.

Not being a fool, Trudeau undoubtedly knew his request was, at the very least, unusual. But he had concluded by June of 1978 that the only way to force the provinces to move on patriatation was to demand it unilaterally from Britain.

This was the 11th Canadian attempt since 1927 to agree on terms for patriation. Had Trudeau not done exactly what he did, the Constitution would almost certainly still be in Britain, and amendments to it would still be subject to approval by Westminster; which would be absurd and, many would say, disgraceful.

Had the premiers not swallowed hard and accepted the Charter of Rights, Trudeau was ready (indeed eager) to go to a national referendum. He knew, and the premiers knew, that Canadians, being constitutional illiterates, would probably support anything that promised them more rights. The obvious possibility that judges as a group are as likely (or more likely) to be as arrogant, political and high-handed as politicians – and unaccountable to boot – may need to be suffered for a long time before most people appreciate it.

In the end, Trudeau and the premiers won and lost in roughly equal measure; which, by the rule of thumb of parliamentary brokerage politics, probably means it was a good deal.

As a result, since 1982 the Canadian Constitution has consisted primarily of:

The Constitution Act, 1867 (formerly the British North America Act), as amended over the years by Britain. This Act establishes the responsibilities and powers of federal and provincial legislatures and courts.

The Constitution Act, 1982. This establishes the Canadian Charter of Rights and Freedoms, aboriginal rights, the principle of Equalization and the constitutional-amending formula.[1]

These together comprise the written Constitution of Canada.

The unwritten, conventional part centres on Parliament. For example, nowhere do the Constitution acts establish the position of a prime minister (though it is referred to in passing twice in the 1982 addendum). Nowhere is our elaborate system of Cabinet government and parliamentary confidence anywhere constitutionally spelled out. Nowhere is it written that the Governor General (vice-regent for our head of state, the Queen) must proclaim any law approved by Parliament. Nowhere do the Constitution acts establish the Supreme Court of Canada; the 1867 framers left its creation to an optional federal statute which could (in theory, at least) be repealed by Parliament tomorrow.

This was not stupidity or laziness on the part of the framers; it is the British system. In Britain, Parliament may, with three simple readings and royal assent, repeal any statute going all the way back to the famous Magna Carta of 1215. (In fact, most of the famous medieval Charter has indeed been repealed over the years.)

Just as a federal parliamentary system was considered a necessary but difficult hybrid by Canada's framers in the 1860s, there is today equal difficulty grafting a judicially enforced Charter of Rights to a system of parliamentary supremacy. It leaves ambiguous who is ultimately in charge of defining and protecting freedom: the courts or the legislatures?

Since England's Glorious Revolution of 1688-89, English constitutional authority has rested on the King in Parliament; that is, the King may enact any law he wants, no matter how cruel or foolish, provided Parliament agrees. Parliament, in turn, is there to protect the civil and political freedoms of Englishmen from unjust encroachment by the King and his executive government. In the British parliamentary tradition, judges do not instruct Parliament in matters of rights; rather, Parliament instructs and compels judges.

Prior to Trudeau's 1982 Charter of Rights, this was how it worked in Canada. The only constitutional role of the courts was to settle jurisdictional disputes between Ottawa and the provinces.

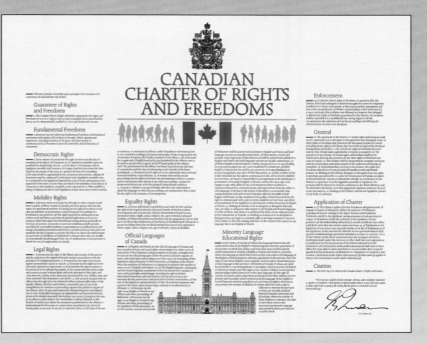

The 1982 Charter of Rights ended the British principle that the King in Parliament has the power to do whatever they believe necessary.

The first quarter century of Charter of Rights experience indicates that the power to define and defend freedom has passed to the judges, as many political leaders in 1982 predicted it would. At the same time, federal-election turnouts have sunk steadily from an all-time high almost touching 80 percent in the Diefenbaker era, to an all-time low barely above 60 percent in the 2004 election won by Liberal leader Paul Martin.

However, such trends have a way of changing, and nothing except a lack of public will prevents Canadians from restoring power to their elected legislatures.

William Dafoe, a famous editor of the *Winnipeg Free Press* in the mid-20th century, once commented: "There are only two kinds of government: the scarcely tolerable and the absolutely unbearable." Democratic systems change only when people in large-enough numbers feel they have gone from the first sort to the second.

---

1. Other historic documents have constitutional authority as well, such as the Royal Proclamation of 1763, the Quebec Act of 1774, the acts creating new provinces after 1867, and the British Statute of Westminster of 1931 declaring the British dominions self-governing.

After seeing the Queen off at the airport, Trudeau celebrated with one of his occasional trademark pirouettes.

Photo - Canadian Press Images

EPILOGUE

Not shown in the famous photograph are the premiers of the "outer" provinces in the West and the Atlantic.

They were undoubtedly more satisfied with the outcome than the constitutional leaders from central Canada. Since 1867, smaller provinces had simply been told how things would be done. That their limited sovereignty had survived a determined and deadly attack by a popular federal government will have been a source of great relief to them, if not celebration.

The sombre front-row faces in the photo were those of Ontario Premier Bill Davis, federal Justice Minister Jean Chrétien, Trudeau, federal Finance Minister Allan MacEachen, and Quebec Premier René Lévesque.

All had, in varying degrees, failed.

Trudeau personally had lost much, and Davis with him. Both had vested their personal political capital in defining (or redefining) Canada as a bicultural union run from the Centre. They fell far short. Lougheed's "7/50" amending formula had severely weakened that. So too had the western "opting-out" section in the Charter of Rights. Trudeau had recovered some last-minute ground by limiting any opt-out to five years unless renewed. But the "Notwithstanding Clause" – Section 33 – was a messy intrusion. It preserved the British principle (or at least the possibility) of parliamentary supremacy in what would otherwise have become the American system of de facto judicial supremacy.

But the centralists had to a considerable degree succeeded. Trudeau at least had his Constitution, complete with individual rights and language guarantees. Davis at least had the satisfaction of knowing he had clinched the final deal, thus saving the country from the referendum that Trudeau could otherwise have subjected it to, with possibly shattering effect.

The only man who went home utterly defeated was René Lévesque. He had lost Quebec's claim to a unilateral veto: the Constitution would be patriated without the support of the Quebec National Assembly, with an amending formula that could bypass Quebec. He had lost his bid for guaranteed financial compensation if Quebec opted out of future social programs. And he had lost the right to deny education rights to English parents in Quebec. He was reported as sobbing and cursing on the plane home.

The frowns on those central Canadian faces may have reflected a realization that Quebec's quest for greater sovereignty might come back stronger than before. How could it not?

Regardless of such forebodings, like Pontius Pilate, what they had written they had written.

On a rainy, windy day – April 17, 1982 – Queen Elizabeth II came to Parliament Hill to sign the royal proclamation that made Canada a fully sovereign nation.

■ ■ ■ ■

In his book on the Meech Lake constitutional fiasco eight years later, Patrick Monahan saw the day Queen Elizabeth signed the new Constitution Act into law, April 17, 1982, as a portent of trouble. When Trudeau proclaimed to 30,000 visitors on Parliament Hill that French and English were united at last, the sky darkened, thunder sounded above the Peace Tower, and the sky poured down rain.

Photo - Canadian Press Images

About the Author

Link Byfield, a long-time reporter, editor, commentator and policy advocate who lives at Riviere Qui Barre near Edmonton, was editor and publisher of the newsmagazines Alberta Report and Western Report from 1985 to 2003. Previous to that, he won consecutive first prizes for political journalism at the Western Magazine Awards. He was also a contributing writer and editor for the history series Alberta in the Twentieth Century.

In 2003 he became chairman of the Citizens Centre for Freedom and Democracy, a nonpartisan advocacy organization for responsible government and constitutional reform.

In 2004 he was chosen by 238,000 Albertans as a senator-elect under the province's Senate nominee law, and was a founding member of the Wildrose Alliance Party in 2008.

Assisting in *Identity Crisis and the Rise of Quebec* were his wife Joanne, a journalist and researcher, his son Eli, and Edmonton freelancer Craig Docksteader.

Photo and Archival Sources

The publisher and author gratefully acknowledge the generous assistance of the sources of the photographs and archival material contained in this volume: The National Archives of Canada, the National Library of Canada, Glenbow Museum and Archives, the Ontario Provincial Archives, Provincial Archives of Alberta, Department of National Defence, The Montreal Gazette, The Calgary Herald.

INDEX

Note: Numbers in italics refer to photographs or captions.

CANADA IN THE 20TH CENTURY

To order additional copies of this book, or others in the series please call CanMedia at 1-888-301-2664 or visit our website at
www.cdnhistory.com

BIRTH OF A NATION
1900 TO 1929

The tumultuous story of Canada's emergence as a modern state - from a frontier of empire to the 20th Century's first economic tiger. The horrors of the Great War, and the forging of a national identity as troops of the young Dominion lead the Allied forces to victory on the battlefields of Flanders, the social and political turmoil of the Roaring 20s, and the looming economic crisis that would end Canada's first great boom. Veteran journalist and author Paul Stanway brings to life the leaders, heroes, villains, and celebrities who left their mark on the on a developing country. All beautifully illustrated with hundreds of rare photographs, many reproduced here for the first time in decades.

TRAGEDY & TRIUMPH
1930 TO 1953

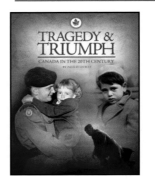

Ravaged by the unemployment and misery of the Great Depression, Canada is once again called upon to stand with Britain in a global war - this one more terrible than any conflict in human history. Punching far above its weight, the country plays a central role in the defeat of the Axis powers, and emerges from the challenges of World War Two reinvigorated and united as never before. The onset of the Cold War and the Korean conflict cast a pall over the post-war years, but the hard times finally give way to an unprecedented period of prosperity that transforms the lives of ordinary Canadians. The tragedies and triumphs that shaped a maturing nation are recalled in vivid detail and lavishly illustrated with unique photographs.